PRAISE FOR CHRISTIANITY IN THE CROSSHAIRS

"Secular elites have placed Christianity—and especially Catholicism—in the crosshairs for decades. Christians and Catholics are their declared enemies. What makes the radicals tick? The answer: threatening, controlling, and smearing Christians. And few have taken fire and flak quite like Bill Donohue. The bold Donohue and his fearless Catholic League have bravely taken on the ruling elites for decades. Now, you can, too. This book will help equip the faithful to fight back."

—Paul Kengor, PhD,
professor of political science, Grove City College, editor of *The American Spectator*, and author of *The Stigmatists* and *The Devil and Karl Marx*

"American society is wrestling with deep cultural rifts. In this timely book, Bill Donohue maps the landscape with clarity—identifying the key actors, the ideas that animate them, and the consequences for our nation. He shows how cultural elites and activist networks often align in ways that marginalize the family and religious faith, with Christianity frequently in the crosshairs of the debate. Whether or not readers share all his conclusions, they will find Donohue's argument carefully researched, lucidly written, and genuinely illuminating. It's a valuable guide for Christians—and for anyone who wants to understand what's driving today's cultural conflicts."

—Tony Perkins,
President, Family Research Council, Washington DC

"With his latest release, *Christianity in the Crosshairs*, Bill Donohue has provided Catholics and other concerned Christians and conservatives with an incredible, yet practical, resource to help us do more than just survive in these tumultuous and divisive times. This book offers a compelling case to fight complacency with a willingness to step out of our comfort zone by going beyond Sunday. With his no-nonsense style, Donohue combines eye opening, real-life stories with solid research of the current decline of our culture. Readers will be encouraged as they see how in the end, despite the many storms that swirl around us, the ruling class and raging radicals are no match for deep faith and strong families."

—Teresa Tomeo,
host of EWTN's Catholic Connection

"There is no better social scientist writing in America today than Bill Donohue. Writing in a bold, direct style, he lays bare how today's "elites"—as they call themselves—and today's radicals have formed an unholy alliance to destroy faith and family—and how those of us who treasure both must fight back. As a leading Catholic layman, Donohue is the head of the Catholic League, and he has been in the front lines of the culture war for decades. He believes that each and every believing Catholic must resist the soft totalitarianism that God-hating progressives want to impose on them and their Church. Read this book and you will answer the call to resist.

—Steven W. Mosher,
President, Population Research Institute

CHRISTIANITY IN THE CROSSHAIRS

Ruling Class and Radicals Find a Common Enemy

Bill Donohue

TAN Books
Gastonia, North Carolina

Christianity in the Crosshairs: Ruling Class and Radicals Find a Common Enemy © 2026 Bill Donohue

Cover design by Jordan Avery

ISBN: 978-1-5051-3669-2
Kindle ISBN: 978-1-5051-3780-4
ePUB ISBN: 978-1-5051-3779-8

Published in the United States by
TAN Books
PO Box 269
Gastonia, NC 28053

www.TANBooks.com

Printed in India

For Bernadette Brady-Egan

CONTENTS

Acknowledgments

Writing a book is an exciting intellectual challenge, something I treasure. Like all authors, there is also the hope and expectation that readers will gain insight into the subject matter, and in this case, that means a greater appreciation for the causes and consequences of the secular war on Christianity.

There are many people who have inspired me to write this book, both professionally and personally.

TAN Books is a success because of the dedication of Conor Gallagher, Kevin Gallagher, and the patriarch, Bill Gallagher. They have assembled a fantastic team that includes Tim Hill, Jason Gale, and Mary Pakaluk. I especially want to thank John Vella, my editor, for his contribution; he has been a joy to work with.

The Catholic League board of directors, led by Michael Schwartz, is always in my corner. On my board of advisors, I would like to single out Paul Kengor and Steve Mosher for encouraging me to pursue TAN. The Catholic League staff deserves a special mention—it is they whom I interact with the most. In particular, I have profited from discussions with Bernadette Brady-Egan, Michael McDonald, and Nicholas Palczewski.

I am blessed to have such a great family and many close friends. Valerie, Caryn, Caitlin, Paul, Jay, and my grandkids, Grant and Nina, are a great source of happiness—as are my favorite relatives, the McGetricks. Among my friends, the standouts are Maggie and Mike Mansfield, and Linda and Tom Boyle. Then there are the boys and girls at Doc's; their never-wavering belief in the power of spirits is profound, especially the kind that quenches our thirst.

Introduction

The average Joe likes to spend time with his family, work hard, party with friends, go to dinner, enjoy sports, take an occasional vacation, etc. He may have an interest in politics, but he is not an activist. Indeed, he pretty much wants to be left alone and not be subjected to someone else's agenda. But too often, he is.

The ruling class is made up of the decision makers who run our institutions, and they are not like the average Joe. They work in government, law, corporations, education, the media, the entertainment business, the healthcare industry, foundations, and the like. They love being in charge. They especially like it when they get the average Joe to follow their lead.

There is another sector of society that is just as active in getting its way. They are radical intellectuals and activists: the former supply the ideas and the latter act on them (for the sake of simplicity, they will jointly be referred to as the radicals). They work in government, nonprofit advocacy organizations, higher education, and the media. Driven by ideology, they want to remake our institutions to fit their vision of society. To do so, they must get the average Joe to buy into their left-wing agenda. If he resists being coaxed, coercion is a viable option.

The ruling class and radicals may appear to be opposites, and in some ways they are, but they share a common purpose: they want power. Whether capitalist or "progressive," they want to control the average Joe. Sometimes they even work in tandem. They are good at cultivating a subdued populace, and they are masters at getting what they want.

George Orwell and Aldous Huxley provided the template. In Orwell's classic book *1984*, written after World War II, Orwell showed how the state takes command of society. Huxley's famous work *Brave New World*, published in 1932, depicted a future society where the people were seduced by the ruling class to do what they were programmed to do. Orwell was a student of Huxley, and while they were concerned about the same subject, their points of emphasis were quite different. Of the two, Huxley's fictional account of what the future would look like more accurately describes our current condition in Western civilization.

The ruling class and radicals mimic what these two English authors wrote. Both are determined to get the average Joe to adjust his sails and dutifully accept their game plan. They use control and seduction to get what they want. They don't want slaves as much as they want a docile citizenry, preferably one that happily accepts their subordinate status. Charles McGrath, who studied Huxley's work, nicely explains his position. The ruling class succeeds "not by oppressing their citizens but by giving them exactly what they want, or what they think they want—which is basically sex, drugs and rock 'n' roll—and lulling them into complacency."[1]

Seeking to subdue the people is an old idea. Under the Roman Empire, the ruling class used bread and circuses: they provided a subsistence living and offered plenty of diversionary activities. In short, when the masses have their bellies full and are eager to be entertained, the ruling class can proceed without resistance. Today, government paternalism is more expansive than ever before, and the obsession with sports has never been greater.

The totalitarian governments of the twentieth century, fascist and communist alike, did not hesitate to kill. Approximately 150 million people died under the regimes of Hitler, Stalin, Mao, and Pol Pot. In the democratic countries of the twenty-first century, violence is eschewed. But the ambition to control the people remains a constant, an end that is pursued as much by the ruling class as it is by radicals. They both prefer a gentler approach, one that nudges the people to accept their fate. Thought control is one of their favorite techniques.

It needs to be said that the ruling class is not monolithic. There are elites who are not mirroring the ideology of the Left and are, indeed, working against them. Donald Trump is certainly not a friend of radical intellectuals and activists. But the wealthiest members of the ruling class gave the vast majority of their donations to Kamala Harris in 2024—her coffers dwarfed his. Goldman Sachs endorsed her candidacy, cheering her support for illegal immigration, low-income workers are a priority.

It is ironic to hear Trump's critics say he is captured by an oligarchy. In fact, as Victor Davis Hanson has pointed out, of the ten wealthiest people in the United States, "until recently, I would say the 2024 election, they were all against the Republican Party and were lavish donors for the Democrats."[2] He is talking about Elon Musk, Jeff Bezos, Mark Zuckerberg, Warren Buffett, Larry Page, Sergey Brin, Larry Ellison, Bill Gates, and Mike Bloomberg. Musk voted for Hillary Clinton in 2016 and Joe Biden in 2020. Bloomberg spent $1 billion of his own money in a losing effort to win the Democratic primary nomination in 2020.

Trump also garnered the opposition of the ruling class in the media, education, and the entertainment industry. They were relentless in their assaults on him. He won not because of the ruling class but in spite of them. He won because he represented the average Joe.

Trump won by such a wide margin—capturing all seven swing states, the Electoral College, and the popular vote—that he stunned the ruling class. Moreover, he even got some in their ranks to reverse course: key players took a fresh look at their positions on migrants, crime, censorship, and other issues. This is significant because it constitutes a cultural shift. Just as markets make adjustments—market corrections are not uncommon—cultural corrections are often made, albeit not as frequently. But it would be naïve to think that the ruling class has given up its quest for control.

Catholicism understands what animates the ruling class and radicals: they are guilty of the sin of pride.

Saints Augustine and Aquinas identified pride as the heart and soul of sin. The desire to dismiss God—to exalt ourselves and think that we are self-sufficient—is a spiritual crime of a monstrous order. C. S. Lewis not only agreed with Augustine and Aquinas, labeling pride "the great sin," but he said, "It was through Pride that the devil became the devil."[3]

The hand of the devil is clearly at work, and this is especially visible when considering what stands in the way of total victory: the two most powerful forces in civil society—namely, family and religion. The average Joe lays anchor in his family and in his church, the two institutions that command his primary allegiance. That's why the ruling class and radicals want to disable them—they can't win if family and religion occupy center stage in the average Joe's life.

That is what this book is about. It identifies the players, makes plain their means and their ends, and details how they work to undermine family and religion. Elites and activists loathe traditional norms and values; they are determined to undermine them. But try as they may, signs of resistance are everywhere. How this culture war ends is uncertain, but what is not in question is the goal of radicals and the ruling class. Driven by power and the need to control, they are the greatest enemy of freedom in Western civilization.

CHAPTER 1

WHAT MAKES THE RULING CLASS AND RADICALS TICK

Throughout history, the ruling class has done battle with its subjects—master versus slave, noble versus peasant, capitalist versus working class, and so on. There have been slave revolts, peasant revolts, and working-class revolts, and some have been successful. But rarely have those in charge broken bread with those who led the opposition. Today, we are faced with something altogether new: the alignment of large sectors of the ruling class with radicals. The elites and activists are not completely united and are often still at each other's throats. But they are more likely to pursue similar strategies today than ever before. They also have a common enemy. To be blunt, they are working together to undermine the dominant culture: they have Christianity in the crosshairs.

What do they want? Large-scale change. Not a total revolution, but close enough. They don't like the status quo, and they desperately seek to reset society. They believe that traditional norms, values, and institutions are more of a problem than a solution to what ails us. We need a major societal facelift, a thoroughgoing reconstruction of the political, economic, social, and cultural order. In today's vernacular, this means we need to "reimagine" society.

Rulers and radicals are not oppressive in the way previous potentates have been. Instead, they want people to be content, subdued, and docile. They don't like it when they are challenged or resisted. They are convinced—and they are right about this—that the biggest obstacle to their rule comes from Christianity. Christian churches, schools, hospitals, agencies, and associations represent the antithesis of their secular vision of society. That is why they must be trimmed, if not excised.

We can't serve two masters. Elites and activists know this to be true and are bent on winning. To win, they must disable the enemy, and that means Christianity. They have been doing a really good job of this, though they realize that victory is not a slam dunk.

Who are these people who want to disable Christianity? Let's take a look at a profile of the ruling class. Then we'll take a look at who the radicals are. Finally, we'll examine how these two competitors found common ground.

The Ruling Class

Pollster Scott Rasmussen surveyed what he calls the elite 1 percent, those individuals who make over $150,000 a year, live in densely populated areas, and have postgraduate degrees. Most of them are super liberals. They are also the decision makers, the ones who call the shots in our most influential institutions. A large segment of these people went to one of twelve elite schools. Rasmussen estimates that "about half the policy positions in government, half the corporate board positions in America, are held by people who went to one of these dozen schools."[4]

If the ruling class were guided by what Catholic teachings say—namely, the common good—this profile may not matter. But they are not. They are motivated by winning and are prepared to cheat to get their way. This is not an opinion. It's what the elites believe. Rasmussen has the data. He asked, "Suppose that your favorite candidate loses a close election. However, people on the campaign know that they can win by cheating without being caught. Would you rather have your candidate win by cheating or lose by playing fair?"

Among all Americans, just 7 percent said they would want their candidate to win by cheating. But among the elite 1 percent, that number was 35 percent. Among the most politically obsessed top 1 percent—those who talk about politics every day—the figure is 69 percent. In other words, seven in ten of the most politically charged elites who run this country would rather their candidate win by cheating than allow another candidate to win fairly.

Economist Stephen Moore, who paid for the Rasmussen survey, offered his own analysis of the data. He concluded that we have two Americas. "First, there are the cultural and over-educated snobs—the kind of people who religiously read the *New York Times*, drive EVs, wear Harvard or Yale sweaters, and have never even heard of NASCAR or eaten at Popeyes or ridden a John Deere tractor. And then there is normal main street America. The snobs thumb their collective noses at the unrefined working-class Americans. The elites believe they are intellectually, culturally, and morally superior to the working class and rural America."[5]

It has often been said that the country is so divided that we live in two different worlds. Moore looked at the data and came to the same conclusion.

"The Grand Canyon-sized divide between the elites in America and ordinary Americans is so profound that it is as if they live in two different countries." That's how Moore sees it. "Silicon Valley, Manhattan, and Washington, D.C. have become bubbles that have lost contact with everyday Americans."[6] It must also be said that these big-time liberals are the first to condemn "white privilege," yet they are overwhelmingly white men and women of privilege. They have nothing in common with the average Joe. They don't take mass transit, and they sure don't live in crime-ridden projects; they more typically live in gated communities.

The elites make sure they live the high life, but they don't want the rest of us to live that way. Rasmussen found that more than two-thirds of the Ivy elite school college grads he surveyed would ban gas stoves, gas-powered cars, air conditioning, SUVs, and "non-essential air travel"—meaning no vacation trips for the average Joe ("non-essential air travel" presumably would not mean traveling by private jet to elite business conferences). When the public was asked if they support a ban on these modern conveniences, less than one in four favored any of these bans.

The elites are not worried about crime—they have their own security—but they are worried about climate change. Indeed, 70 percent of them say they would pay $500 or more each year in taxes and higher costs to reduce climate change.

Contrast that with what the average American is prepared to do: 72 percent said they would be willing to pay $100 or less. The elites really do live in their own world.

Moore notes just how much the ruling class despises the working class. He opines, "You won't see too many elites at a Trump rally with 30,000 people."[7] He's right.

Most of the left-leaning members of the ruling class wanted nothing to do with Trump in 2024. But that didn't stop him from doing better than he had in 2016 with virtually every segment of the population. The exceptions were notable: those who made over $100,000 a year; those with a postgraduate degree; and the religiously unaffiliated. These are among the most defining characteristics of the ruling class. Therefore, even if Trump succeeded in getting some elites to rethink their positions, it would be folly to think that most of them have fundamentally changed their views. They may be in retreat, but they are not prepared to do a 180.

Registered Democrats are so full of hatred for Trump that nearly two-thirds (64 percent) admitted that they should "oppose everything" he does; he was in office for just one month.[8] Worse, a poll by the Network Contagion Research Institute found that a majority (55.2 percent) of self-identified "left of center" adults said that murdering Trump is justified.[9]

Just before Memorial Day weekend in 2024, Trump held a rally in a poor neighborhood in the Bronx, drawing tens of thousands. Kathy Hochul, the governor of New York, dismissed the event, saying it was of no consequence for "Donald Trump to be the ringleader and invite all his clowns to a place like the Bronx."[10] The people she called "clowns" were overwhelmingly Puerto Rican, working-class people. Hochul and her husband are multimillionaires.

Hochul's smugness and her condescending attitude toward the "clowns" who live in "a place like the Bronx" are so typical of the way rich liberals think. That's why they have no problem justifying cheating in an election: the masses are fundamentally stupid and don't know what's in their own best interest anyway. But the elites know what's in their best interest, and that's all that matters. There is nothing new about their contempt for the average Joe. Longshoreman philosopher Eric Hoffer opined on this subject in the 1960s, saying "self-appointed elites" will "hate us no matter what we do," and that "it is legitimate for us to help dump them into the dustbin of history."[11]

Hochul's "clowns" are seen by Hillary Clinton as a "basket of deplorables." President Joe Biden called them "garbage." Nancy Pelosi, the former Speaker of the House, was even more contemptuous of the average Joe. In an Oxford debate in 2024, she slammed those who are drawn to the populist movement, branding them "poor souls who are looking for some answers." The problem with these people, she said, is that they don't listen to the elites. "We've given [answers] to them, but they're blocked by some of their views on guns. They have the three Gs: guns, gays, God."[12]

It really bothers the ruling class that the average Joe looks to God and not the government for answers. Obama and Hochul see religion, especially Christianity, as a force that blocks the reach of government, thus standing in their way of exercising maximum control. They prefer religion to be a purely private matter. But it is not—it has grave public implications—and they know it.

Why do these elites hate the average Joe? For one thing, they have nothing in common with him. Clinton's net worth is estimated at $120 million. Pelosi's is estimated to be as much as $413 million. But it's more than money that separates them from the average Joe. John Podesta knows Clinton as well as anyone; he ran her presidential campaign. In a 2016 email to Jennifer Palmieri, the communications director for the Clinton campaign, he wrote that she "has begun to hate everyday Americans."[13] Why? Because, as Pelosi said, the average Joe doesn't listen to the answers they've been given.

Former Florida Senator Marco Rubio, who was named Secretary of State by Trump, also knows how the ruling class thinks. He identifies with the people, but many of those in government do not. "Despite claiming to love democracy, many liberal elites distrust the vast majority of the American people—even despise them."[14] The hatred the liberal elites have for the average Joe is exactly what Orwell and Huxley feared would happen, thus necessitating the thought police. The masses must be manipulated for their own good. The elites are convinced that they know where our shoes pinch us better than we do.

If the ruling class settled for making decisions that the average Joe wants them to make—decisions that positively affect their everyday lives—there would be no controversy. But that is not the case. The elites believe they have a calling, a vocation, and they are destined to fulfill it. They are convinced that it is their job to remake the world.

At the top of the ruling class hierarchy is a class of super elites who are committed to global governance. Robert F. Gorman is a political scientist who specializes in international studies, and he understands them as well as anyone. They are interested in obliterating national sovereignty and in seeking to "establish an entirely secular order in which activities such as education, health care, economic development, and justice are fashioned by global experts rather than by the leaders in their natural local and national contexts." He identifies them as "secularists who are at best suspicious of but often outright hostile to religion and traditional culture as influences on civilization."[15]

The global elites do not see all religions as a threat to their rule. "The traditional teachings of Christianity, rooted in the gospel of Jesus Christ, are a major target for advocates of global governance. They have adopted the mantle of peace, justice, human rights, and humanitarian advocacy—the social gospel of the Church—but have systematically attacked the Church as an institution, the traditional family and traditional moral values, and love of country and love of God."[16] Most consequentially, "They are opponents of religious liberty and even of freedom of conscience."

Gorman is correct. The global elites see Christianity as a hurdle to clear if their rule is to be consolidated. They try to hijack the great outreach programs established by the Church to serve the dispossessed, setting themselves up as secular saviors. But their hostility to traditional norms and values, and their disdain for family and religion, outweigh whatever good their programs do. The poor need more than food, clothing, and shelter. They need what the state cannot provide—a sense of community where they are valued for who they are, independent of their station in life. Christians understand this, but the elites do not.

Seamus Bruner calls the ruling class Controligarchs. He is speaking about "a new breed of philanthropists, entrepreneurs, and tech titans seeking to impose an unprecedented system of control not only in the U.S., but around the world." His concern is that these elites are "making investments that will micromanage every aspect of your life."[17]

If there is one person in elite quarters who is quite open about his ambitions, it is Klaus Schwab, the German engineer and economist who founded the World Economic Forum. He invites elites from all over the world to meet in Davos, Switzerland. Their goal in life is to generate the "Great Reset," to set in motion ideas that will radically transform the way we think and behave. "What we do in Davos," he explained, "is to push the reset button."[18] In 2025, before he stepped down from heading this organization, he told the crowd, "The future is shaped by us, and particularly shaped by us here in this room."[19]

Yuval Noah Harari, a senior advisor to Schwab, envisions a society where artificial intelligence will replace the Scriptures and create unified "religions that are actually correct." His arrogance is stunning. "AI *can* create new ideas; [it] can even write a new Bible." He adds that "in a few years, there might be religions that are actually correct . . . just think about a religion whose holy book is written by an AI." Someone needs to introduce this genius to Christianity.

Who elected these people to do this? No one. Whom do they consult with, outside their privileged circle? No one.

What motivates them? Control. According to Scott Walter, who has studied the role that elites play in shaping our society, there are plenty of organizations like Arabella, a "dark money" operation whose funding sources are hard to trace, that exercise incredible influence. Yet the average Joe has never heard of them. Walter maintains that what motivates left-wing donors and operatives more than anything else is "a lust to control others."[20] They are obsessed with control.

In the 1950s, long before Arabella was founded, sociologist C. Wright Mills wrote his famous book *The Power Elite*. He maintained that there was a ruling class comprised of well-educated persons who occupy the command centers in government, the corporate world, and the military. They go to the most prestigious schools, both secondary and collegiate; they work together; they fraternize with each other; they intermarry. This is no conspiracy, Mills said. The elites may not even be conscious of just how powerful they really are.

Effective as the power elite are, they are not solitary rulers. They depend on advisors, technicians, and opinion-makers to carry out their duties. Immediately below them are those in Congress and in the sprawling bureaucracies of the federal government, what we now call the administrative state. Today, they command a level of power that would have astonished Mills.

Jason Chaffetz, a former congressman, wrote a book about these people: he calls them "puppeteers." "Increasingly," he writes, "the work of government is being done by people outside of government—people who are invisible to the American public, but who pull the strings, set the agendas, create the incentives, and write the rules we must all live by. They rotate their own people in and out of the bureaucracy, leverage their vast resources on behalf of the Democratic Party, and they inject a globalist agenda none of us ever voted for."[21] A globalist agenda that has no tolerance for Christianity.

Those who work in the federal government and staff the important jobs are known as the B Team. When a congressman sought to meet with a Senate-confirmed cabinet secretary but was instead granted a meeting with his senior staff, he expressed his dismay by having to meet with the B Team. "It's true—we are the B Team," he was told. "You are meeting with the right people. We 'B' here before you, we 'B' here after you, and we 'B' the ones who make the decisions."[22] Rubio says it's even worse than this. He notes that "some government employees are acting of their own accord, as opposed to carrying out the policies of their elected bosses."[23] In effect, Washington is rife with these unelected fiefdoms, the so-called Deep State.

As Philip Hamburger points out, these unelected officials are not exactly religion-friendly. The Columbia University professor of constitutional law notes that "administrative bureaucrats, especially administrative experts, are not representative of the United States and on average are intolerant of religion, especially relatively orthodox opinions." Yes, they are nothing like the average Joe. "Administrative power, in other words, is slanted against traditional Catholics, Protestants, Jews, and others who adhere to their inherited faiths."[24]

In addition to the perennial bureaucrats, the power elite are supported by celebrities. They play the role that Huxley wrote about, keeping the masses happy. They love to mingle with the power elite, Mills says, because they love to be on display. "If such celebrities are not the head of any dominating hierarchy," he said, "they do often have the power to distract the attention of the public or afford sensations to the masses, or, more directly, to gain the ear of those who do occupy positions of direct power."[25] Yes, they are very good at that. Kamala Harris's presidential campaign broke all records in giving prominence to celebrities, so much so that it backfired, making her look like an unserious candidate.

Radicals

Radicals, in the first half of the twentieth century, were known as communists. In the second half, they were called the New Left. Some were later dubbed cultural Marxists. Today, they are called progressives. All of them are radical egalitarians: they hate hierarchies of all kinds, allowing an exception for themselves—they are too indispensable not to be in charge. Their hatred of Christianity is their signature.

What animates the Left is power. They can't get enough of it. Saul Alinsky, the Chicago radical, was very good at organizing. He was fond of instructing his followers to keep their eye on the big prize, not the particular issue they were pursuing. "You want to organize for *power*!"[26] Everything was subordinate to mobilizing the people to achieve power. Revolution is the ultimate goal, not reform.

To appreciate what they stand for, we can do no better than to understand exactly what the communists in the United States have long sought to accomplish.

In 1958, two years after Mills's book on the power elite was published, W. Cleon Skousen, a student of communism, published *The Naked Communist: Exposing Communism and Restoring Freedom*. Looking back at the book with the benefit of hindsight, it is stunning how accurately he was in describing how the communist agenda would unfold. Only now the ones carrying it out are known as progressives. Almost all are nonbelievers, and many are atheists.

Skousen detailed forty-five communist goals. Many of them dealt with warfare, Russia and China, the U.N., and the communist apparatus. In some cases, what he predicted was modified by contemporary radicals. For example, he said the communists wanted to "discredit and eventually dismantle the FBI."[27] Instead, what we've seen is a progressive takeover of elite positions within the agency. From the phony Russian collusion attributed to Trump—Hillary Clinton was the leading protagonist—to spying on ordinary Catholics, the FBI has been weaponized by politically driven progressives.

One communist goal that has had more than a measure of success is socialism. "Support any socialist movement to give centralized control over any part of the culture—education, social agencies, welfare programs, mental health clinics, etc."[28]

The largest labor union in the nation is the National Education Association. It not only gives most of its enormous contributions to the Democrats, but the issues it favors are classic radical goals: it has a Zinn Education Project, named after radical historian Howard Zinn, that supplies teachers with anti-American resources. It was two far-left professors,

Frances Fox Piven and Richard Cloward, who mobilized the welfare state to crash the economy, hoping to usher in socialism.

"Infiltrate and gain control of big business." Mission accomplished. Skousen asks, "*infiltrate to do what?*" He had a ready response. "The answer is the consolidation of power."[29] From the Rockefellers and the Fords to Bill Gates and George Soros, big money capitalists have funded some of the most extremely radical programs in the nation. "Big Philanthropy," as those who track this issue have said, typically funds left-wing projects and organizations, and this is done "at the expense of funding for traditional charitable causes most Americans would personally associate with the word 'philanthropy.'"[30] It makes one wonder whose side they are on.

"Capture one or both of the political parties in the United States."[31] That left-wing extremists have captured the Democratic Party is contested by no one. Indeed, the Biden administration, together with the Democrats who run left-wing cities such as Portland, Seattle, San Francisco, Los Angeles, Minneapolis, Chicago, New York, and Philadelphia, have proved they have nothing in common with the platform and policies of JFK and LBJ, nor, for that matter, Jimmy Carter and Bill Clinton. The drift left started with Obama and crystallized under Biden.

"Infiltrate the press."[32] Virtually everyone concedes that the mainstream media—ABC, CBS, NBC, CNN, MSNBC, PBS, NPR, the *New York Times*, the *Washington Post*, the Associated Press—are the mouthpiece of the left. Then there are any number of internet and social media outlets that tilt sharply left. Looks like this communist objective is in the bag.

"Create the impression that violence and insurrection are legitimate aspects of the American tradition; that students and special-interest groups should rise up and use 'united force' to solve economic, political or social problems."[33]

Education, especially higher education, has been indoctrinating students with anti-American propaganda since the 1960s, though the pace has quickened more recently. Students didn't take over college campuses in 2024 because they were bored—they did so because they were drunk on ideology. Their radical professors did a splendid job filling their heads with a false and dark picture of Western civilization, all the while trashing Christianity. Yet, had it not been for the outsized role that the Catholic Church has had on Western civilization, we would not enjoy the liberty and prosperity that are the world's envy. Migrants from all over the world crash our borders not to experience oppression but to escape it.

"Weaken the police."[34] That's exactly what we have been witnessing. Those who started the "defund the police" movement were not African Americans—it was mostly white radicals, some of whom were funded by the ruling class—who sought to destroy urban America. After years of demonizing the police, cities across the nation are finding it increasingly difficult to recruit new members. The armed forces were faced with the same problem under the Obama and Biden administrations, but it improved markedly under President Trump. To these communist goals must be mentioned the plan to disable the family and religion. This will be given extensive treatment in the second half of this book. They command our attention because they are the two biggest obstacles standing in the way of the radical agenda.

Americans not only have to worry today about these communist goals being foisted on us by progressives, but they have to keep an eye on what Communist China is doing. According to Peter Schweizer, China is flooding the United States with illicit guns as part of their "Disintegration Warfare" strategy. They are targeting our "soft underbelly," exploiting "the spirit and psychology of [its] people." They are implementing the plan of an ancient Chinese strategist, General Sun Tzu. He taught how to win a war without fighting. Victory will be achieved, he counseled, by breaking the "national will, values and cohesion" of a nation.[35]

Rulers and Radicals Unite

The alignment of rulers and radicals did not occur overnight. In the aftermath of the tumultuous 1960s, it became clear that we were witnessing something new.

As was pointed out, the Communist Party in the United States set its eyes on capturing one of the two political parties, and they settled on the Democratic Party. This didn't happen until one of the mainstays of the party, working-class Catholics, was dislodged from power. That was evident by 1972.

Columbia University professor Geoffrey Layman cites 1972 as the pivotal year when secularists took command. Two political scientists from Baruch College, Louis Bolce and Gerald De Maio, agree.[36] That was the year when Catholics were effectively driven out of command positions in the party.

After Senator Hubert Humphrey lost to Richard Nixon in 1968, the McGovern Commission (named after failed presidential candidate Senator George McGovern) was established to reform the way presidential candidates were chosen. "Catholics had made up about one in four Humphrey votes in 1968" observed author Mark Stricherz, "yet they received only one in fourteen slots on the commission in 1969." When the voters went to the polls in 1972, secular Americans chose the Democrats by a margin of 3–1.[37]

Fast forward two decades to 1992. According to Layman, "the Democratic Party now appears to be a party whose core of support comes from secularists, Jews, and the less committed members of the major religious traditions." Similarly, Bolce and De Maio said, "60 percent of first-time white delegates at the [1992] Democratic convention in New York City either claimed no attachment to religion or displayed the minimal attachment by attending worship services 'a few times a year' or less."[38] Indeed, at the convention, Pennsylvania Governor Robert Casey, a Catholic, was treated as a pariah because he was proudly pro-life. Anti-Catholic bigots publicly mocked him.

Why did this happen? Mike McCurry, former press secretary to President Bill Clinton, explained it this way: "Because we want to be politically correct, in particular being sensitive to Jews, that's taken the party to a direction where faith language is soft and opaque."[39]

There was another reason why the working class abandoned the Democratic Party. In the 1980s, the young, urban professionals, or yuppies, were drawn to the Democrats, the consequences of which proved to be profound. According to Tom McGrath, who wrote a book about this development, the yuppies "helped shift the Democratic Party's focus away from its labor coalition and toward the hyper-educated liberal voters it largely represents today, eventually creating an opening for Trump to cast Democrats as out-of-touch elites and draw the white working class away from them. In fact, if it weren't for the 1980s yuppies and the way they shifted America's political parties, the modern MAGA GOP might never have arisen in the first place."[40]

Some of the yuppies were former yippies. Yippies were those who, in the 1960s, identified with the Youth International Party (YIP), a group of radicals cofounded by Jerry Rubin. He was known for his extreme left-wing politics, calling for a communist victory in Vietnam and other "guerrilla theater" causes. He played an integral role in the 1968 riots during the Democratic National Convention and was subsequently named as one of the "Chicago Eight" who went on trial for their offenses. He later donned a dress suit and became a successful capitalist.

Rubin was only one of many radicals who exchanged their "Che" Guevara T-shirts for a suit and tie. Hillary and Bill Clinton were both caught up in the radical hippie culture, but they didn't stay there for too long. They quickly morphed into the ruling class. In short, in the 1980s, many of yesterday's radicals became ruling class contemporaries.

So, while it is true that the ruling class and the radical elite have historically been at odds, that is no longer the case. They share many things in common, among them a contempt for the average Joe.

Some of the elites not only look down their noses at the common man, but they regard him as a "useless" human being. World Economic Forum superstar Yuval Noah Harari is not happy with what he sees down the road with these people. "The biggest question maybe in economics and politics in the coming decades will be what to do with all these useless people."[41] As Seamus Bruner observes, "these twenty-first century 'useless people' are not disabled or unfit; they are simply bored and superfluous."[42] From where Harari is sitting, the ones who are "useless" are the people who can't do much to help the "useful" ones—namely, elites like him. Hence, they are a drag. It would be hard to find a conviction more out of step with the Catholic Church's emphasis on the human dignity that inheres in every human being than this.

Radicals also have no respect for the "useless." Marx hated the "lumpenproletariat," or what he regarded as the "scum of the earth." They include what we would today call the underclass—drug addicts, alcoholics, prostitutes, the homeless, and the like. Often, they live in a zombie-like state and are rendered useless because they are unable to organize and become revolutionaries.

Herbert Marcuse, the influential German cultural Marxist, spoke with derision of the working class, the very people Marx banked on to carry out the revolution. In the 1960s, he said, "They find their soul in their automobile, hi-fi set, split-level home, kitchen equipment."[43] In short, because they like the good life, this makes them useless to radical causes.

Divide and Conquer

One of the many tactics employed by the ruling class and radicals is to "divide and conquer." If the American people, who are mostly Christians, can be divided, it provides a buffer zone for the ruling class; it also allows radicals to pursue their political agenda with limited resistance.

This is a very old idea. "If a kingdom is divided against itself, that kingdom cannot stand. And if a house is divided against itself, that house will not be able to stand" (Mk 3:24–25). The Roman historian Sallust argued that the nobles were able to prevail over the masses because the former were organized and the latter were divided. The Roman imperial strategy during the reign of Tiberius was a classic divide and conquer gambit. The tribes collapsed under the discord that was fomented by the rulers.

Harvard scholars who have studied the divide and conquer scheme throughout history explain why it works. It is attractive "because it is cheaper to set factions within the latent opposition to fighting among themselves, and if necessary to defeat them piecemeal, than it is to defeat them as a unified enemy."[44] Today, divide and conquer game plans originate in radical intellectual quarters, but it could not succeed without the blessing of the ruling class.

America's national motto, *E pluribus unum*, "out of the many, one," is treated with disdain by the Left. They don't want assimilation—they want division. That is why they gave birth to the ideology of multiculturalism in the 1980s.

Multiculturalism, in theory, its proponents say, means respect for diverse cultures and peoples. This is a ruse. Pope Benedict XVI saw right through it. He said that multiculturalism has led to "a peculiar Western self-hatred that is nothing short of pathological."[45] What makes this such a travesty is that no civilization in the history of the world has given birth to more liberty, equality, and prosperity than

Western civilization. Moreover, the reason it has proven to be so successful is because it is rooted in our Judeo-Christian tradition.

In practice, multiculturalism is a tool used to divide us. Ryan P. Williams, president of the Claremont Institute, sees it as the very opposite of our motto. "It seeks to divide and conquer Americans, making many groups out of one citizenry. The modern Left, accustomed to running the campuses according to the new social justice diktats of multiculturalism, now wants to run the world that way."[46]

Williams is right. The way they want to run the world is by promoting the international cousin of multiculturalism, mass migration. The elites know that when certain cultural groups are allowed to migrate to Western nations—steeped in the Judeo-Christian ethos—assimilation is going to be a real problem.

In 2024, Eva Vlaardingerbroek, a young Dutch political commentator, spoke at a Hungarian convention on this subject. After noting that migrants to Europe have brought a spike in crime and an unwillingness to assimilate, she warned that if it continues, it "will go down in history as the time in which Western nations no longer had to get invaded by hostile armies in order to be conquered. This time will then go down in history as the period in which the invader was actively invited in by a corrupt elite, and not only did this corrupt elite invite the enemy in, they made the native population pay for it too." This, she said, is what the New World Order looks like. "So what's the antidote? A strong Christian Europe of sovereign nation states."[47]

Less than two months before he died, a prominent member of the ruling elite who used to encourage mass migration changed his mind. After the Hamas attack on Israel in October 7, 2023, there were celebrations in the streets of Germany. This had a profound effect on Henry Kissinger, the 100-year-old professor and diplomat. "It was a grave mistake to let in so many people of totally different culture and religion and concepts, because it creates a pressure group inside each country that does that."[48] He was an honest man—he admitted he gave the wrong advice.

The Woke Agenda

There is no question that the influx of migrants from parts of the world who do not share the Judeo-Christian vision of man and society has wreaked havoc throughout Canada, the United States, and Europe. Those who come with the intention of assimilating—of adopting the language, norms, and values of Western nations—are not a problem. The problem is those who adamantly reject our heritage and who are steadfast in pursuing their own agenda.

According to Carlon Howard, Chief Impact Officer at the Equity Institute, the convergence of rulers and radicals has been evident since the early twentieth century. He cites Dr. John Harvey Kellogg, founder of the cereal giant, as an early example of corporations gone "woke." For decades, the Kellogg Foundation has been a major sponsor of radical programs.

But why? Why would the ruling class adopt the radical agenda? According to Howard, "Companies may use their participation in social initiatives as a way of distracting from other issues that could limit their profits, such as low wages and poor working conditions."[49] Following Huxley, distracting the masses is one of the most prized ways that elites use to maintain control. Corporate involvement in social media has added to this condition—it makes elites appear to be socially conscious.

If there is one person who personifies both the ruling class and radical politics, it is George Soros. There is hardly a left-wing cause that the atheist billionaire doesn't sponsor or promote, both foreign and domestic. For him, there is no inconsistency between the interests of rulers and the objectives of radicals—they are one and the same.

Soros uses his Open Society Institute to help "reset" America's priorities. He contributes to "dark money" organizations that make it hard to trace the origins of their funding sources. He is not alone in doing so. For example, the Gates Foundation, the Ford Foundation, and the Rockefeller Foundation fund Arabella, a powerful left-wing operation. Soros also contributes to the Sixteen Thirty Fund, another "dark money" entity; it specializes in reshaping the political landscape. The average Joe has no idea who these organizations are and how much power they have in restructuring American society.

Left-wing causes include crusades against traditional values and organizations. Take the Boy Scouts. Their foes began their assault on them in the early 1990s when Levi Strauss Company, Bank of America, and Wells Fargo yanked their donations over the exclusion of homosexuals. The United Way of DeKalb County, Illinois, and the United Way of the

San Francisco Bay Area did likewise (at that time, the United Way contributed roughly 25 percent of the Boy Scouts' budget). It was not the average Joe who declared war on the Boy Scouts—it was the ruling class. They succeeded. The organization went from over 4 million members in the 1990s to approximately 1 million today.

Disney, a traditionalist stalwart, shocked millions by embracing the politics of the Left. Their commitment to the radical LGBTQ agenda has led them to create transgender characters for children and support laws that undermine parental authority. The pushback from organizations like the Catholic League, which produced a documentary on Disney exposing its sexually corrupt agenda, has had some effect in getting the elites at the company to hit a different sort of "reset" button, though the temptation to lean left is extant.

Today, left-wing professors are teaching their impressionable students that sex is not binary and that men can get pregnant. This not only flies in the face of what Christianity teaches, but it flies in the face of science. They are wrong on both counts, but it hardly raises an eyebrow to learn that they actually believe this stuff. More surprising is when corporations, pressured by such investors as Blackrock and Vanguard, teach their employees the same nonsense. That's what they do at Meta (formerly Facebook): since 2014, they've been telling their workers that in addition to male and female, there are fifty-eight other options, such as genderfluid and agender. They just make up these terms and expect everyone to get on board. This is another example of the way rulers and radicals come together.

More recently, Kansas City Chiefs' kicker Harrison Butker was condemned by establishment organizations, the media, and left-wing activists because of a commencement address he gave at Benedictine College in 2024. Rulers and radicals had at him because he defended traditional moral values.

Butker is a practicing Catholic who gave a Catholic speech at a Catholic college. The students gave him two standing ovations. But to those unaffiliated at the school, his speech was labeled offensive because he is a traditionalist. Nothing he said was incendiary or insulting, but because he spoke positively about moms who elect to work at home taking care of their children, an online petition was started demanding that the Chiefs fire him. The left-leaning elites who run the NFL—and who have a cozy relationship with the Chinese Communist Party—quickly distanced themselves from Butker. Had he spoken about the virtues of Hamas or gender ideology, his critics would have lauded him.

Make no mistake, those who waged the attacks on Butker were driven by anti-Catholicism. The Associated Press unleashed a string of red flags about Benedictine College being "part of a constellation of conservative Catholic colleges that tout their adherence to church teachings and practice—part of a larger conservative movement in part of the U.S. Catholic Church."[50] Moreover, it was astonishing to read that three in ten Americans (29 percent) disapproved of his First Amendment right to express his religious beliefs—at a Catholic school, no less!

The spring of 2024 witnessed many attacks on tradition. In fact, what happened on elite college campuses was a celebration of hatred, violence, anti-Americanism, and Jew hatred. It was another example of the way the ruling class elites work in tandem with radical activists.

The pro-Hamas demonstrators who took over their campuses burned the American flag, harassed Jewish students, and praised Hamas terrorists. They were aided and abetted by outside activists, and many of them were paid by the ruling class. Among the most prominent organizations to do so was the Tides Foundation.

According to the Capital Research Center, "If the Left does it, Tides funds it."[51] It receives its money from Soros, the Ford Foundation, Rockefeller Brothers Fund, Rockefeller Foundation, Rockefeller Philanthropy Advisors, William and Flora Hewett Foundation, Silicon Valley Community Foundation, and K. Kellogg Foundation. It specializes in "pass-through funding," a mechanism that shuffles money to communist-inspired organizations such as the Working Family Party.

Tides managed to underwrite two of the most pro-Hamas organizations responsible for the campus riots: Jewish Voice for Peace and IfNotNow. Another source of funds for this crusade was the Wall Street king, Goldman Sachs.

Here's how the elites play their game.

Goldman Sachs Philanthropy Fund funnels money to The People's Forum, a left-wing entity with ties to the Chinese Communist Party. It is backed by American businessman Neville Roy Singham, who is well-known to the Communist dictators. He uses Goldman Sachs' charity arm as a pass-through to The People's Forum. Though Goldman Sachs maintains it has no direct ties to this group, in a circuitous way, it does.

Singham lives in Shanghai, but he is active in the U.S. For example, he took the $785 million he made in the sale of his Chicago software company and invested it in Marxist groups in America. He bankrolled The People's Forum, led by Monolo De Los Santos, enabling them to lead the protests at Columbia University in 2024. De Los Santos has said that after the radicals defeat Israel, they will set their sights on the U.S. He has been traveling to Cuba for decades, getting advice from the Communist elite.

The protesting students on campus have much in common with their well-heeled donors. The rich live a pristine lifestyle, unaffected by the consequences of their ideas. Meanwhile, the student stooges take over university buildings with impunity, having food delivered to them by Uber drivers.

In essence, the difference between rulers and radicals has mostly vanished, despite what elites say. By contrast, the teachings and policies of the Catholic Church have nothing to do with supporting radical causes funded by the ruling class. Which explains why it is hated by both groups.

Chapter 2

The Quest for a Compliant Citizenry

Beware the "Quiet Men"

On March 8, 1983, President Ronald Reagan addressed the National Association of Evangelicals. This is when he made his famous "evil empire" speech, calling out the Soviet Union for its monstrous legacy. But he also said something that day that gets closer to what this book entails. He quoted from C. S. Lewis's *Screwtape Letters*.

"The greatest evil is not done now in those sordid 'dens of crime' that Dickens loved to paint. It is not even done in concentration camps and labor camps. In those we see the final result. But it is conceived and ordered (moved, seconded, carried and minuted) in clear, carpeted, warmed, and well-lighted offices, by quiet men with white collars and cut fingernails and smooth-shaven cheeks who do not need to raise their voice."[52]

It is the quiet men who comprise the ruling class whom we must guard against. As we have seen, many have adopted the radical political agenda, so they are increasingly one and the same. While some of the more extreme radicals take to the streets and are not averse to resorting to violence, most of them more closely resemble the quiet men who run establishment organizations.

Notice that Lewis referred to this kind of elite behavior as evil. The late journalist Lance Morrow knew this subject well. "Many people believe evil doesn't exist. That view is especially common among the rational and enlightened, who insist that events always have a scientific, clinical or political explanation. They are mistaken. Evil is real, with a spooky, inscrutable life of its own."[53]

The quiet men who are capable of evil want an obedient populace. They like it when the average Joe falls in line, single file. Here's a real-life example.

In 2016, Bill Ivey, chairman of the National Endowment for the Arts under President Bill Clinton, sent an email to John Podesta, the manager of Hillary Clinton's presidential campaign, suggesting how Clinton could make inroads against Donald Trump. He noted that "we've all been quite content to demean government, drop civics and in general conspire to produce an unaware and compliant citizenry."[54]

Ivey and Clinton are convinced that the American people are basically stupid. They see this as a fortuitous moment ripe for exploitation. If the masses are unaware that they are being manipulated, it would make it easier for elites to secure their compliance. But if they look for guidance from sources other than government—from Christianity—that would pose a problem.

Contemptuous. Arrogant. Yes, what Ivey said is both. But it is worse than this: the advice he offered is what these people really believe. Dangerous would be a more accurate description of this mindset. After all, the people we are talking about are not ordinary zealots—they are the elites who occupy the command centers in society.

Catholicism Disdains Compliant Citizenry

Standing against the quiet men who want a compliant citizenry is the Catholic Church. Some may find it hypocritical for the Church to insist that its members show fidelity to its teachings but not extend the same courtesy to the state when it demands compliance with its strictures. But the Church is a voluntary organization; those who find its mandates overbearing can leave. In the kind of society that Huxley, and to a lesser extent Orwell, portray, there is no escape path. When the people are seduced and manipulated by the state, they are rendered impotent.

The Catholic Church has always supported a vibrant civil society, one where the people find community in the mediating institutions of the family, church, voluntary organizations, and the like. This cannot be achieved by a passive populace. On the contrary, it relies on participation.

In 1971, Pope Paul VI noted that the desire for equality and participation "grow stronger to the extent that modern man becomes better informed and better educated."[55] Catholic teachings stress that the dignity of the human person is contingent on the ability of citizens to participate in the affairs of their community. The American bishops, in their pastoral letter on the economy, noted that the "ultimate injustice" is "for a person or group to be actively abandoned as if they were non-members of the human race. To treat people this way is effectively to say that they simply do not count as human beings."[56]

This is what we are up against. Following what Huxley feared, there are some elites, and radicals as well, who do not want a society that prizes participation; they want one that prizes passivity. In 1985, Pope Saint John Paul II gave his World Day of Peace Message, saying, "It is essential for every human being to have a sense of participating, of being part of the decisions and endeavors that shape the destiny of the world."[57] Six years later, in *Centesimus Annus*, he reaffirmed the Church's commitment to the mediating institutions, essentially underscoring the need for men and women to create social institutions that "have their own autonomy with a view to the common good."[58] In other words, we should not look to the state to fulfill our duties to our fellow man; we should look to each other.

The Catholic Church's embrace of a participatory democracy is conditioned on our obligation to promote the good society; it does not apply to policies that are fundamentally unjust. Indeed, Catholics are permitted to engage in civil disobedience when the government egregiously violates basic human rights. This is the kind of participation that the rulers envisioned by Huxley feared most. We must be guided by our conscience, the Church instructs, and when the government shows nothing but contempt for natural law and natural rights, we are obliged to oppose it.

The United States Conference of Catholic Bishops (USCCB) issued a document in 2023 titled "Forming Consciences For Faithful Citizenship" that underscores the Church's commitment to participatory democracy. "In the

Catholic Tradition," the bishops said, "responsible citizenship is a virtue, and participation in political life is a moral obligation." They maintain that this obligation is "rooted in our baptismal commitment to follow Jesus Christ and to bear Christian witness in all we do."[59]

The Catholic conception of a healthy society assumes the individual will be guided by a well-formed conscience and participate vigorously in the political affairs of his nation. He will not assume a passive position, letting the elites determine his thoughts and deeds. This explains why the ruling class, following the totalitarian impulses of radical intellectuals and activists, always has Christianity in its crosshairs.

Soft Totalitarianism

The vision of society that excites Ivey and Clinton—inducing compliance—is an example of "soft totalitarianism."

Many writers use the term "soft totalitarianism" to distinguish between the "hard totalitarianism" associated with Hitler, Stalin, and Mao, and the more insidious variety that seeks to undermine such basic institutions as marriage and the family. For Catholic theologian George Weigel, "soft totalitarianism" harms civil society, undermining "the social and cultural foundations of democracy."[60] When the state intrudes on those institutions that stand between the individual and the state—most notably the family and the church—it weakens them, making the people more susceptible to government agents. To those whose goal is to create a compliant citizenry, the appeal of "soft totalitarianism" is irresistible.

Rod Dreher, also writing from a Christian perspective, sees "soft totalitarianism" as offering a therapeutic approach, one that operates under "the guise of helping and healing." But it is no less a threat to liberty than earlier, more violent expressions of totalitarianism. "Today's totalitarianism demands allegiance to a set of progressive beliefs, many of which are incompatible with logic—and certainly with Christianity. Compliance is forced less by the state than by elites who form public opinion, and by private corporations that, thanks to technology, control our lives far more than we would like to admit."[61]

More than any institution, religious or secular, the Catholic Church has the richest and most impressive record of combating totalitarianism, be it of the "hard" or "soft" variety. Pope Pius XII did more to resist Hitler and rescue Jews than any other leader in the 1930s and 1940s. He won the plaudits of the editorial board of the *New York Times* and the international Jewish community for doing so. This was before revisionist accounts appeared.

Pope Saint John Paul II not only wrote about totalitarianism, but he played a major role in bringing about its demise in the USSR. He faced the kind of regime that Orwell wrote about—namely, the "hard totalitarianism" made famous by Hitler and Stalin (and later Mao). Orwell described their rule as a police state, marked by an all-consuming surveillance. To achieve order, torture and execution were the chosen weapons.

Less well-known is what John Paul II had to say about the softer variant being played out in the democracies. This is closer to what Huxley feared: the ability of the ruling class to appease the masses, resulting in a subservient populace. To avoid this, the pope was insistent on the need for the democracies to be guided by truth, not power; otherwise, they will turn into a "thinly disguised totalitarianism."[62] This is the specter that is haunting the West today.

The fundamental problem with "soft totalitarianism" is its ability to manipulate the masses without drawing attention to its means and its ends. For example, those who lived under totalitarian rule in the twentieth century knew exactly what to fear—their henchmen were brutally open about their monstrous deeds—but those subjected to a softer form of rule are often unable to see it for what it is. It is for this reason that Catholic philosopher Joseph Pieper regarded it as the most dangerous form of totalitarianism. It never appears to be what it is.

Democratic Despotism

The French Enlightenment philosopher Charles Louis de Secondat, Baron de La Brède et de Montesquieu, is known for his writings on democracy, specifically his conviction that without a separation of powers, no functioning democracy could ever work. Less well-known was his admonition that democracies were prone to despotism. He warned against the comforts that a bourgeois culture spawned, one that made the people unaware of the political ambitions of its rulers. The masses, he said, were easily manipulated, making the use of force unnecessary. The "'perfect subject' in a despotism demands to be dominated without being consulted."[63]

What Montesquieu envisioned sounds remarkably like the kind of society that Bill Ivey recommends, one where a compliant citizenry is the norm. We all know our place, acceding to the strictures of our rulers without dissent or fanfare. Spoiled and seduced, our reticence is precisely what allows the quiet men to be despotic. It's a home run for the rulers and a strike out for their subjects.

A century later, another French writer, Alexis de Tocqueville, wrote his masterpiece, *Democracy in America*. His understanding of the uniqueness, and the genius, of the American experiment in democracy is unparalleled. But he also drew attention to what he called "democratic despotism."

Unlike living under the absolute rule of a monarchy, democratic despotism is "mild despotism." No one is executed, but everyone conforms their thinking and orients their behavior, to comply with the agenda of the ruling class. The people willfully cooperate in their own subservience, a dream come true for their masters.

"It is in the nature of absolute power in democratic ages not to be savage or cruel," Tocqueville observed, "but meddlesome in detail."[64] Those who would micromanage the lives of the people would not be tyrants, he said; rather, they would more resemble schoolmasters. "Thus I think the kind of oppression which threatens democracies is different from anything there has ever been in the world before."[65] What makes this oppression so troubling is the immense power afforded to the ruling class. "That power is absolute, thoughtful in detail, orderly, provident, and gentle." The goal is to keep the masses "in perpetual childhood." Indeed, "it likes to see the citizens enjoy themselves, provided that they think of nothing but enjoyment."[66] The rulers see to it that the people are taken care of, but it comes with a price—their dignity.

Give Them Plenty of Bread

The ruling class is very good at taking care of people, just as Tocqueville noted. But their interest is guided by politics, not charity. It's about keeping the people, especially the poor, satisfied and in their place. This is exactly what the ancient Roman poet Juvenal predicted—give the people "bread and circuses," and they will be content. In essence, the average Joe can be bought.

Economist Richard K. Vedder notes that the New Deal in the 1930s provided bread to the masses in the form of welfare, as did the Great Society programs of the 1960s.[67] This was augmented by Obama and Biden when they expanded these welfare programs beyond recognition, particularly the federal food stamp rolls (known as the SNAP benefit).

John Keane, an Australian political scientist, is more critical. He says welfare programs in democratic nations are "among the favored strategies of despots." He says, "These handouts and programs have a vassalage quality, resembling the medieval European practice of lords handing out benefice in exchange for their subjects' loyalty." He contends that the ruling class buys the loyalty of "the powerless" by "using a range of welfare measures," and that the quid pro quo works just fine.[68] The rulers are also buying subservience, which is exactly what Huxley feared would happen.

There is little doubt that welfare recipients give up a good measure of their autonomy in exchange for government largesse. This was not the case in the preindustrial era when local churches formed a bond with the recipients of their charity. But when the state provides the "bread," no such bond exists between bureaucrats and their faceless recipients. Regrettably, the state is not only buying loyalty but also generating dependency. The cost of this condition comes at a big price, both economically and personally. But it secures the kind of social stability that at least some members of the ruling class want. Huxley said that social stability was so important to the ruling class that he called it "the primal and the ultimate need."[69]

Recall that in Tocqueville's analysis of "democratic despotism," he warned us about the masses being kept "in perpetual childhood" by a power that is "absolute, thoughtful in detail, orderly provident, and gentle." This is about as good a summary of the welfare state today as there is in print. Dependency is a hallmark. Those who are dependent are not in a position to challenge the ruling class, and they typically become complacent in their subservience. They also lose their civic spirit, rendering them politically impotent.

Tocqueville came to his conclusion based on the behavioral consequences of the first government program to provide for the poor—namely, the eighteenth-century British policy initiative known as the Speenhamland system. He wrote a prescient statement on the characterological effects of state-sponsored welfare programs. "Any measure which establishes legal charity on a permanent basis and gives it an administrative form thereby creates an idle and lazy class."[70]

Welfare, he said, induces the pauperization of the masses. This is the cost of throwing "bread" at the poor. It should be noted that Tocqueville did not witness pauperism in Spain and Portugal, where there were a lot more poor but little in the way of moral delinquency. That's because they had no state welfare program.

We should have learned by now that, although there are good humanitarian reasons to assist those who cannot provide for themselves, programs that allow able-bodied persons to avoid work by enrolling them in welfare programs are doing a disservice to them and society. What we have created is more akin to a master-slave relationship than anything else. This is the kind of scenario Huxley saw coming.

The latest scheme to expand the welfare rolls is called Universal Basic Income (UBI). It is already being tested in some cities, and some political elites want it to go national. It had the support of Pope Francis—he wanted to help the poor and was a foe of income inequality—though it is not certain he truly understood how this policy plays out in real life.[71]

There are three aspects to UBI. The first is that it is a cash transfer, not a service-based program. Recipients are given money that they decide how to spend; this is quite different from programs that offer in-kind assistance for housing and food. Second, it is universal, meaning that everyone is included; it is not targeted at some specific demographic group. Third, it is unconditional and not dependent on recipients meeting some criteria.

This sounds novel, and in many ways, it is, but the outcomes have already been assessed, and they are not fortuitous. Indeed, the kind of docility that Huxley feared, and the kind of behavioral consequences that Tocqueville noted in the Speenhamland experiment, have come true.

Nicholas Eberstadt is a dogged researcher and political economist at the American Enterprise Institute. He and a research assistant, Evan Abramsky, analyzed the data from the American Time Use Survey, an initiative of the Bureau of Labor Statistics. They detailed self-reported information on roughly ten thousand prime-age men who are not in the labor force, meaning they are neither working nor looking for work. "By examining the self-reported patterns of daily life of these grown men who do not have and are not seeking jobs, we may gain insights into the work-free existence that some UBI advocates hold to be a positive end in its own right."[72]

What they found was disturbing but predictable. What did these men do during the day? They could have helped doing housework, cooking, or doing home maintenance. But they didn't. When compared to unemployed men and women with jobs, they actually spent significantly less time doing these things. They also spent a lot less time helping to take care of other household members.

So what exactly did they do with their time? Watch TV? Yup. They spent their days "socializing, relaxing, and leisure." Regarding the latter, these men spent about seven and a half hours a day on leisure activities, most of it (over five hours) spent watching TV. That comes to about 1,900 hours a year, which the researchers note is "almost equivalent to the time commitment of a full-time job."[73]

The researchers cite a study by Alan Krueger, who also studied these men. Their capsule summary of his work is worth repeating. "The rhythms of life for a great many of the prime-age men in America currently disengaged with the world of work is defined not simply by days and nights sitting in front of screens—but sitting in front of screens numbed or stoned."[74]

Eberstadt and Abramsky observe that "there would seem to be no shortage of anomie, alienation, or even despair in the daily lives of men entirely free from work in America today." They're right.

I see it almost every day in New York City. In the Penn Station area where I work, there are a countless numbers of men who appear to be able-bodied but who are simply hanging out, doing nothing. Many are stoned. This has grave implications for UBI, as the researchers note. "Why, then, would we not expect a UBI—which would surely result in a detachment of more men from paid employment—to result in even more of the same?"[75]

The ruling elites are the ones who are pushing UBI. To some extent, they are just giving up on the underclass and want to "take care of them." But in doing so, they are creating more of them. That, no doubt, fits into their game plan: the more docile this segment of society is, the more secure the elites feel. We are already at a stage in American history where more are reliant than ever before on government aid, so it is troubling to see elites wanting to go down this road even further.

Since UBI has no restrictions—people can spend the money any way they want—would this not incentivize irresponsible behavior? It already has.

Washington, D.C., mayor Muriel Bowser experimented with a UBI program of her own. She gave 132 mothers monthly payments of $900 or $10,800 lump sum to see if it would lead to "economic improvement." She called it her "equitable economic recovery strategy."[76] But there was nothing equitable about the way Canethia Miller spent her dough. She had a rollicking good time.

Miller took her stash and went on a "five-day, $6,000 trip to Miami." She said she put some of the money aside but decided, "I wanted to blow it. I wanted to have fun." She reportedly had lots of fun, but not before she treated herself to a makeover: she spent $180 to get her hair and nails done.[77]

This is an example of the "circus" end of the "bread and circuses" gambit introduced by the Romans. Huxley predicted this would happen, and he was right.

Count the Catholic Church Out

When it comes to treating work as a tonic to soothe the masses and treating welfare as a means to keep the poor subservient, count the Catholic Church out. It takes a much more positive and robust approach to these subjects. Unlike the ruling class and radicals, it has no hidden agenda.

Pope Francis was adamant in his conviction that "there is no poverty worse than that which takes away work and the dignity of work."[78] This is the mirror opposite of the position taken by contemporary proponents of the Roman give-them-bread approach to work. Pope Saint John Paul II understood that, unlike all earthly creatures, only man is capable of work. Indeed, he is "*called to work*."[79]

Our saintly pope touched on something all Americans can identify with. In many ways, we are defined by the work we do. When we meet someone for the first time, we typically ask, "What do you do?" No one says they walk, talk, eat, and sleep, though that is what we all do. They give an occupational answer. The pope believed that work is good for man because he *achieves fulfillment* as a human being. Those in the command posts who want a compliant citizenry are more interested in satisfying man's needs without engaging him in the workplace. They are prepared to offer "bread" in return for acquiescence, thus denying man the kind of fulfillment the pope said we need.

The Catholic Church believes in a "preferential option for the poor." It is biblically based. "You shall not oppress the poor or vulnerable" (Ex 22:20–26). "Speak out in defense of the poor" (Prv 31:8–9). "What you do for the least among you, you do for me [Jesus]" (Mt 25:34–40). "Blessed are the poor, theirs is the kingdom of Heaven" (Lk 6:20–23). Tradition holds the same. The U.S. bishops' conference explains, "The prime purpose of this special commitment to the poor is to enable them to become active participants in the life of society."[80] That is why the Catholic understanding of work and welfare is "a much more positive and robust approach" than the one posited by rulers and radicals.

No one epitomized the Catholic approach to working with the poor more than Saint Mother Teresa. If ever there were an altruist, it was her. She selflessly gave of herself for decades, helping the sick and dying, picking them up off the street, securing medicinal care, and comforting them in their closing days. And she never asked anything in return.

Those she ministered to were the most destitute of them all: children who survived abortions, the malnourished, lepers, AIDS patients, the physically and mentally handicapped, elderly cripples—she never turned anyone away. Indeed, she implored those who would abandon the dispossessed—this included hospital staff—to "give them to me."[81]

In the 1980s, Mother Teresa founded the first AIDS hospice in New York City. The mayor, Ed Koch, was astonished by her compassion. "She said that when AIDS patients were near death, she would sit at their bedside. Often they would take her hands and place her fingers on their faces wanting her to feel their lesions and to close their eyelids for the last time."[82]

She never thought of herself as a miracle worker. Her goal was to comfort the sick and dying, but she also provided medical assistance. She gave them the love we all crave, something modern welfare systems cannot ever give. When British Prime Minister Margaret Thatcher touted her welfare program, the saintly nun replied, "But do you have love?"[83]

Radicals claim to champion the cause of the poor. In fact, they do nothing for them, save to promote more poverty with their socialist prescriptions. That is what I told Christopher Hitchens, the English atheist who hated Mother Teresa. Why would the Left have such animosity toward the diminutive Albanian nun? Because her approach to the poor was based on a private, voluntary effort grounded in Christianity. Atheist socialists, therefore, saw her as a threat. They were right about that.

Pope Saint John Paul II warned us about the effects of a bureaucratic state trying to alleviate poverty. He was not opposed to welfare programs, per se, but he was concerned about concentrating too much power in the hands of the state.

The American bishops have a different but related concern, and it is one that addresses the prospects of democratic despotism. "Welfare policy should reduce poverty and dependency, strengthen family life, and help families leave poverty through work, training, and assistance with child care, health care, housing, and transportation."[84] As they quite rightly noted, poverty has a cultural dimension, not just an economic one. If we are to make progress, welfare programs must address those factors that lead to family breakdown and that, paradoxically, would include these very programs.

What Mother Teresa embodied, and what John Paul II and the American bishops were getting at, is what the Church fathers call subsidiarity. Those who are closest to the problem are best suited to fix it. In other words, while there is a role for government welfare programs, those who work at the local level are better situated to deal with the indigent than those who are not near them.

The Catholic Church does not see the poor as a segment of society that needs to be tamed and subdued. It does not see them as an entity to be exploited for political gain. It sees them as human beings whose needs must be met. That sounds rather simple, but when compared to the ambitions of elites and radicals, it is anything but pedestrian.

Placating the Masses

It takes more than "bread" to appease the average Joe; it is important to keep him entertained. Orwell knew this to be true when he observed that the goal of the party is to cultivate docility. The working class, called the "proles" (proletariat), are trained to enjoy the types of entertainment created for them and to subordinate their interests to the interests of the party. Similarly, Huxley said what mattered most to the elites was how to keep the people happy. Not only would sex and drugs be plentiful, euthanasia would be widely practiced, thus minimizing unhappiness in the population. The Controller in *Brave New World* put it succinctly, saying the goal is "to shift the emphasis from truth and beauty to comfort and happiness."[85]

The ruling class has been quick to pick up on this thinking. There is a marketing company in Abu Dhabi that is run by the government, Flash Entertainment, whose motto is, "Put simply, we make people happy."[86] They do that by bringing in major singers and musicians from the United States.

A more dramatic exposition of this strategy to keep the people happy was unveiled in 2016 at a World Economic Forum event in Davos. Ida Auken, a former Danish environment minister, said, "Welcome to 2030. I own nothing, have no privacy, and life has never been better." This was quickly interpreted and posted on a WEF video as, "You'll own nothing. And you'll be happy."[87]

WEF superstar Yuval Noah Harari says his vision of the future includes anti-depressant "happy pills" that will keep the average Joe in his place.[88] Recall that Harari is the same guy who is worried about what to do with all the "useless people" in society. In his mind, they are a drag. It would be hard to find a conviction more out of step with the Catholic Church's emphasis on the human dignity that inheres in every human being than this.

To guard against the boredom that the average Joe experiences, there must be plenty in the way of fun and distractions, or what the Roman elite called "circuses." What's different today is that the elites have succeeded to such an extent that the average Joe has managed to entertain himself, unmanipulated by the ruling class.

It is astonishing how many Americans are in constant need of being entertained. When I was a young man, most of the passengers on the Long Island Rail Road were reading a book or a newspaper. Now, few do. They are on their phones, talking to whomever, playing video games, watching a TV show or movie, doing puzzles, shopping, listening to music, gambling online—but few are reading.

Worse, when many people meet their friends in bars, restaurants, and clubs, after a quick hello, they go right back to their phones. As soon as they actually get together, they can't wait to converse with someone who is not with them. And as soon as they get together with that person, they contact someone else. Even more maddening is the sight of family members sitting in a restaurant not talking to each other. The kids have their videos, and the adults are texting away.

Sports can be a great way to have fun, but they can also be a great way to divert attention from the machinations of the ruling class. For example, the elites who run the National

Football League are very good at exploiting our preoccupation with sports (the NFL is also run by those who are knee-deep in the politics of the Left). It used to be Sunday games. Then they added Monday games. Then they added Thursday games. They keep adding more regular season games and playoff games. Predictably, government elites are partnering with the NFL elites. Between 1970 and 2020, state and local governments spent $33 billion in public funds to build stadiums in North America; the median public contribution covered 73 percent of the costs.

Lyman Stone, a social scientist, studied this subject and found something else at work. "Modern governments actively promote sports, not only for nationalist reasons but as benign, politically nonthreatening entertainment to accompany the welfare state. Bread and circuses is not only an ancient Roman phenomenon but also the actual function of modern sports."[89]

Educator Neil Postman sees what is happening to our society and how right Huxley was. "When a population becomes distracted by trivia, when cultural life is redefined as a perpetual round of entertainments, when serious public conversation becomes a form of baby-talk, when, in short, a people become an audience, and their public business a vaudeville act, then a nation finds itself at risk; culture-death is a clear possibility."[90] Or, as one of the members of the ruling class puts it in *Brave New World*, "We condition the masses to hate the country. But simultaneously we condition them to love all country sports."[91] Entertainment can also divert attention from serious threats to the ruling class.

When Rev. Martin Luther King Jr. was murdered in 1968, protests turned violent in several cities. The mayor of Boston, Kevin White, sought to avoid a riot by asking African American rock star James Brown to let his scheduled concert at the Boston Garden air on local television, hoping to induce black youths to stay home and watch him perform. Brown agreed. Few showed up to see him perform in person, but most watched him on TV. There were no riots.

In the 1980s, as a way of getting young black men to stay off the streets at night, "midnight basketball" debuted in Chicago and later in many other cities. It was invented to reduce crime between 10 p.m. and 2 a.m. Did it work? For the most part, yes. A 2006 study of "midnight basketball" games held in predominantly black neighborhoods between 1990 and 1994 found that crimes declined markedly. Property crimes, drug-related crimes, and violent crimes declined.[92]

Drugs

If there is one proven way the ruling class induces docility, it is by facilitating drug use.

Huxley said the inhabitants of the *Brave New World* would be enslaved by "soma," meaning drugs. As noted, the goal of the ruling class is to craft a compliant citizenry, one where the people will be complacent and happy. Drugs do the job. As Huxley put it, soma is there to "calm your anger, to reconcile you to your enemies, to make you patient and long-suffering." It is no longer necessary to work hard to achieve these outcomes. "Now you swallow two or three half gramme tablets, and there you are. Anybody can be virtuous now. You can carry at least half your mortality about in a bottle. Christianity without tears—that's what *soma* is."[93] To put it differently, when we experience adversity, there is no need to "offer it up" to Christ—just reach for a joint, a needle, or a crack pipe. Bingo, the pain is gone.

Municipalities and states are making it easier to buy marijuana, and in some cities, they are allowing much stronger drugs. Only the naïve thought it would slow demand. All the talk about decriminalizing drugs, or legalizing them altogether, was based on the assumption that it would end the black market. In fact, it grew. Who needs to pay taxes for drugs when they're available on the street for much less? Moreover, Uncle Sam will never legalize all drugs, and there will always be a cap on how much anyone can buy. But none of this applies to the black marketers. The net result: more people are becoming addicted, and that means more of them are increasingly dysfunctional, dependent on government. It would be hard to write a better script to promote docility.

Here again, elites and radicals have something in common. The radicals want liberty without limits, and that includes partaking in as many drugs as they fancy. Their motto was well said by psychologist Timothy Leary in the 1960s: "Turn on, tune in, drop out." The one-time Harvard professor loved LSD, becoming the most famous advocate of psychedelic drugs. But some in the ruling class like drugs too.

Rep. John Boehner was Speaker of the House, and in 2011, the Republican stalwart proclaimed that he was "unalterably opposed to the legalization of marijuana."[94] After he retired in 2015, he joined the board of a cannabis company and soon became the poster boy for legalizing marijuana.

Money has a way of persuading people. In 2019, it was reported that he stood to make $20 million hawking weed. In 2024, in a spirit of bipartisanship, the Biden administration pushed hard to deemphasize the negative effects of marijuana, putting it in a new classification that no longer treated it as a serious drug.

In the mid-nineteenth century, the British used opium to destabilize China. More recently, China has been flooding the U.S. market with fentanyl to destabilize America. According to Peter Schweizer, who has studied this issue carefully, China is out to beat the U.S. with drugs, not guns. The fentanyl it is distributing is thirty to fifty times as powerful as heroin. In 2024, the House Select Committee on the Chinese Communist Party released a report that was damning. "The fentanyl trade boosts China's economy has allowed Chinese organized crime to become the world's premier money launderers with US law enforcement finding evidence indicating that money laundering schemes involved Chinese government officials and the Chinese Communist Party elite."[95]

There we have it. Elites in the United States and Communist China align to make money and induce docility in the masses. Getting what they want makes them happy, and drug users are happy to indulge their base appetites.

The Catholic Church's Conception of Happiness

Catholics love sports and entertainment as much as anyone, and there is nothing in Catholic social teaching that is censorious about them. Drugs are a different story—the Church is firmly opposed to them. Where the Church and the ruling class differ on sports and entertainment is over their reasons for liking them: the elites see them as a control mechanism, making it easier to produce a compliant citizenry; the Church has no ulterior motive. Moreover, unlike the ruling class, which has a sinister idea of making the average Joe "happy," the Church's understanding of happiness has nothing to do with manipulating the masses.

Father John A. Hardon asked, "How it is possible what everyone is looking for, so few seem to find?"[96] He is speaking about true happiness, and what he has to say is very different from what the ruling class and radicals believe. He mentions three characteristics.

"True happiness does not consist in sex indulgence. That brings its victims only remorse and degradation and disease and an early grave." Second, "true happiness is generosity. People who are generous are happy people." Third is the "most important condition of true happiness, namely, its relationship with God."[97]

The Catholic understanding of happiness is the total opposite of what elites and radicals believe. It embraces self-discipline, self-giving, and fidelity to the Almighty. It has nothing to do with creating a society where subservience to the elites is the preeminent goal. If anything, it wants a citizenry where the people are participatory.

It's bizarre. The myth that the hierarchy of the Catholic Church nurtures a mindless obedience in the faithful is still prevalent in some quarters. This is pure nonsense. Fidelity, yes; subservience, no. In truth, it is the ruling class, following the advice of radicals, that are the supreme control freaks. As we will see in the next two chapters, that involves thought control and behavioral control.

Chapter 3

Thought Control

Tradition means something special to all peoples, and for most Americans, it is intimately tied to our patriotic history. But there are some members of the ruling class, coached and coaxed by radicals, who see tradition as anathema, as something worthy of being discarded. They are more interested in erasing the past than in preserving it. That way, they can take command and institute their agenda. Attempts to delegitimize our history inevitably pits elites and radicals against Christianity, the font of our traditions.

Both Huxley and Orwell saw erasing the past as a priority for ruling elites. It remains so today in many elite quarters.

Huxley's *Brave New World* is set in London, six hundred years in the future. It is a society without war, hunger, and disease, but there are other elements that made it a disaster. The past would be scrubbed free, with no recollections of history, art, and literature. Most important, religion would be eliminated, thus setting the table for the power brokers to secure the total allegiance of its subjects. The average Joe would be stripped of his primal fidelity to God, making him susceptible to the overtures of the ruling class. What follows should ring a bell. The parallels with our country today are striking.

The Controller in Huxley's story declares, "History is bunk," explaining, "That's why you're taught no history."[98] When he is asked by a dissenter why some books, such as those written by Shakespeare, are prohibited, he is told, "Because it's old; that's the chief reason. We haven't any use for old things here."[99] Similarly, museums have been closed and historical monuments have been blown up.

Orwell depicted a similar reality. If someone was caught with a diary—that represents the past—he could be punished by death.[100] The ruling class, known as the Party, wiped out the past. "Every record has been destroyed or falsified, every book has been rewritten, every picture has been repainted, every statue and street and building has been renamed, every date has been altered."[101] Why? The Party slogan is, "Who controls the past controls the future; who controls the present controls the past."[102]

In *1984*, Winston Smith, an unhappy low-ranking member of the Party, worked at the Ministry of Truth, altering historical documents to fit the ideological predilections of Big Brother. Much the same is being done today in the United States, whether by government bureaucrats or college professors. Rewriting history is emblematic of "soft totalitarianism" and "democratic despotism."

Some of those who work in government and education, as well as the high tech industry, are already using artificial intelligence (AI) to reshape the past. Two students of this phenomenon, Jacob N. Shapiro and Chris Mattmann, note that "history can be a powerful tool for manipulation and malfeasance. The same generative AI that can fake current events can also fake past ones." This does not bode well.

"The prospects of political actors using generative AI to effectively reshape history—not to mention fraudsters creating spurious legal documents and transaction records—are frightening."[103] Indeed, Google's AI chatbot Gemini has already faced a mountain of criticism for revising history, offering a left-wing understanding, of course. AI is grist for propaganda merchants.

Members of the ruling class, especially those in government, have been working hand in hand with radical activists to scrub our history clean of anything that puts a positive face on Christianity. Statues and monuments of historical figures in the annals of Christianity have been targeted by vandals for defacement or destruction. The persons they choose to defile are judged unfairly, applying today's standards to yesterday's understandings. It is essentially an ahistorical exercise.

The bishop of Madison, Wisconsin, Donald Hying, was so alarmed by the trashing of iconic figures that he asked, "Should certain statues be placed in museums or storage? Perhaps. Should we let a group of vandals make those decisions for us? No." He also made a good historical point by criticizing radicals who claim that Christianity represents "white supremacy." He cogently notes that "in the Catholic Church, every culture, country, ethnicity, and race has claimed Jesus and the Blessed Virgin Mary as their own."[104]

Columbus and Fr. Serra

When it comes to erasing the past, one of the most popular historical figures to beat up on is Christopher Columbus.

Today's radicals, aided and abetted by many in the ruling class, would have us believe that he destroyed the Garden of Eden created by the Indians. This is bunk.

Robert Royal, the Catholic scholar, has written a great deal about Columbus and the Indians, and he offers a more mature understanding of what happened. "Long before Columbus," he writes, "indigenous peoples practiced slavery, human sacrifice, torture, racism, sexism, imperialism, colonialism, and much more that we would object to today alongside their great achievements." He further notes that those who believe that the Indians "were innocents living in perfect harmony with God, nature, and one another, have set themselves up for deep disillusion when they actually look into the record."[105]

Columbus, Royal says, was no saint, but he was inspired by his Catholicism. This was not lost on Fr. Bartolomé de las Casas, the sixteenth-century Dominican priest known as the "defender of the Indians." He understood Columbus's shortcomings but he also noted his "sweetness and benignity" of character and his deep faith. He never questioned his motives. "Truly, I would not dare blame the admiral's intentions, for I knew him well and I know his intentions were good."[106]

Carol Delaney, a former professor at Stanford and Brown universities, wrote an informative book on Columbus wherein she noted that Columbus not only had good relations with the Indians, calling them "very intelligent," but he "fervently believed it was the duty of every Christian to try to save the souls of non-Christians." His religious convictions were evident when he ordered the settlers to "treat the native people with respect."[107] He meant what he said. On his third voyage in August 1500, he hanged men who disobeyed him by harming the native people.[108]

None of this is discussed by radicals who want to erase the past by demonizing Columbus. Their goal is to rid from the public mind any good deeds done by him, treating him as some kind of monster who oppressed his subjects. They also seek to implant an intellectually dishonest account of indigenous peoples, portraying them as angelic. It would be more accurate to say that there were noble and ignoble people in all camps.

While frying Columbus is the big fish for radicals, their gross attacks on Fr. Junípero Serra are even more dishonest. With good reason, Pope Francis canonized Serra in 2015: The eighteenth-century Spanish priest courageously defended the human rights of Indians in North America. With malice, radicals effectively turned a saint into Satan, something which is not simply immoral but evil.

In August 2017, "Murder" was written on a statue of Saint Serra. His hands were painted red, and a swastika was depicted on the statue of the child standing next to him. The defacement took place near the San Fernando Mission outside of Los Angeles. Two months later, a second statue was defaced at the Old Santa Barbara Mission. A statue of Serra was decapitated and splashed with bright red paint. In June 2020, a statue of him was toppled in San Francisco's Golden Gate Park, and the next day another statue of the legendary priest was torn down at Placita Olvera in Los Angeles. Four months later, demonstrators pulled down a statue of Serra in

San Rafael, California, as part of an Indigenous Peoples Day protest. The statue was taken down after being painted red.

While radicals were destroying property, the ruling class was erasing history by renaming sites originally named after Saint Serra. In September 2018, Stanford University decided to rename many places on campus that gave tribute to him. Serra Mall was renamed "Jane Stanford Way" in honor of Jane Stanford, cofounder of the university. Campus buildings were also slated to be renamed. In 2021, California governor Gavin Newsom signed legislation to remove a statue of Serra from the state capitol in Sacramento. A few weeks later, Los Angeles mayor Eric Garcetti announced that the park across from Union Station, which was commonly referred to as Fr. Junípero Serra Park, would be renamed.

Did any of these radicals or elites know anything about Saint Serra other than left-wing propaganda? If they had read books about him—I read many of them and published a monograph based on them, "The Noble Legacy of Father Serra"—they would never have acted the way they did.[109] Their ignorance was stunning. Here's a quick look at what I found.

Junípero Serra was born on the island of Majorca, off the coast of Spain, in 1713. He died in Monterey, California, in 1784. Partly of Jewish ancestry, this young and sickly boy applied to enter the Order of St. Francis of Assisi; he became a Franciscan in 1731.

He is known as the greatest missionary in U.S. history, traveling 24,000 miles, baptizing and confirming thousands of persons, mostly Indians (in 1777, the Vatican authorized Serra to administer the sacrament of Confirmation, usually the reserve of a bishop). He had but one goal: to facilitate eternal salvation for the Indians of North America.

Culturally, the Indians appeared inferior, but they were not seen as racially inferior. For example, when Serra first met the Chumash Indians of Southern California, he and the Franciscans were struck by how different they looked and behaved. The women were partially naked, and the men were totally naked. Moreover, the Indians had no written language and practiced no agriculture. They lived by hunting, fishing, and gathering. They ate cats and dogs, owls and rats, but none of this stopped them from getting along with the Franciscans.

The primary reason they got along well is because the Catholic Church led the protests against inhumane treatment of the Indians; the Spanish crown ultimately agreed with this position. It cannot be said too strongly that the principal mission of the Franciscans was not to conquer the Indians but to make them good Christians. The missions were supposed to be temporary, not some permanent takeover.

Radicals claim that violence decimated the Indians. Wrong. Diseases did. It was diseases contracted from the Spaniards that accounted for the killings. Radicals also claim that the Indians were treated the way Hitler treated the Jews. Wrong again. Hitler committed genocide against Jews; there was no genocide committed by Serra and the Franciscans against the California Indians. Hitler put Jews in ovens; the missionaries put the Indians to work, paying them for their labor. It is also wrong to argue that the Indians were treated as slaves. Slaves in the U.S. had no rights and were not considered human. The missionaries granted the Indians rights and respected their human dignity.

A total of twenty-one missions were established by the missionaries, nine of them under the tenure of Serra; he personally founded six missions. He baptized more than six thousand Indians and confirmed over five thousand; some ten thousand were baptized overall during the mission period. Impressive as these numbers are, it was his personal characteristics that made him so special.

Professor Gregory Orfalea has done yeoman's work on Serra. "To the Indian," he writes, "he [Serra] was loving, enthusiastic, and spiritually and physically devoted." His devotion was motivated by his embrace of Christianity and his strong sense of justice. To put it another way, his love for the Indians was no mere platitude. "Love thy neighbor as thyself" was routinely put into practice; he knew no other way. But it was his humility, coupled with his merciful behavior, that distinguished him from other missionaries.[110]

Serra was so merciful that he said, "in case the Indians, whether pagans or Christians, would kill me, they should be pardoned." This was not made in jest. He insisted that his request be honored as quickly as possible and even declared, "I want to see a formal decree" on this matter.[111]

Father Serra deserved to be made a saint. Shame on those who seek to erase his noble legacy by depicting him as the enemy of the Indians. That is a malicious lie.

The most malicious of lies told about Serra were told by the *New York Times*. I took them on, and they could not answer me.

A week after Pope Francis canonized Serra on September 23, 2015, the *Times* maligned him in a front-page story by Laura M. Holson, "Sainthood of Serra Reopens Wounds in Colonialism in California." She said, "Historians agree that he [Serra] forced Native Americans to abandon their tribal culture and convert to Christianity, and that he had them whipped and imprisoned and sometimes worked or tortured to death."[112]

This was a bald-faced lie. On the same day that Holson's news story was published in the newspaper, September 30, 2015, I emailed her the following: "You said that 'Historians agree' that Fr. Serra had Indians 'tortured to death.' I have done research on Serra and written about him, yet I know of no historian who makes such a claim. Please name them. I can name many who never made such a claim."[113]

When Holson did not respond, I contacted the "Corrections" section on October 1, asking for a correction; I also contacted the public editor.

"This is a serious issue: when a reporter blithely says that 'Historians agree,' readers take it that there is at least a consensus among historians about the subject. But such is not the case on this issue. The only persons given to such an accusation are radical activists, not professional scholars." I even emailed a list of "the most authoritative books on Fr. Serra." I pointed out that none of the authors whom I cited ever accused Serra of torture.[114]

After a week went by with no response, I wrote the newspaper again. I asked if someone could "name the historians who say Fr. Serra tortured Indians."[115] Finally, I received a response from Gregory E. Brock, Senior Editor for Standards at the

New York Times. He said the editors had discussed my complaint but were waiting for Holson to return from Oregon, where she had been on assignment. His response was a gem.

"Certainly you have very strong views on this issue and have written extensively about it. But after many discussions, a review of past Times coverage and other resources, I agree with Ms. Holson's editors that 'historians' is accurate, and therefore no correction is required." He closed by saying that after reading my correspondence, "I cannot think of anything we could do or say that would convince you that our coverage was fair and accurate—or that the reference to 'historians' is accurate."[116]

In response, I said the following. "Thank you for taking my complaint seriously. I have just one question: Who are the 'historians' who claim that Fr. Serra tortured Indians?"[117]

The same accusation was made in 2020 in an online opinion column by Elizabeth Bruenig, "'Racism Makes a Liar of God.'" Bruenig wrote that Serra's "eager participation in the conquest of North America" included "torture, enslavement of and murder of some of the Native Americans he intended to convert."[118] Note that she embellished the lies that Holson told.

I challenged her on the torture accusation and provided her email address to the Catholic League's email subscribers. She got so bombarded—"I received a flood of ill tidings via email"—that she was forced to write a second account on this subject.[119] While her second installment was more balanced, nowhere did she disprove my claim that Serra never tortured a single Indian.

The *New York Times* carries significant weight with the ruling class and radicals alike. That is why I felt the necessity of contesting these unfair attacks on this saintly priest. Rewriting history is what communist dictatorships are famous for doing. It is even more disturbing when it happens in democratic nations.

Thought Control

Erasing the past is symptomatic of a much larger issue—thought control. Orwell foresaw a totalitarian society where Big Brother and the Thought Police were ubiquitous and where the Party had total control. The masses would be indoctrinated with Newspeak, a propaganda-induced language called "doublethink." The Party's slogans, "War is peace" and "Freedom is slavery," were drilled into people's heads, making them prime subjects for manipulation. Winston, who became a slave to the Party, wrote in his diary that "freedom is the freedom to say that two plus two make four."[120]

There is nothing more totalitarian than thought control. History is replete with dictators, but most were content to call the political shots, having no interest in controlling the mind of the average Joe. Orwell nicely illustrated this new, much more invidious brand of tyranny.

Party officials had to lecture Winston to get in line and accept that "reality exists in the human mind, and nowhere else." The individual mind can make mistakes, he was told, but not the mind of the Party. "Whatever the Party holds to be truth *is* truth. It is impossible to see reality except by looking through the eyes of the Party."[121] To put it differently, those who insist that truth is found in Christianity simply cannot be tolerated. The ruling class will see to that.

More insight into the future was given by Huxley upon the publication of Orwell's book in 1949. He wrote to his student commending him for his work, focusing on the central aspect of *1984*—namely, the "ultimate revolution." Both of them, Huxley said, foresaw a society that "went beyond politics and economics, and which aims at the total subversion of the individual's psychology and physiology," but that does not have to rely on force to win. "My own belief is that the ruling oligarchy will find ways of governing and of satisfying its lust for power, and these ways will resemble those of which I described in *Brave New World*."[122]

Huxley was not sanguine about the future. "Within the next generation I believe that the world's rulers will discover that infant conditioning and narco-hypnosis are more efficient, as instruments of government, than clubs and prisons, and that the lust for power can be just as completely satisfied by suggesting people into loving their servitude as by flogging and kicking them into obedience."[123] Grim but true. In fact, when Huxley was interviewed in 1958, he said, "It is rather alarming to find that only twenty-seven years [after writing *Brave New World*] quite a number of those forecasts have already come through with vengeance."[124]

Three years later, Huxley was even more pessimistic about the future. Speaking before the California Medical School in San Francisco, he said, "There will be in the next generation or so a pharmacological method of making people love servitude and producing dictatorship without tears, so to speak, producing a kind of painless concentration camp for entire societies so that people will in fact have their liberties taken away from them but will rather enjoy it."[125] In other words, "democratic despotism" will have delivered on the quest for a "compliant citizenry."

Communist Roots

Thought control has long been a staple in the arsenal of the Left. Following the Russian Revolution in 1917, the term "political correctness" was used by Marxists to profess allegiance to the Communist cause; no other thoughts were allowed. While the French Revolution was the first totalitarian revolution, this was the first time a regime sought to institute thought control.

Solzhenitsyn was critical of the Czars who ruled Imperial Russia, but they were angelic compared to what Stalin did. Under the Czars, people were at least free to think what they wanted. Not so under Stalin. As the Russian freedom fighter said, the first freedom is freedom of conscience, a right inextricably tied to freedom of religion. It was this that Stalin sought to crush.

Thought control was not perfected until Mao Zedong took over in China in 1949. In the 1950s, journalist Edward Hunter was among the first to alert the public to Mao's brainwashing tactics. He aptly described this as a process to "change a mind radically so that its owner becomes a living puppet—a human robot—without the atrocity being visible from the outside."[126] But it wasn't until the Cultural Revolution in the 1960s, as detailed by Yale psychiatrist Robert Jay

Lifton, that Mao unleashed a huge brainwashing campaign, making sure that the only correct thought was that of his own. Those who resisted Maoism were punished, and tens of millions perished.

Xi Van Fleet lived under Mao's totalitarian regime, and she says that there are some unfortunate parallels with what is going on today in America. She specifically cites "the woke revolution." She regretfully notes that too many Americans don't know about what happened during the Cultural Revolution in communist China. "Anything traditional, anything that's old needs to be dismantled. And that is what we are seeing here is the same thing." The goal is the same, she says: "absolute power."[127]

She's right. In fact, the Communist Party in the U.S., as detailed by Skousen in the late 1950s, made the eradication of anything traditional one of its goals. "Discredit the American Constitution by calling it inadequate, old-fashioned, out of step with modern needs, a hindrance to cooperation between nations on a world-wide basis."[128] The Left picked up on this, insisting that the Constitution was a "living" and "malleable" document, one that could be altered, of course, to serve their interests.

"Discredit the American founding fathers. Present them as selfish autocrats who had no concern for the 'common man.'"[129] That was a related Communist goal. This has been the staple propaganda of American left-wing historians such as Howard Zinn, who was himself a member of the Communist Party. His bestselling history book, *A People's History of the United States: 1492—Present*, has poisoned the minds of millions. It has also been seriously debunked, but that matters little to true believers.

"Belittle all forms of American culture and discourage the teaching of American history on the ground that it was only a minor part of 'the big picture.'"[130] This is very much the agenda of multiculturalism: denigrate the West and celebrate Third World nations, all in the name of "diversity." This has nothing to do with scholarship; it has everything to do with politics.

The Communist Party also advocated its followers to "use technical decisions of the courts to weaken basic American institutions by claiming their activities violate civil rights."[131] After the people voted down gay marriage proposals all over the nation, even in uber-liberal California, prominent members of the ruling class listened to their radical allies and upended the institution of marriage as it had been known since the beginning of time.

Another Communist goal which fits with its thought control agenda was to "continue discrediting American culture by degrading all forms of artistic expression. An American Communist cell was told to 'eliminate all good sculpture from parks and buildings, substitute shapeless, awkward and meaningless forms.'"[132] Little doubt this is another box the Left can check—the artwork that dots the trendier parts of urban America proves it. As early as 1959, John Canaday, art critic at the *New York Times*, noted that "freaks, charlatans and the misled" had surrounded the truly creative, thereby granting legitimacy to the work of phonies. "Let us admit," he wrote, "that the nature of abstract expressionism allows exceptional tolerance for incompetence and deception." He aptly concluded, "We have been had."[133]

"Dominate the psychiatric profession and use mental health laws as a means of gaining coercive control over those who oppose Communist goals."[134] There is little doubt that many of those in the mental health field are militant secularists who are bent on giving their radical agenda a veneer of scientific credibility. Indeed, those in the psychiatric profession who oppose the left-wing goals of the elites who run the various associations are treated as pariahs, and some have been banished.

For thought control to succeed, the Communist Party said, its activists must "get control of the schools." One way to do this is to dumb down academic standards, or, as they put it, "soften the curriculum." It was also important to "Get control of teachers' associations."[135] Is there anyone who doubts that these goals have been met? The National Education Association not only continues to water down standards, but it is the largest labor union in the nation, and its politics are decidedly left-wing.

Catholicism Abhors Thought Control

Free will is central to Catholicism, making it the very antithesis of thought control schemes. It may have demanding strictures, but it covets conscience rights, something radicals and many in the ruling class oppose. Indeed, the *Catechism of the Catholic Church* teaches that "conscience is man's most secret core and his sanctuary." It is also tied to truth. "The truth about the moral good, stated in the law of reason, is recognized practically and concretely by the prudent judgment of conscience."[136] To radicals, this is heresy. Not only do they deny the existence of truth, but they see the "prudent judgment of conscience" as a threat to their agenda. They are right about that.

The bishops' document on conscience formation can be seen as a full-throated rejection of thought control. It did not mention thought control directly, but its insistence on religious liberty made plain its predilections. Central to its thinking was the admonition that "no one is to be forced to act in a manner contrary to his own beliefs, whether privately or publicly, whether alone or in association with others, within due limits."[137] No proponent of thought control could agree with this dictum.

Pope Francis knew how sinister thought control can be. He saw it as an expression of what he called "polite persecution." Typically, it is "disguised as culture, disguised as modernity, disguised as progress." It centers on thought control. "God made us free," he said, "but this kind of persecution takes away freedom." It is the devil, he added, who is the sponsor of "polite persecution." The devil's hand is at work when "the powerful want to impose attitudes, laws against the dignity of the children of God, persecute them and oppose God the Creator."[138]

Jack Phillips knew exactly what the pope was talking about. He made a name for himself when he stuck to his Christian convictions and refused to personalize a wedding cake for two homosexuals who planned to get "married." He never denied service to someone because he was a homosexual; it's just that in this instance, he was asked to affirm a ceremony he could not in good conscience perform.

His religious liberty objections were eventually upheld in the Supreme Court, but the lawyer for the gay men made crystal clear that he was not content to have their case decided by the courts. The goal was to get inside the head of Jack Phillips. The attorney admitted that his goal was to "correct the errors of Jack's thinking."[139] Spoken like a true Maoist.

Thought Control Abroad

Thought control is not simply a feature of the ruling class and radicals in the United States; it has infected our neighbor to the north and our neighbors across the Atlantic.

Jordan Peterson is a well-respected Canadian psychologist who rejects the woke culture. An independent-minded scholar, he has been victimized by the College of Psychologists of Ontario for his beliefs, even to the point of forcing him to undergo "remedial social media training," a form of thought control.[140] Restrictions on individual rights are so strong that an appeals court rejected his petition. Simply because he refuses to accept the anti-science lexicon of gender ideologists—calling a person "they"—he is targeted by the masters of "polite persecution."

Free speech has deteriorated so far in the United Kingdom that people are being arrested for praying in public. Isabel Vaughan-Spruce is the director of the U.K. March for Life. She was arrested for the crime of silently praying outside an abortion clinic. Her attorney, from the United

States, said her case "is remarkable because she was punished not for what she said, but for what she thought." Taking a page right out of Orwell's *1984*, law enforcement officers confronted her and asked, "What are you thinking? Are you praying in your mind?"[141]

Dr. Hilary Cass cannot use public transportation in England for fear of being harassed. What set off the radicals? She issued a report critical of transgenderism medicine. The online assault on her was so vicious that she feared for her life, impelling her to forego public transportation.[142]

Scotland is home to some of the most totalitarian expressions of thought control in the world. When legislation against hate speech was enacted in 2024—strengthening existing law—there were approximately eight thousand accusations made in the first week alone. Virtually anything said that might upset LGBTQ persons was now criminalized. The eight thousand complaints were greater than the annual total for hate crimes in general in any full year in Scotland.[143]

Päivi Räsänen, a Christian member of Finland's parliament, tweeted her objections to her church's involvement in an LGBTQ parade. She was prosecuted for "hate speech."[144] When she won in court, the prosecutors became persecutors by continually appealing her case to higher courts.

In 2024, a thirty-year-old Belgian man, Dries Van Langenhove, was sentenced to a year in prison for espousing his beliefs on a private online group chat with his friends. The government didn't like what he said and labeled his speech a "hate crime."[145] Conditions are so bad in Belgium that a conference of conservative speakers was banned by Brussels mayor Emir Kir. The cops surrounded the venue barring access to the event. His order said that some of the speakers "are reputed to be traditionalists." He was right about that. One of them was Cardinal Gerhard Müller. Though the courts overturned Kir's ban and allowed the conference to be held, the German cardinal noted that he felt it was "like Nazi Germany."[146]

Ruling Class Endorses Radicals on Free Speech

Left-wing radicals deplore free speech, making them prime supporters of thought control. Many don't want to admit to this, but one of their heroes, Herbert Marcuse, made no bones about it. In the 1960s, he penned an essay, "Repressive Tolerance," justifying censorship. He did not buy the liberal line about the answer to bad speech being more speech. He made the case to discriminate against those whose speech worked against the radical agenda. He even justified violence. Those who were oppressed, he said, were victims of a system which used violence against them. Therefore, their use of violence is a just reaction against them.

Marcuse's position pitted radicals against the ruling class. But over time, many members of the ruling class came to see free speech as a problem. They may not have adopted his more extreme views, but they clearly moved in his direction. For example, when corporations adopt "ESG" policies—environmental, social, and governance—their interpretation of governance is no ode to free speech. According to one CEO, Daniel Cameron of the 1792 Exchange, this is very much what Orwell predicted. Speaking of governance, he said, "This is Big Brother inside the corporations, telling people how to speak and ultimately to not express their First Amendment rights."[147]

What Cameron said is no exaggeration. Consider the findings of a 2023 poll by RealClear Opinion Research. The good news is that "9 in 10 voters in the U.S. think First Amendment protections for freedom of speech is a good thing, while 9% think it is a bad thing."[148] Guess who the ones are who hate free speech? The ones who claim to be the princes of tolerance.

The poll found that "the most glaring gap is between conservatives and liberals, i.e., between Republicans and Democrats." On the issue of free speech, "Republicans are not the authoritarian party. That distinction belongs to the Democrats." Here are some examples.

- 34 percent of Democratic voters say Americans have "too much freedom." Only 14.6 percent of Republicans agree.
- A majority of Democrats (52 percent) believe it is okay for the government to censor speech that protects the national security, a view shared by a third of Republicans.
- When asked if they agreed with the statement, "I disapprove of what you say, but I will defend to the death your right to say it," a majority of Republicans (51 percent) "strongly agreed" but this was true of only 31 percent of Democrats.
- 75 percent of Democrats believe government has a responsibility to limit "hateful" social media posts; the figure for Republicans is 50 percent.[149]

So much for the myth about liberals being the tolerant ones.

Some may say that this rejection of free speech on the part of liberals is certainly not accepted by such proponents of the First Amendment as the American Civil Liberties Union. They are wrong.

The ACLU was founded in 1920, and in the 1930s, it threatened a libel suit against *The American Mercury* magazine simply because the author was critical of it. Nothing libelous was said. When both the magazine and the ACLU agreed to have a neutral party assess the article and render a judgment, the famed Baltimore journalist H. L. Mencken agreed to do it. He came down solidly on the side of the magazine. The ACLU promptly labeled him a "fascist."[150]

Even on the subject of thought control, the ACLU is not the champion of free speech that many think. In 1978, I interviewed the founder of the ACLU, Roger Baldwin, in his home in New York City. It was part of my Ph.D. dissertation on the organization, which I subsequently turned into a book.

When Baldwin, who was an atheist, told me that it was not acceptable for a student to say a prayer in school, I asked, "Well, whose rights are being infringed upon if there is a silent prayer voluntarily said by a student?" He said, "They've tried to get around it even further than you by calling it meditation." To which I responded, "What's wrong with that?" He said that "it's a subterfuge, because the implication is that you're meditating about the hereafter or God or something." And that is not something that the founder of the ACLU could stand—the average Joe's kid meditating about God in school. I had to ask him, "Well, what's wrong with that? Doesn't a person have the right to do that? Or to meditate about popcorn for that matter?" He said, "I suppose that—it sounds very silly to me because it looks like an obvious evasion of the constitutional provision."[151] Prayer obviously scared the daylights out of him.

The Role of the Media

The ruling class and radicals merge again in their control of the media. But this is a relatively new development.

In the middle part of the twentieth century, the big media in the United States, both print and electronic, was liberal leaning, but most reporters and broadcast journalists strived to be objective. For the most part, they succeeded. This changed dramatically in the twenty-first century. Cable television, internet news, podcasts, and social media gave rise to the advent of partisan commentary. To be frank, the distinction between hard news and editorial opinion has been lost as the latter has bled into the former. Newspapers have also succumbed to partisanship, taking on the role of fact checkers. The problem is their fact checking is more likely to evince a political preference than an objective outcome. It is also selectively employed.

Radicals didn't change; elites in the media did. This takes on heightened significance when we consider that in the early 1980s, fifty companies owned 90 percent of the media in the United States. Forty years later, six companies controlled almost all the media: five side with liberal politics and one with conservative politics. Add to this the influence that

Facebook, Apple, Amazon, Netflix, and Google have and the dominance that liberal outlets have is overwhelming. Even sports channels such as ESPN are no longer apolitical, having adopted the politics of the Left.

The Associated Press has outsized influence, especially with a decreasing number of newspapers. Most papers cannot afford to pay for a reasonably large pool of reporters, meaning they have to rely on big wire services like AP for news coverage. The problem is the nation's largest wire service is in part bankrolled today by millions of dollars from left-wing foundations. When the likes of the Rockefeller Foundation, the Charles Stewart Mott Foundation, and the William and Flora Hewett Foundation shell out millions—for whatever liberal cause they choose—they expect something in return. AP doesn't disappoint them.

AP has a style book that is more akin to promoting thought control than it is objective journalism. Crisis pregnancy centers, which give women contemplating an abortion a choice, are referred to in AP stories as "crisis pregnancy centers."[152] The scare quotes are designed to delegitimize these entities.

Reputable journalists still exist, but they often pay a price for maintaining their integrity. James Bennet was the editor of the *New York Times* editorial page, but he resigned in 2020 after he was lambasted by dozens of the paper's staffers for publishing an op-ed article by Sen. Tom Cotton earlier in the year that they did not like (he called for the military to step in to control urban riots after the death of George Floyd). Bennet initially defended running the article but later said it was wrong to do so. Cotton said the paper had caved into a "mob of woke kids."[153]

In 2024, NBC News had no sooner hired Ronna McDaniel, the former head of the Republican National Committee, when it dumped her following an outcry from its left-wing employees. National Public Radio suspended one of its veteran journalists, Uri Berliner, after he published an essay in the Free Press that argued NPR has lost its reputation of being open-minded and no longer allowed a diversity of viewpoints. Liberal bias, he said, was now the rule. He resigned after accusing the new CEO of confirming the very problems he cited in his article. He was right. The new chief, Katherine Maher, does not believe in objective journalism. She believes that "the truth, by definition, is malleable."[154] She is wrong. By definition, truth is not malleable—opinions are. But to postmodernists who believe that truth is a fiction, people like Berliner are a threat to their quest for thought control.

The Role of Higher Education

I have said many times on radio and TV that there is more free speech allowed in your local pub than in your local college campus. There are no "Free Speech Zones" in pubs, and patrons are rarely shouted down. But such reserved spaces for free speech exist on many campuses, and speakers—they are *always* conservatives—are routinely shouted down. Pubs also allow diversity of thought, but most colleges do not. Instead of colleges and universities being beacons of free speech, they have become beacons of thought control.

When I was an undergraduate at New York University, I had just finished a four-year stint in the U.S. Air Force.

I wrote satirical articles—going after liberals and conservatives—for the student newspaper, all of which were published. After a while, I noticed that my pieces making fun of conservatives were published but not my ones poking fun at liberals. I confronted the students who ran the paper. I quit after being lied to—they denied any bias.

At about the same time, I took issue with one of my professors. The course was on Latin America and every assigned book was published by the Monthly Review Press. When I asked him in class why he only assigned books published by the Communist Party of the United States, the students were surprised to learn of this. He got angry. It convinced me that diversity of thought was not going to be tolerated.

Many other such examples could be offered. Suffice it to say that when I became a professor, I joined an organization in the 1980s that sought to do something about this condition, the National Association of Scholars. I soon joined the board of directors and became the president of the Pennsylvania chapter, as well as the Pittsburgh chapter. NAS is still fighting the good fight today.

The elites who run higher education are indistinguishable from the Left. Nowhere in American life is the nexus between the ruling class and radicals as strong. Professors who have lived under totalitarian regimes know this better than anyone.

Igor Efimov is a biomedical engineer at Northwestern University. He grew up in the Soviet Union and sees disturbing parallels in higher education here in America. He is particularly alarmed about the push for diversity, equity, and inclusion, especially as it affects science, technology, engineering, and mathematics, what is known as STEM education. He says the USSR had a "good STEM education system," but "it was poisoned by [M]arxist identity politics, which was primarily based on social class and ethnicity." He does not like what he sees on campus. "My everyday experiences as a chemistry professor at an American university in 2021 bring back memories from my school and university time in the USSR. Not good memories—more like Orwellian nightmares."[155]

No one seriously doubts that radicals have captured the administration and faculty on most campuses, including many Catholic ones. Faculty have been punished for accepting the Catholic Church's teachings on sexuality, and students have been forced to undergo "diversity sensitivity training" and partake in "remediation training" for committing the same offense.[156] This is thought control.

The University of California, Berkeley, is home to the 1964 free speech movement on campus. It was a fraud from the beginning. One of the students involved was Sol Stern, who later turned out to be a brilliant conservative student of education. He is right to observe that Berkeley now "exercises more thought control over students" than ever before. But as he points out, this is less a perversion than a perfection of what radicals actually sought. He says the idea that students were fighting for free speech "was always a charade." Indeed, "the struggle was really about clearing barriers to using the campus as a base for radical political activity."[157] Matters have only gotten worse. In 2022, Berkeley students banned supporters of Zionism from campus. The dean of the law school, Erwin Chemerinsky, rightly protested, arguing that this was viewpoint discrimination.

Those who promote thought control are not shy about their ambitions. Michael Bérubé is a literature professor at Penn State, and Jennifer Ruth is a professor of film studies at Portland State. They are the authors of a book that brazenly argues that academic freedom no longer serves its original goal, "the abstract pursuit of an ever-contested truth." They say that academic freedom is the invention of white males and represents "institutional racism," "white supremacy," and "settler colonialism." They want faculty on every campus to form Orwellian committees that would police speech, ensuring that it does not run afoul of radical ideas about race.[158]

These ideas spell the demise of higher education. They are put to use at places like Harvard. In 2021, evolutionary biologist Carole K. Hooven and biostatistician Tyler J. VanderWeele found out firsthand how the censors operate.

Hooven taught that sex is binary, which is exactly what evolutionary biology holds to be true. She was immediately denounced by the graduate student director of her department's Diversity, Equity, and Inclusion task force. No graduate students agreed to serve as her teaching fellow, making it untenable for her to continue teaching. The faculty in her department failed to support her, so she resigned. VanderWeele, a practicing Catholic, signed an amicus brief opposing a federal right to gay marriage in favor of states, right position; he also opposes abortion. Though they did not succeed, his graduate students in public health demanded that he be fired.

The Role of Government

No institution is better able to achieve the Orwellian goal of thought control than government. Nor is there any institution that has more power to punish those who resist. Naturally, the ruling class denies it is promoting thought control, but when they admit to policing what they call "disinformation," they are showing their hand.

"Disinformation" is defined as the intentional dissemination of false information. It is different from unintentionally spreading false information, or what is called "misinformation." The problem as played out in real life is: Who decides what is false, and how can motive be discerned? Most important, what if it is determined that these "fact checkers" are politically motivated, using their mantle to squash information they find disagreeable? How can they be dislodged?

In 2024, European Commission President Ursula von der Leyen spoke at the World Economic Forum in Davos. Following the lead of WEF Chairman Klaus Schwab, she called for increased cooperation between governments and big business in enacting censorial speech codes. She identified the enemy as "disinformation."[159] In the name of protecting the average Joe from the "wrong" information, they are deciding what he can see and read. "Government Knows Best" should be the motto of these masters of thought control.

In the United States, Barack Obama is known for his war on "disinformation." In April 2022, the former president gave a keynote lecture at Stanford University, where for over an hour, he railed against "disinformation," calling it "a threat to democracy." He urged private businesses to perform "content moderation," or what some have called "a new Orwellian euphemism for mass censorship." This involves the use of algorithms to "slow the speed" of "wrong" information.[160] Among those who support Obama in this effort is George Soros; he has spent a small fortune trying to censor speech.

If Obama is known for rhetorically declaring a war on "disinformation," President Joe Biden is known for implementing it. In 2022, he appointed Nina Jankowicz as head of the Department of Homeland Security's "Disinformation Governance Board." She was selected on April 22 as "Disinformation Czar," but owing to the incredible public backlash, she resigned on May 17. Fox News said her goal was "intended to censor Americans' speech." She sued, claiming she was defamed, but on July 22, 2024, her case was dismissed. As George Washington law professor Jonathan Turley noted, the judge "demolished the claims of figures like Jankowicz that they are really not engaged in censorship." The judge explicitly said that the post she was given "was formed precisely to examine citizens' speech."[161]

The Biden administration was not deterred. Though it gave up on trying to institutionalize an office to police speech, it never gave up on using existing agencies to do the job. Just hours after Biden began his presidential term, the White House website was revamped to allow users to choose their pronouns. The new list allowed people to identify themselves as "she/her, he/him, they, them, other, or prefer not to share."[162] This was just the beginning.

Seven months into his term, the administration rolled out new guidelines for transgender employees that threatened to punish those who violated them. "Continued intentional use of an incorrect name, pronoun, and/or honorific – also known as misgendering – could, depending on its severity and pervasiveness, contribute to a hostile work environment allegation, and constitute misconduct subject to disciplinary action, up to and including separation or removal."[163] This was not simply another example of thought control—employees must call someone "they" if he or she insists—it is a declaration of war against nature and nature's God. Despite what these totalitarians say, human nature does not change, sex is binary, and protestations to the contrary are anti-science.

Communist societies have a long history of deprogramming their people. Totalitarian dictators are very good at purging the past and forcing those who hold to traditional norms and values to scrub their minds free, thus enabling them to inculcate the norms and values of the ruling class. Deprogramming is the penultimate expression of thought control. Its proponents literally want to remake its subjects.

When Tocqueville spoke of democratic despotism, he did not envision it reaching the point where deprogramming would be operative. Incredibly, even in democratic countries, there are calls to deprogram those who hold contrary ideas.

Donald Trump's supporters have been targeted by elites for deprogramming. They are not content to disagree with Trump and his fans—they are bent on making them undergo a psychological makeover.

In October 2023, Hillary Clinton, who lost to Trump in 2016, said the time had come for a "formal deprogramming" of what she called Trump's "cult members."[164] Two years earlier, the longtime NBC co-host of the "Today" show Katie Couric, rhetorically asked, "How are we going to really almost deprogram these people who have signed up for the cult of Trump?"[165] In 2020, failed Trump White House communications director Anthony Scaramucci opined that Trump supporters, and especially those who worked in the administration, should be considered candidates for deprogramming. A few days later, failed CNN host Don Lemon commented on those who voted for Trump in 2016, saying "a lot" of them "need to be deprogrammed, right now, before they cast their next ballots."[166]

Former Labor Secretary Robert Reich showed his fondness for Stalinist tactics a few weeks before the 2020 election. "When this nightmare is over," he said, "we need a Truth and Reconciliation Committee." After the election, David Atkins, a prominent California Democratic operative, wondered aloud "how 'do' you deprogram 75 million people?" He said, "We have to start thinking in terms of post-WWII Germany or Japan." Senator Bernie Sanders insisted "we need to send all the Republicans to the reeducation camps." Eugene Robinson, an African American columnist for the *Washington Post*, said, "There are millions of Americans, almost all white, almost all Republicans, who somehow need to be deprogrammed."[167]

Harvard students, who never consider themselves to be the unwitting dupes of brainwashing, called for reeducation and moral rehabilitation camps. No one beat Michael Beller, an attorney for Public Broadcasting Services (PBS). He set his sights on kids, imploring Homeland Security to take the children of Republican voters away. "And then we'll put them in reeducation camps."[168] He was subsequently fired. He should have moved to North Korea.

These people mean it. If they could find a way to legally deprogram the average Joe who disagrees with them, they would send him off to a reeducation camp. Their contempt for individual liberty and tolerance for diversity of thought is monumental. Indeed, they are an existential threat to democracy.

On June 25, 2024, I wrote a letter to Alejandro Mayorkas, Secretary of Homeland Security, wanting to know if I am on a watch list for domestic terrorism.

The occasion for writing was a news report saying that internal files from the "Homeland Intelligence Experts Group" had been made public, and that although the group was now defunct, the contents of the second batch were disturbing. In looking at who might be a threat to national security, when all else fails, the group said, agents should look for "indicators of extremists and terrorism."[169] They named those who were in the military and were religious as indicators. A third indicator was supporters of Donald Trump.

I wanted to know what Homeland Security was going to do with these records. "Where is the evidence that being in the military, being religious and being a supporter of Donald Trump is a threat to national security? I ask these questions because according to these criteria, I check all three boxes."[170] I then gave the date when I was honorably discharged from the United States Air Force, the date when I began my tenure as president of the Catholic League, and the date when Trump tweeted kind remarks about me regarding comments I made about him on CNN and in an article I wrote for Newsmax.

I ended by saying, "This begs the question: Am I on a watch list? My family, friends and Catholic League members would like to know if I may be considered a domestic terrorist."[171] He never replied.

Chapter 4

Behavioral Control

The Gift of Covid

The goal of changing the thinking of the average Joe is important, but it is incomplete: he must change his behavior. That was very much on the mind of Klaus Schwab when he convened the World Economic Forum in Davos in 1971. He told the gathering it was time to think more about stakeholders than shareholders. The former represents a socially conscious group of investors who will reset society, both at home and abroad. Two decades later, globalist Strobe Talbott proudly proclaimed that "nationhood as we know it will be obsolete; all states will recognize a single, global authority."[172] Then the control freaks will rule the world.

Where did the ruling class get these ideas? From radicals, of course. Michael Woronoff writes that "support for stakeholder capitalism has largely sprung from the mouths and pens of academics and progressive activists."[173] UCLA law professor Stephen Bainbridge notes that stakeholder advocates are often statists, those who believe that government should be used to usher in a new economic order, imbued with the politics of the Left.[174]

Economist Charles Gasparino says the origins of corporate wokeness can be traced to the late 1980s and the 1990s when corporate CEOs "began running companies along the lines of so-called corporate responsibility, using shareholder money to donate to various charities, or end world hunger." Then came stakeholder capitalism. He says much of what happened is due to "a heavy dose of Wall Street CEO guilt."[175] Pressured by radicals and the Obama administration, the ruling class in business gave the ruling class in government what it wanted.

There are signs, however, that the politicization of Wall Street is cooling. For example, Jamie Dimon, CEO of JP Morgan, has gone from a defender of stakeholder capitalism back to shareholder capitalism. This suggests that the cooperation of the ruling class with radicals is sometimes less than what meets the eye. When the corporate biggies embraced Black Lives Matter, for instance, they did so largely to get radicals off their back. It was more political than genuine. Moreover, the Trump victory moved some elites to change course, and even if this was done for reasons that were not entirely principled, the outcome was important nonetheless.

Following the economic crash of 2008, urban specialist Richard Florida wrote an insightful book, *The Great Reset*, that maintained that the financial crisis was one in a series of failures that bedeviled the nation. We experienced depressions in the 1870s and 1930s, both of which required a "Great Reset." We were now ready for another one. This was music to the ears of the WEF. In 2014, the elites who met at Davos listened to Schwab announce that it was time "to push the reset button."[176] Six years later came Covid, giving elites an opportunity they could milk for years. And they did it all in the name of stakeholder capitalism.

Covid was a nightmare for millions of people, but for the ruling class, it was the gift that kept on giving. In 2020, Schwab knew he had a remedy. "I see the need for a Great Reset." He told the Davos audience that his "Great Reset" would "recreate a global framework which really is in line with the requirements of a society in the twenty-first century."[177] They always pitch their schemes globally; that way they achieve maximum power.

The Davos ruling class foresaw a hi-tech world that was different in substance, but not in principle, from what elites before them envisioned. "Strip away the Davos jargon," writes John Tierney, "and the Great Reset is Plato's dream of a philosopher king society. Intellectuals have always yearned for a world run by intellectuals, and politicians have always found reasons to give themselves more power."[178]

Belgian clinical psychologist Mattias Desmet contends that "the coronavirus crisis did not come out of the blue. It fit into a series of increasingly desperate and self-destructive societal responses to objects of fear: terrorists, global warming, coronavirus. Whenever a fear arises in society, there is only one response and one defense in our current way of thinking: increased control."[179]

Radical activists epitomized what Desmet said. In particular, Obama advisor Rahm Emanuel echoed what his fellow Chicagoan Saul Alinsky first broached when he opined, "Never let a crisis go to waste."[180] Two months into the Covid crisis, Hillary Clinton joined the fray, arguing that "this would be a terrible crisis to waste."[181] Communist sympathizer Jane Fonda gushed, "I just think Covid-19 is God's gift to the Left."[182] California Governor Gavin Newsom was more specific. "There is opportunity for reimagining a progressive era as it pertains to capitalism, a new progressive era and opportunity for additional progressive steps. So, yes, absolutely, we see this as an opportunity to reshape the way we do business and how we govern."[183] No one needed to be consulted.

After the Covid scare was over, political scientist Jeffrey H. Anderson nicely captured what happened to the average Joe. "It's still hard to believe that Americans lived through a period in which executive officials, with no legislative involvement, ordered churches, shops, and schools to be closed, forced Americans to hide their faces behind masks, and even demanded that they be fired for not taking experimental vaccines."[184] How this happened is a sad tale.

The architects of this authoritarian response were public healthcare bureaucrats Anthony Fauci and Deborah Birx; they were neither practitioners nor scholars. Less than three weeks on the job, the advice they gave triggered a White House series of federal guidelines that locked down the schools and put severe restrictions on restaurants and gatherings of ten or more. Three days later, California governor Newsom was the first to lock down his state.

Scott Atlas, who had been chief of neuroradiology at Stanford University, was added to President Trump's Task Force in the summer of 2020, but he was outnumbered by Fauci, Birx, and CDC director Robert Redfield, none of whom were an epidemiologist. At a Task Force meeting some six months into the pandemic, Atlas asked Fauci about the lockdowns. "So you think people aren't frightened enough?" Fauci replied, "Yes, they need to be more afraid." It is for reasons like this that Atlas said that "the administration had elevated a couple of government public health bureaucrats to effectively be in charge of public policy." What it yielded was "one of the greatest public health failures in history."[185]

Standing with these authoritarian public health bureaucrats was Bill Gates. He spent more than $3 billion on various programs run by Fauci and Birx, and he was a big supporter of the lockdowns. Face masks, social distancing, quarantines, temperature checks, travel restrictions—he wanted it all. More important, he strongly opposed making these measures voluntary; he insisted that they must be imposed. "Normalcy only returns," he said, "when we've largely vaccinated the entire global population."[186] Gates profited monetarily from his investments in vaccines, but as Seamus Bruner said, what he really profited from was his quest for "social control." He notes that this has worked before. "The Rockefellers, after all, had profited immensely from taking over entire countries' health-care system for purposes of 'disease control.'"[187]

No one was more enthusiastic about forcing people to get vaccinated than Fauci. He even went so far as to say that it was important to bully them. "It's been proven that when you make it difficult for people in their lives, they lose their ideological bulls***, and they get vaccinated." This led Select Committee Pandemic chairman Brad Wenstrup to call out Fauci to his face when he testified. "Americans were aggressively bullied, shamed, and silenced for merely questioning or debating issues such as social distancing, masks, vaccines, or the origins of COVID."[188]

The role that Fauci played was key. He funded the Wuhan Institute of Virology's gain-of-function bat research that genetically alters organisms to enable the spread of viruses into new species. MIT professor Kevin Esvelt asked in 2021, "Why is anyone trying to teach the world how to make viruses that could kill millions of people?"[189] To make matters worse, the Wuhan Institute had a very poor safety rating. In 2012, Fauci admitted that it was "unlikely but conceivable" that gain-of-function research would "trigger a pandemic."[190] Richard Ebright, a Rutgers professor of chemical biology, declared that "Fauci likely caused the COVID-19 pandemic, by first opposing, and then repeatedly and flagrantly violating, US-government policies" on this kind of research.[191]

When Fauci was hammered by Senator Ted Cruz for repeatedly denying that the U.S. government had funded the gain-of-function research at the Wuhan Institute, he replied with characteristic arrogance that his critics are "really criticizing science because I represent science. That's dangerous."[192] Yet Mr. Science admitted that his promotion of the six-feet rule for social distancing "sort of just appeared" without a solid scientific basis.[193]

The Lockdowns and the Catholic Response

The Catholic response to vaccinations was mostly positive, though the American bishops called for ethical guidelines in their production. They singled out AstraZeneca for criticism, saying it was found to be "more morally compromised" and should therefore "be avoided" if alternatives were available.[194] At issue was the distribution of vaccines that might have some connection to cell lines that originated with tissue taken from abortions. A joint letter from Catholic leaders, clergy and laity alike, appealed to pharmaceutical companies to pursue cell lines that are morally acceptable. Regrettably, there were few non-Catholic leaders, religious or secular, who made this issue a priority.

The Catholic response to the way the ruling class and radicals treated people of faith during the pandemic was not as positive, with good reason: left-wing intellectuals blamed Christians for Covid. Katherine Stewart, writing in the *New York Times*, said that religious conservatives, especially Christian Nationalists, were impeding the response to Covid by giving President Trump bad advice. As evidence, she cites an innocent comment that Trump made: he said that he hoped that his ramped-up efforts to combat Covid meant we are "just raring to go by Easter." What's wrong with that? "He could have said, 'by mid-April.'"[195] Such paranoia on the part of the Left is not uncommon, but this quip takes the cake. It also shows how much Christianity terrifies them.

Here's further proof. In May 2020, Howard County Maryland Executive Calvin Ball sought to ban sacramental wine *and* the Eucharist at Mass. "There shall be no consumption of food or beverage of any kind before, during, or after religious services, including food or beverage that would typically be consumed as part of a religious service."[196] In doing so, he went beyond Prohibition, which allowed for sacramental wine and the Eucharist.

I immediately issued a news release asking Catholic League supporters to contact Howard County spokesman Scott Peterson (we found his email address). He quickly got the message and the order was rescinded. It was a happy ending, but Catholics should never have been targeted in the first place.

The notion that Covid was a crisis too good to waste was made manifest in a public debate over what kinds of medical procedures should be given a priority at a time of limited resources. Surely those suffering from complications arising from Covid, for instance, should qualify, but those seeking elective surgeries were not in the same boat. Surely they could wait. Chethan Sathya, a pediatric surgeon and journalist in New York City, explained what was at stake: "Surgeries are resource-intensive—requiring surgeons, anesthesiologists, nurses, transport teams, medical beds and equipment such as ventilators. Suspending elective surgeries will free up those doctors, and other medical personnel, and rooms and equipment."[197]

Sounds reasonable. Guess who objected? The abortion industry. NARAL and Planned Parenthood insisted that abortion was not elective surgery and must be provided at all times. But is it?

Take two women, Joy and Jane. Joy has a life-threatening heart problem and is scheduled for surgery. Jane wants an abortion. No one in his right mind would equate the two. If Joy doesn't get heart surgery, she will probably die. If Jane is denied her abortion, she lives (as does her baby).

It comes down to this: Joy has a need; Jane has a want. No woman *needs* an abortion—it is, as they like to say, a matter of choice.

Does this mean that abortion is like any other elective surgery, such as a facelift (rhytidectomy) or a tummy tuck (abdominoplasty)? No. In those cases, only the person's face or tummy is affected. In the case of abortion, another person is affected. And there is nothing elective about that person's fate.

The pandemic raised important questions about religious liberty and public health concerns. When two goods collide, the resolution should not eviscerate either of them; balancing the two is the proper way to proceed. To put it differently, whenever religious liberty collides with public health, the government is obliged to put the least restrictive measures on religion. If that is done, and the motive is purely to protect the public, then in a crisis situation, temporary bans may be legitimate.

Motive counts. Why? Because we must always consider the source of an objection to religious exemptions. If the source is the medical community, and reasonable temporary restrictions are called for in a crisis situation, that is one thing; if the source is a hostile force, that is another. Unfortunately, there were plenty of examples of the latter during the pandemic.

Freedom From Religion Foundation, Americans United for Separation of Church and State, and the Center for Inquiry all issued statements against allowing religious exemptions for bans on large gatherings. Their motives were not benign. Indeed, they were malicious.

Covid gave them an opportunity to crush religious expression, and they seized on it with alacrity. Some of those in government heeded their advice. This was another example of how radicals influence the ruling class.

These atheist activists helped create an environment where government officials provided disparate treatment of religious and secular institutions. In fact, one liberal blogger, Nate Silver, observed that "it's kind of crazy (and it tells you a lot about who was writing the restrictions) that churches in some jurisdictions were subject to more restrictions than museums."[198] He was right. The average Joe is more likely to frequent churches than museums, but he is not on the mind of elites.

Bans were issued in many parts of the country on drive-in church services. In some cases, such as in Louisville, Kentucky, these bans did not apply to drive-through restaurants and liquor stores, making plain the animus against religious expression. In California, the entire state was subjected to a ban on chanting and singing in churches. But there were no restrictions on those protesting racism; social distancing rules were ignored. Similarly, Illinois placed restrictions on houses of worship, but none on protesters. Even when the most draconian restrictions were curbed, Governor J. B. Pritzker urged that singing and "group recitation" be curbed. In Pennsylvania, Governor Tom Wolf put restrictions on public gatherings, limiting them to 25 people indoors and 250 outdoors. Yet as many as 20,000 attendees were allowed to attend an auto show and flea market outdoors. Wolf even participated in a Black Lives Matter protest that violated the letter of his emergency order.

Massachusetts placed many restrictions on religious and secular events, but Governor Charlie Baker made one exception: "outdoor gatherings for the purpose of political expression are not subject to this Order."[199] In Minnesota, restrictions were placed on faith-based services, but none were demanded of protesters. In New York, four pages of mandated limitations on worship services were issued, including a ban on chanting or yelling. All ethnic parades were banned in New York City, but Mayor Bill de Blasio made an exception for Black Lives Matter protests. In the state of Washington, restrictions were placed on religious and faith-based organizations. The government even sounded the alarms by warning that "frequent reports of spiritual gatherings" can become "COVID-19 'superspreader' events."[200] But when it came to demonstrators, these assemblies were not seen as "superspreader" occasions.

Supporting this hypocrisy were 1,300 epidemiologists and health workers who signed a May 30 letter saying that those who protested stay-at-home orders were "rooted in white nationalism and run contrary to respect for Black Lives Matter." But when it comes to protesters, they said, "we do not condemn these gatherings as risky for Covid-19 transmission. We support them as vital to the national public health."[201] This incredible statement proved how utterly politicized many in the medical profession had become. It also demonstrated how vacuous the restrictions were—they obviously meant very little if they could be lifted for political purposes.

The ruling class was so obsequious and craven in its response to radical demands that it literally became their advocates. Fortunately, U.S. District Judge Gary Sharpe saw right through this scheme. He issued a preliminary injunction on June 26, 2020, saying de Blasio and New York Governor Andrew Cuomo exceeded their authority by putting severe restrictions on houses of worship while treading easily on demonstrations. By allowing the protests, he said, they were "encouraging what they knew was a flagrant disregard of the outdoor limits and social distancing rules." In doing so, they "sent a clear message that mass protests are deserving of preferential treatment."[202] What made this so perverse is that literally three months earlier, Cuomo ordered still recovering Covid patients to be sent to nursing homes. It led to over 4,300 deaths (before he rescinded his directive). Dr. Daniel Choi of Hofstra University's School of Medicine branded his decision a "death sentence."[203]

Covid caused dramatic economic harm to most institutions, which is why federal programs were instituted to distribute funds to help bolster them. Covid did not discriminate between religious and secular entities, but when the Small Business Administration (SBA) awarded federal funds to religious bodies, militant secularists went wild. Three law professors, one from Cornell and two from the University of Virginia, wrote an article in the *New York Times* decrying what they called the "quiet demise of the already ailing separation of church and state."[204] They may as well have been shouting at the moon. The SBA's Paycheck Protection Program was included in the Coronavirus Aid, Relief, and Economic Security (CARES) Act. It unanimously passed in the Senate and was approved by voice vote, without opposition, in the House. There was nothing unconstitutional about it.

This didn't stop efforts to discriminate against religious institutions. Washington granted Pennsylvania a grant of $471 million. Of that amount, $66 million was to be spent on private and religious schools, but Governor Wolf allotted only $19 million. This is the kind of money grab that the ruling class is very good at.

A similar game was played by New York City. It provided money to public school students to be tested for Covid but denied funds to parochial schools. The Archdiocese of New York sued and won. Michael Deegan, the superintendent of schools for the archdiocese, found it "peculiar that the Catholic schools of the Archdiocese of New York would need to go to court to vindicate this basic legal principle, especially in the middle of a public-health emergency."[205] The "basic legal principle" he was referring to had to do with treating public and nonpublic schools equally when it comes to health and safety issues. The ruling was appealed but it failed: the Catholic schools were reimbursed by the City of New York.

San Francisco was worse than New York in instituting discriminatory policies. Throughout most of the pandemic, the city limited outdoor worship to twelve participants. In September, 2020, it increased the number to fifty but capped indoor worship to "one individual member of the public." While churches in San Francisco had to limit their admittance to one person at a time, the city's hotels were fully open, and most retail stores were allowed to operate at 50 percent capacity. Similarly, during the same time, hundreds of Black Lives Matter protesters marched across the Golden Gate Bridge.

The animus against Catholics was so extreme that public officials in San Francisco did a headcount of parishioners attending Mass. The San Francisco city attorney, Dennis Herrera, sent a cease-and-desist letter to the Archdiocese of San Francisco ordering it to stop indoor religious services. He said nothing about doing a headcount at Protestant churches, Jewish synagogues, or Muslim mosques. He was only interested in policing Catholics.

Fortunately, the Archdiocese of San Francisco was led by a courageous archbishop, Salvatore Joseph Cordileone. He demolished the city's position in a splendid piece in the *Washington Post*. He said "the scientific evidence" was incontrovertible. The measures he employed in the churches made the city's concerns a nonissue. "These safeguards are working. As three infectious-disease specialists who reviewed evidence on more than 1 million public Masses over the past few months concluded, there have been no documented outbreaks of covid-19 linked to church attendance in churches that follow the protocols."[206]

The U.S. Supreme Court initially disappointed friends of religious liberty but later corrected itself. In a 5–4 decision in July, 2020, it upheld a Nevada order that restricted attendance at churches more than at casinos or movie houses; the lawsuit was filed by Calvary Chapel Dayton Valley. In his dissent, Justice Neil Gorsuch aptly noted that the pandemic poses "unusual challenges," but, he said, "there is no world in which the Constitution permits Nevada to favor Caesars Palace over Calvary Chapel."[207]

Matters changed at the end of November. Just before midnight on Thanksgiving eve, New York State Governor

Cuomo, a professed former altar boy, took it on the chin when the U.S. Supreme Court ruled 5–4 that his executive order limiting occupancy in houses of worship could not stand. It was blocked pending a review by the 2nd Circuit Court of Appeals.

The Supreme Court said that "even in a pandemic, the Constitution cannot be put away and forgotten." It was a win for the Diocese of Brooklyn and Agudath Israel of America. They argued that declaring religious services to be "*non*essential," while labeling pet stores, hardware stores, and other secular entities "essential," was a serious First Amendment infringement on their religious liberty. Cuomo dug himself a hole when he admitted in a press conference that his order was "most impactful on houses of worship."[208]

One of the more interesting aspects of this case was the reaction to the ruling. Americans United for Separation of Church and State went ballistic. It admitted to filing forty other amicus briefs in courts across the country seeking to deny religious exemptions from Covid orders. Most illuminating was the response of liberal religious publications and organizations. *America* and *Commonweal*, two liberal Catholic media outlets, said nothing. Neither did the *National Catholic Reporter*, a dissident publication that rejects the Church's teachings on marriage, the family, and sexuality. *Sojourners*, the liberal Protestant magazine, and Religion News Service, which hosts a variety of liberal religious writers, also went mute. So telling.

A few days later, the high court also ordered U.S. District Court Judge Jesus Bernal to reconsider his support for occupancy limits imposed by California Governor Newsom.

He was told to review its 5–4 decision from the week before striking down Cuomo's draconian edict.

The Masketeers

I live on Long Island and work in New York City. During the pandemic, I noticed many more people walking around with masks in the city than in the suburbs. When I left in the early morning, few were wearing masks outdoors, but as soon as I got to the Big Apple, it changed: people were wearing masks walking down the street, on bicycles, and in cars (often with no one in them).

What explains the difference? For one, liberals dominate urban America, and it is they—the masketeers—who are enamored of masks. They are not like the average Joe, who fortunately knows better.

California is one of the most liberal states in the country. Not surprisingly, its big cities were heavily populated with masketeers. Dennis Prager noticed in early 2021 that "where I live (the Los Angeles area), I am usually the only person on the street not wearing a mask."[209] He added that "you do not need medical or scientific expertise to understand the foolishness of outdoor mask-wearing."

But Prager is in the minority. Pundits noted that one of the reasons why California Governor Newsom easily fended off a recall challenge was because of his stringent Covid policies. The masketeers love him.

Newsom authorized a veritable lockdown of the state and did not end his stay-at-home order until June 15, 2020. His health officials ordered all unvaccinated persons age two and over to wear a mask in indoor public spaces and businesses. Los Angeles County went further, mandating that those age two and over wear masks in indoor settings regardless of their vaccination status.

Californians loved it. Fully two-thirds said they approved a universal mask mandate for indoor public spaces; only 25 percent were opposed. A majority, 51 percent, said they liked masks so much that they would personally choose to wear one indoors in public *even if not required to do so*. Similarly, a majority were in favor of the state forcing everyone in California to get vaccinated.[210]

Then again, liberals wouldn't be liberals unless they didn't embrace statist prescriptions: they adore mandates as much as they do cancelling those who disagree with them. And they can always make exceptions for themselves.

College students, most of whom have been taught by the Left, were enthusiastic about mask mandates. They would recoil in horror from any adult who asked them to practice restraint in their sex life, but they jumped for joy when college administrators ordered them to wear a mask.

In September 2021, a College Pulse survey of college students found that eight in ten favored mask mandates for indoor settings. In February 2022, dozens of students walked out of class at the University of Nevada, Reno, to protest the repeal of the mask mandate. This is a classic example of how thought control abets behavioral control. The average Joe was never so obliging.

Tyler Cowen is a Bloomberg opinion columnist who noticed the rank hypocrisy of the masketeers during Covid. After attending some conferences and public events, he observed that "the wealthier attendees are usually not wearing masks, but the poorer servers and staff almost all were."[211] None were more hypocritical than liberal politicians.

Nancy Pelosi was Speaker of the House during the pandemic, and she was an ardent advocate of mask mandates and other restrictions. But she was caught on tape visiting her hair salon in San Francisco breaking rules that were meant only for service outdoors. Moreover, she was seen with a face mask around her neck rather than over her mouth.

Governor Newsom enjoyed an NFC Championship game between the Rams and the 49ers, but he was pictured with basketball superstar Magic Johnson without a mask, even though everyone was supposed to be wearing one unless they were eating or drinking.

Michigan Governor Gretchen Whitmer is a big fan of masks, which explains why she mandated wearing them in enclosed public places. That was on a Friday in April 2020. On Monday, she appeared at a Lansing news conference without a mask. Nor did any of those who spoke, which included doctors and health executives.

In August 2021, Barack Obama threw himself a huge three-day birthday party on Martha's Vineyard. Hundreds of guests showed up, but the only ones wearing a mask were their servers. Two years later, President Biden walked into the White House State Dining Room without wearing a mask. Some members of the press who were there were taken aback, and what did he do? He joked about it.

If masks work, as the ruling class insists, why would they place themselves at risk by not wearing one? That would make them irrational. But they are not. For them, the great value in mandating masks for the average Joe is a matter of control, which is why they exempt themselves. In short, forcing the masses to wear masks makes it easier for them to accept their destiny as compliant citizens.

What Covid Policies Wrought

Worldwide, one in three people lost a job or a business during the lockdowns, and half saw their earnings decline. But not everyone was a loser. The richest members of the ruling class did great, grabbing more than $1 trillion, while the middle class and small-business owners lost approximately the same amount. No one did better than Joe Biden. The pandemic allowed him to run his presidential campaign from his basement, eschewing press scrutiny.

Florida and California did about equally well in avoiding Covid deaths, but residents in California paid a big price for nothing. Under Florida Governor Ron DeSantis, his state had half the unemployment rate of Governor Newsom's California, far fewer business closures, and many more business start-ups. Comparing Florida to New York highlights the consequences of inept leadership. New York Governor Cuomo forced nursing homes to accept Covid patients while DeSantis authorized Covid-only facilities and forbade nursing homes from taking Covid patients. Cuomo's edict resulted in thousands of body bags.

In New York City, the Covid czar under Mayor de Blasio, Dr. Jay Varma, implored everyone to abide by the most severe restrictions, yet he made a joke of them himself. He admitted in 2024 that at the height of the Covid craze, he attended drug-fueled sex parties with his wife; more than two hundred people were at the orgies that he hosted.

The effects of the Covid lockdowns had a severe impact on churches. Church attendance decreased, and while the post-pandemic members increased, they never returned to where they were before Covid. Not only that, but some got used to watching church services on TV, which is a poor substitute for in-person worship, to say nothing of the effect on declining funds for church expenses. And as detailed earlier, ridiculously harsh restrictions on churches represented a real diminution in religious liberty.

It wasn't just the First Amendment guarantee of religious liberty that took a hit during Covid; free speech was also decimated. The lockdowns and the punitive response to houses of worship took place in 2020. It was in 2021 that free speech was targeted, and no one paid a bigger price than experts who refused to accept the conventional wisdom.

Ben Weingarten is known in England and America for his stellar research. At the beginning of 2022, he accurately sized up what was happening. "The year 2021 closes as the year of the *crackdown*, when the Ruling Class weaponized its powers to crush dissenters from its Wokeist-Scientist orthodoxy in arguably the most far-reaching, brazen and lawless assault on Americans by the state and its private-sector adjuncts in our nation's history." He was particularly upset with the way civil society reacted; it cooperated with the onslaught. "Censorship, algorithmic suppression, deplatforming, cancelation, social media mobs, sackings, subpoenas, show trials, surveillance—these became part of the daily drumbeat, desensitizing us to what we would usually recognize as both abnormal and un-American."[212]

Weingarten does not exaggerate. The pandemic was exploited by the ruling class and its radical allies in furtherance of their quest for control. While there were crazies who offered delusional ideas about the integrity of the 2020 presidential election, those who raised legitimate questions about the way some election results were tallied were treated as if they were nuts. Ditto for those who questioned the origins of Covid. The mad push for critical race theory—itself a racist idea (all white people are inveterate racists)—led to a crackdown on anyone who dissented. Free speech was under assault.

Desmet, the Belgian psychologist, characterized this response as an example of mass formation, and by that he means "radical intolerance of other opinions and a strong tendency toward authoritarianism."[213] He cites elite response to the pandemic as an exemplary case. When research published in scientific journals is censored on social media, that is a serious problem. When prominent doctors dissent from the reigning orthodoxy and are sanctioned for doing so, that is a serious problem. This happened on both sides of the Atlantic.

What Desmet described continued well after the pandemic was over. In 2024, Dr. Martin Kulldorff, a longtime professor of medicine at Harvard University, was fired, after a lengthy suspension, for what he said was "clinging to the truth" about Covid lockdowns and vaccine mandates. He was fired by Harvard-affiliated Mass General Brigham hospital system for daring to question the accepted wisdom.[214] Before he was canned, he co-authored the influential, and scientifically astute, Great Barrington Declaration. This was in October 2020; he was joined by Dr. Sunetra Gupta of Oxford University and Dr. Jay Bhattacharya of Stanford University; the latter was blacklisted by Twitter. The three argued for Covid restrictions that, as Kulldorff wrote, "protect the elderly, while letting children and young adults live close to normal lives."[215] They also implored government officials to open the schools. As events unfolded, what they said was vindicated. Yet they were treated as pariahs.

In 2025, Meta CEO Mark Zuckerberg revealed that the Biden administration was relentless in putting pressure on Facebook to censor posts about Covid that they disliked. He said they "would call up our team and like scream . . . at them and curse." These were senior members of the Biden administration. "I believe the government pressure was wrong, and I regret that we were not more outspoken about it," he said.[216] Such bullying is repugnant when it emanates from the private sector—it is positively outrageous when it comes from the White House.

I was not surprised that the ACLU would fail to protect free speech, though many others, including conservatives, were. The ACLU's first response to Covid, issued March 2, 2020, stated that "individual rights must sometimes give way to the greater good." It contended that "people can sometimes be deprived of their liberty through quarantine," noting "this is how it should be."[217]

This is not an indefensible position. But it is strange coming from an organization that defends the distribution of child pornography as a free speech right and routinely treats national security interests as subordinate to free speech interests, even in the most serious cases. Quite frankly, the

ACLU has never shown much interest in balancing individual rights with the common good. Roger Baldwin, the founder, said he would not serve on a jury because he did not want to be part of convicting anyone. When I asked him how society could function without punishing offenders, he answered, "That's your problem."[218]

The ACLU's interest in protecting the public health is also new. In the 1980s, it passed a policy against state laws that criminalized the intentional transmission of AIDS to an innocent unsuspecting person. When I asked one of its officials, Gara LaMarche, to explain this policy, all he could say was "homosexuals have rights." He froze in silence when I asked if it was okay for someone to intentionally put a toxic substance in the water supply of a city.[219]

Prior to the 2020 riots, the ACLU supported the stay-at-home orders by governors. The ACLU of Minnesota said that "measures like this have overwhelming support from public health experts trying to protect our collective well-being during this unparalleled crisis."

When the Wisconsin Supreme Court struck down Governor Tony Evers's extension of a stay-at-home order, the Wisconsin affiliate condemned the court for ignoring health warnings, thus "jeopardizing the health of all Wisconsinites."[220] But when it came to left-wing anarchists who took to the streets to protest the death of George Floyd, the ACLU saw this as an expression of free speech.

Students were among the most glaring victims of the lockdowns. "Today," the *New York Times* wrote in 2024, "there is broad acknowledgment among many public health and education experts that extended school closures did not significantly stop the spread of Covid, while academic harms for children have been large and long-lasting."

The newspaper's analysis of the data found that "the longer schools were closed, the more students fell behind."[221] Students who were taught remote or hybrid did the worst.

By contrast, Catholic students across the nation continued to learn in school, and their academic performance did not take a hit. Moreover, Sweden, which went against the grain and did not cave in to Covid hysteria, kept the schools open. No students died and almost none got sick. They also did not witness a dramatic decline in academic scores.

The ruling class, which adopted radical policies, has apparently learned little from its Covid policies. Francis Collins, the former head of the National Institutes of Health during the pandemic, and an advisor to President Biden, later admitted that he and his colleagues demonstrated an "unfortunate" myopia. He said that while Covid was raging, those who challenged the conventional medical opinion were "dismissed as reckless nihilists who didn't care if their fellow citizens died en masse." He confessed that focusing exclusively on stopping the disease allowed health professionals to "attach zero value to whether this actually totally disrupts people's lives, ruins the economy, and had many kids out of school in a way that they never quite recover from."[222]

Journalists Joe Nocera and Bethany McLean wrote a book on this subject, and their assessment is not rosy. They write that "the public health establishment" has learned nothing. "If only we had masked up more and earlier. If only we had locked down harder and longer." This is the kind of stupidity that led the authors to conclude that "if such people are in charge again the next time there's a pandemic, or even during a worse-than-usual seasonal virus, their authoritarian and data-denying impulses will be back in full display."[223]

Not only have many in the ruling class learned nothing, but they are itching for another crisis to milk. As John Tierney says, the "crisis industry" of politicians, technocrats, activists, and journalists has fomented "an endless series of alarms," whether it be the "population bomb" or the "energy crisis."[224] Others contend the big crisis waiting to be politicized is climate change.

Marc Morano specializes in tracking climate change developments. Speaking of the ruling class, he says, "They are lusting after what they saw in Covid." To be specific, he warns that "if you could declare a Covid emergency or you can declare any kind of public health pandemic, you can now call climate change that. And that's what they're looking for, bypass democracy, and that's the whole setup."[225]

Sad but true. The ruling class has teamed with radicals to transform America, and nothing allows the government the opportunity to exercise thought control and behavioral control better than a "crisis." The manipulation of the masses, in service to a compliant citizenry, is their best bet to maintain control. It is the essence of "soft totalitarianism."

Chapter 5

The Family Under Fire

The democratic despots need the allegiance of the masses, but this cannot be done if the average Joe finds a sense of community elsewhere. It is in his family and his religion that he finds wholeness, both psychologically and socially, and the ruling class is well aware of this. While this is a plus for the average Joe, it is a decided negative for elites. With regard to family ties, the power brokers seek to decouple his allegiance by weakening the authority of parents, especially the father. That paves the way for turning his allegiance to them.

The Roman Empire fell because it was under attack externally and internally. From the fourth through the sixth centuries, it could not control its borders and succumbed to barbarian invasions. But this collapse of authority did not take place in a vacuum: it was crashing morally within.

In his classic book *The Decline and Fall of the Roman Empire*, Edward Gibbon cited the breakdown of the family and religion as major contributing factors to Rome's decline. But as Saint Augustine persuasively demonstrated, it was not Christianity that abetted the fall; it was paganism. A permissive attitude toward sex saw the ruling class shun marriage: it was no longer regarded as a sacred obligation. Men and women married for financial gain, if at all. Married men took mistresses, the birthrate declined, and divorce, homosexuality, prostitution, and abortion flourished. Sound familiar?

The society that Orwell saw emerging in *1984* was one in which children were taught to give their allegiance to the Party and Big Brother, not their parents. Indeed, they were expected to spy on their parents for the good of the ruling class. Promiscuity was encouraged for the working class, or the "proles," but discouraged for members of the Party. Drugs, divorce, and prostitution went unpunished for the proles, but were not permitted for the ruling class. Those who belonged to the Party were treated like geldings: they were cultivated to concentrate entirely on the good of elites, turning their desires away from sexual escapades.

In Huxley's *Brave New World*, the family would become obsolete. Men and women would not procreate; that job would be done by state control of reproductive technology. There would be test-tube babies, incubators, and artificial wombs. Some would be mass produced in bottles or in a machine, making mothers and fathers unnecessary. In fact, the term "mother" was cast as an obscenity. Children were required to play outdoors in the nude, thus facilitating sexual experimentation. This way, it would be more difficult for them to form deep familial bonds, making it more likely for them to follow the dictates of the ruling class. No one would live beyond the age of sixty: euthanasia was mandatory.

Is there anyone who doubts that we have the means, and increasingly the will, to pull this off?

Classics scholar Victor Davis Hanson sees some parallels between Orwell, Huxley, and the World Economic Forum.

He sees the WEF as embracing Orwell's Big Brother scenario laced with the soma [drugs] of Huxley's anti-utopian society. "No wonder licentious sex and untrammeled pharmacology, commingled with brutal physical punishment, have loomed so large in the leftist pantheon; the lust comes naturally."[226] The specter of control surely looms large.

Canadian author Janice Fiamengo notes that in their book, *COVID-19: The Great Reset*, WEF founder Klaus Schwab and Thierry Malleret believe that the pursuit of social justice means exposing the "fault lines of the world," and that means an embrace of radical feminism. "The single most important plank of feminist Reset ideology involves breaking the link between women and mothering by asserting that looking after children is primarily a form of 'unpaid labor' and that families (or, at least, progressive women) are best served when children are farmed out to persons who feel no deep familial or affective bond with them."[227] Shades of what Huxley envisioned.

WEF elites adopting the politics of the radical Left is to be expected these days—the two have established a symbiotic relationship. Regarding the latter, it was evident in the mid-twentieth century that the U.S. Communist Party had adopted an anti-family agenda. One of its forty-five goals was to "discredit the family as an institution. Encourage promiscuity and easy divorce."[228] Thus did they take a page from both Orwell and Huxley.

This Communist Party goal has been realized. Fewer young people are getting married, and those that do typically have few, if any, children. Divorce laws have long been relaxed, the consequences of which are undeniable. Sexually transmitted diseases have led to an early death for millions, especially for homosexuals. Some parents are struggling to keep their family together after learning that one of their children has decided to "transition" to the other sex. Loneliness, depression, and suicide rates are spiking, another reflection of the collapse of family bonds.

Another goal of the Communist Party in the 1950s was to "eliminate all laws governing obscenity by calling them 'censorship' and a violation of free speech and free press."[229] Not only have laws against obscenity been weakened to the point where they no longer matter, but it is commonplace for left-wing politicians to invite entertainers to sing the most offensive lyrics while performing, grabbing their crotch while doing so. Just as bad is falsely tagging parents as "censors" when they rightly object to obscene books being assigned to their children. No, they are demanding that books for children be age-appropriate—they are not banning books.

"Break down cultural standards of morality by promoting pornography and obscenity in books, magazines, motion pictures, radio and TV."[230] This Communist goal has been realized by Hollywood moguls and Silicon Valley entrepreneurs. TV shows and movies continue to feature raunch, and the internet is even worse, much of it easily accessible by minors. Those who object are stigmatized for doing so.

If there is one institution that has done more to combat these disturbing trends, it is the Catholic Church. From the time it checkmated the moral destitution that marked the paganism of the Roman Empire, to the latest morally depraved fare, it has stood against sexual misconduct and the exploitation of women and children. Its support for the integrity of marriage and the family is legendary. Indeed, its promotion of an ethic of sexual reticence stands in sharp contrast to the culture of sexual recklessness that has engulfed the United States and the West in general.

Every pope in modern times has spoken forcefully about the key role the family plays in the making of the good society. None, however, was better at understanding the kinds of threats to the family that Huxley and Orwell prophesied than Pope Saint John Paul II.

In his 1981 encyclical *Familiaris Consortio*, John Paul II warned that the family was under attack by both civil society and the state. In his 1988 apostolic exhortation on the laity, *Christifideles Laici*, he contended that "totalitarian politics" was working to undermine the family. Three years later, in *Centesimus Annus*, he specifically said that "a democracy without values easily turns into open or thinly disguised totalitarianism."[231] He meant by that the decline in respect for moral absolutes and the concomitant rise of moral relativism. This is the "soft totalitarianism" that was overcoming the West.

His successor, Pope Benedict XVI, was also alarmed about this phenomenon. What keeps the state at bay are the mediating structures that separate the individual from the state. "The family is an intermediate institution between individuals and society, and nothing can completely take its place." The family is good not only for parents and children, but it is good for society. Indeed, he said it is "an indispensable foundation for society," providing a secure place for children. He also stressed the importance of recognizing the "complementary characteristics" of men and women. Both possessed equal dignity, but it was their different, yet supportive, attributes that brought about "a community of love and life."[232]

If only we heeded their words. Our society devalues marriage and the family, accepts secular state edicts on these institutions as if they were the word of God, celebrates moral relativism, and pretends that men and women are essentially unisex in form and practice. This is madness. No wonder the family is reeling, the biggest victims of which are children.

Intellectuals Against the Family

Leave it to the intellectuals. Behind every assault on common sense and common decency lies a swath of intellectuals. Perennially alienated and always thirsting for power, the men and women who traffic in ideas can be counted on to screw things up. Not all of them, of course, but too many.

Why are they prone to mishap? They live in a world of imagination, one in which they carefully craft the good society. Ever confident of their own abilities, they have no need for God. Nor do they need to learn from those who came before them, save for the most radical theoreticians. Because they are driven by an insatiable appetite for control, and a strong contempt for the average Joe, they see the family as an obstacle standing in their way. This explains why they abhor it.

To be sure, there are intellectuals such as Aristotle and Tocqueville who celebrated the family, seeing it as the fertile soil of freedom and democracy. However, such minds are not well represented these days in colleges and universities. But Karl Marx is.

Writing in a similar vein before Marx were the Utopian socialists Charles Fourier and Robert Owens. Owens said marriage was "evil," and Fournier celebrated promiscuity, encouraging women to seek "as many lovers as she chooses."[233] As profound as their writings were in the early nineteenth century, it was left to Marx and his colleague Friedrich Engels to make family bashing a sport among the Left.

Marx and Engels were convinced that the good society—a communist one—depended on the abolition of the family. In his famous *Manifesto of the Communist Party*, Marx wrote, "The bourgeois clap-trap about the family and education, about the hallowed co-relation of parents and child, becomes all the more disgusting, the more, by the action of Modern industry, all the family ties among the proletarians are torn asunder, and their children transformed into simple articles of commerce and instruments of labour."[234] He never bothered to cite any evidence for his extravagant conclusions, and his followers have never criticized him for it. Whatever he asserted was, and still is, taken at face value.

In Marx's communist wonderland, children would no longer be taught and socialized by their parents; that would be the job of the public schools. Engels, in particular, wanted to nationalize the rearing of children, giving the state more authority than parents. This was in keeping with what Fourier, and especially Owens, wanted. Removing children from their parents allowed for "proper" socialization, as determined by the ruling class. This was an early embrace of the ruling class absorbing the idea of radical intellectuals. Communal rearing of children is still a dream of the Left.

Raising children in a collective setting also made it possible for their parents not to worry about shotgun marriages: women did not have to worry about caring for their child as it was to be done communally. In the communist society, parents might still have a special affinity for their children, but there was no structural provision for it. Consensual sex between men and women would be freed from traditional moral norms, allowing for greater experimentation.

Not surprisingly, Marx and Engels were not role models of parenting. Marx fathered a son with his maid, Lenchen, and Engels conveniently assumed paternity for Freddy, lest the great humanitarian be publicly embarrassed. Marx was so detached from his daughters that both committed suicide. Engels was a philanderer who bounced from one woman to another. Like his hero, Karl, he lived a bourgeois life but chose to bed the working class. He lied about marrying an Irish illiterate working-class woman, and after she died, he married her sister on her deathbed. Classy guys these communist icons were.

The effect that Marx and Engels have had on left-wing activists has been profound. Black Lives Matter initially listed thirteen principles, one of which was the promotion of "Black Villages." What did they mean by this? "We disrupt the narrow Western prescribed nuclear family structure expectation. We support each other as extended families and villages that collectively care for one another, especially 'our' children."[235] Perversely, it is the weakening of the nuclear family, especially among African Americans, that has generated so many social problems. But to these radicals, it must be wrecked even further. Just as perverse, Black Lives Matter raked in tens of millions from corporate titans—most of it so ill-spent that it generated a slew of lawsuits. This proves once again the nexus between radicals and the ruling class.

Wanting to destroy the family is one thing; knowing how to do it is quite another. One way to do it is to attack the institution of marriage. Every society in the history of the world—there are no exceptions—makes a provision for (a) the constructive channeling of the sex drive and (b) a stable and patterned setting for the rearing of children. That's why marriage is universal. This being the case, it stands to reason that if the sex drive is not constructively channeled, as the Catholic Church has long said it must be, promiscuity follows, the results of which are not auspicious, especially for women and children.

Those who champion libertinism, the ideology that essentially sanctions a sexual free-for-all, are delusional. Pope Benedict XVI declares that "libertinism is not freedom but rather freedom's failure." He beckons us to weigh the truth of Saint Paul's admonition. "Do not use your freedom as an opportunity for the flesh, but through love be servants of one another (Gal 5:13)." The pope further notes that "flesh" is "the absolutization of the self," or what he calls a preoccupation with the "I." This represents the "degradation of man."[236] To put it differently, those who live a promiscuous lifestyle are not exuding love—they are exuding hedonism. And they pay for it emotionally, physically, and spiritually.

Marriage, the family, and sexuality are being attacked by radical intellectuals and their ruling-class allies. The push for same-sex marriage and gender ideology are two of their most successful efforts.

The American people were never in favor of two men marrying until members of the ruling class relentlessly thrust it upon them. In state after state, including the most "progressive" ones, same-sex marriage was voted down. Traditional Catholics, evangelical Protestants, Orthodox Jews, Mormons, and Muslims successfully resisted gay marriage, even in liberal California. Then the ruling class stepped in by challenging ballot initiatives in the courts, eventually taking their case to the Supreme Court, where they won a narrow victory. Only then did public opinion begin to change.

Similarly, the American people never sanctioned gender ideology, the unscientific notion that the sexes are interchangeable and that more than two genders exist. It was not the average Joe who bought into the idea that boys who identify as girls, and vice versa, automatically make them members of the opposite sex—it was elites in government, education, and the medical profession. The ruling class, following the ideology spawned by radical intellectuals and activists, is responsible. Future generations may look back at this time as a period when the elites abandoned science, common sense, and decency, yielding to child abuse on a massive scale.

African cardinal Robert Sarah warns that the LGBTQ agenda reflects the pernicious idea that God no longer matters. When this happens, "Good becomes evil, beauty is ugly, love becomes the satisfaction of sexual primal instincts, and truths are all relative." He is particularly concerned about the advent of transgenderism, the false belief that we can change our sex. "Nowhere is this clearer than in the threat that societies are visiting on the family through a demonic 'gender ideology,' a deadly impulse that is being experienced in a world increasingly cut off from God through ideological colonization."[237]

Radical intellectuals and activists bent on destroying the family are always attacking men. Patriarchy is their devil. One of the most significant feminists to do so was Kate Millett. She was an author, a bisexual, and a drug abuser. Bipolar, she suffered from depression and had to be involuntarily hospitalized. She was also suicidal. Not only was her personal life a mess, but so were her ideas.

Kate's sister, Mallory, recalls that in 1969, Kate invited her to come to New York City to take part in a "revolution." By that she meant the founding of the National Organization for Women, which happened three years earlier. Mallory agreed to go and took part in a "consciousness-raising-group" that was eerily reminiscent of what was being practiced in Maoist China.

Kate took to the floor asking a series of questions. "Why are we here today?" The participants answered, "To make revolution." "What kind of revolution?" she replied. "The Cultural Revolution," they chanted. "And how do we make Cultural Revolution?" she demanded. "By destroying the American family!" they answered. "How do we destroy the family?" she replied. "By destroying the American Patriarch," they cried exuberantly. To do that, Kate said, they had to take away his power and destroy monogamy.

Apparently, Mallory was the only normal person in the room. "Was I on planet earth?" she later asked herself. She recalls those at the meeting bleated out that their goal was to promote "promiscuity, eroticism, prostitution and homosexuality."[238] They left nothing on the table. All of this must be done to destroy patriarchy, which would then destroy the family. And once that is done, the quest for the compliant citizenry will be advanced. There will be no authority other than the state. This meant the demise of the average Joe, the proverbial bad guy.

However, destroying patriarchy is a tall order. Sociologist Steven Goldberg published a book in 1974 that has stood the test of time, *The Inevitability of Patriarchy*.[239] His research revealed that patriarchy, or male domination, is universal. There has never been a society anywhere in the world that has failed to associate authority and leadership with men. To be sure, there have been many cases where women have been the head of government, but in all cases, authority is overwhelmingly in the hands of men, in and out of government. Moreover, every society gives higher status to male roles than to nonmaternal roles of females.

Feminists try to refute Goldberg's findings by citing the work of anthropologist Margaret Mead. She is said to have found instances where patriarchy does not exist, and many sociology textbooks continue to mention her work. But this is intellectually dishonest. "In every known human society," Mead said, "the male's need for achievement can be recognized. Men may cook, or weave or dress dolls or hunt hummingbirds, but if such activities are appropriate occupations for men, then the whole society, men and women alike, votes them as important."[240]

In her early writings, Mead did take the position that feminists attribute to her today, but they fail to mention that after conducting more research, she revised her thinking.

"Nowhere do I suggest that I have found any material which disproves the existence of sex differences." When asked specifically about Goldberg's conclusions, she said, "It is true, as Professor Goldberg points out, that all the claims so glibly made about societies ruled by women are nonsense. We have no reason to believe that they ever existed."[241]

Goldberg attributes male dominance to hormonal factors such as the higher levels of testosterone that males have. Testosterone is linked to aggression, and aggression engenders male dominance. The Left finds this disturbing because they discount biological explanations in favor of environmental ones. Yet as Goldberg explicitly notes, "*the hormonal renders the social inevitable*."[242] In other words, it is nature, not nurture, that accounts for the universality of patriarchy.

Leaving aside the biological basis for patriarchy, the truth of the matter is that those feminists who railed against it never represented most women. They represent the thinking of radical intellectuals and activists, as well as members of the ruling class.

In 1966, the feminists who founded the National Organization for Women explicitly called for "a sex role revolution for men and women which will restructure all our institutions: childrearing, education, marriage, the family, medicine, work, politics, the economy, religion, psychological theory, human sexuality, morality and the very evolution of the race."[243] The average Jane never wanted anything to do with any of these absurd goals. She wanted to be treated fairly in all walks of life, but she never aspired to be a zealot in pursuit of a radical agenda.

Most women have always wanted to be loved by their husbands and children and to live a normal lifestyle. But this is not what feminists want for them. Feminists think they know what is in their interest better than they do, which is why they don't need to be consulted, just dictated to. This includes legislative efforts that foster their egalitarian agenda, such as the Equal Rights Amendment (ERA).

Soon after women won the right to vote, radical feminists decided that the franchise was too modest a goal. They wanted full-throated equality between men and women in every aspect of life, allowing no exceptions. But the average Jane did not. In fact, most liberal women did not want the ERA.

Eleanor Roosevelt opposed the ERA because it would eviscerate labor laws that protected women from doing dangerous and demeaning work. She was supported by the American Association of Women Professors and the League of Women Voters. Even the ACLU fought the ERA. It argued that the "Unequal Rights Amendment," as it was called, was too extreme and sweeping, disallowing differential legislation that women supported.

It took this position in the 1920s and fought every effort to pass the ERA in the 1930s, 1940s, 1950s, and 1960s; it flipped in 1970.[244] Up until that time, only the most radical feminists wanted it. In 1980, matters had changed so drastically that when a woman ran for senator in Florida, Paula Hawkins, the National Organization for Women worked against her, simply because she opposed the ERA. So much for the feminist shibboleth about the need for more women in government. She won anyway.

The differential legislation that most women supported, until the latter half of the twentieth century, included the family wage. Married men, it was reasoned, should be paid enough to support their wives and children, and this meant that they should get paid more, for doing the same work, than single men and women. The emphasis was on the best interest of the family, not individuals.

The family wage first arose during the industrial revolution in the West in the latter part of the eighteenth century. It was the considered judgment of liberal intellectuals such as John Stuart Mill that women were needed most in the home, raising children. Even socialists such as Friedrich Engels advocated for the family wage. More importantly, most women embraced it as well. Led by middle-class women, they wanted their husbands to be paid enough to support their family, enabling them to work at home caring for their children.

Catholic educators and theorists led the way campaigning for the family wage. According to historian Allan Carlson, this was "their proudest achievement"—namely, the "liberation of married women from toil in the factories, so that they might care for the home and children and so prevent the full industrialization of human life."[245] This required, he said, wage discrimination against women.

Pope Pius XI, in his 1931 encyclical *Quadragesimo Anno*, didn't pull any punches. "Mothers, concentrating on household duties, should work primarily in the home or in its immediate vicinity. It is an intolerable abuse, and to be abolished at all cost, for mothers on account of the father's low wage to be forced to engage in gainful occupations outside the home to the neglect of their proper care and duties, especially the training of children. Every effort must therefore be made that fathers of families receive a wage large enough to meet ordinary family needs adequately."[246]

Our culture, led by radicals and the ruling class, no longer puts the family at the center of public policy. By adopting a culture of radical autonomy, the individual takes center stage. The signs are all around us, and the outcome is not pretty. This is what Harrison Butker was getting at when he spoke positively about the role that women play in rearing their children. That he was chastised for doing so is a sad statement on our society.

Chapter 6

Whose Children Are They?

Controlling Children

It seems axiomatic: children belong to their parents. Parents know this to be true, and so do most people. But left-wing intellectuals and activists don't agree. Children, they say, belong to all of us.

Why would they say such a thing? Remember, the Left has one ambition—to control. They can't control the average Joe if he is raised by his parents. When that happens, the average Joe naturally inclines to accept their norms and values, and the problem with that is they are not likely to be the notions of right and wrong as entertained by radicals and the ruling class. Therefore, parents should not have first dibs on raising their own children. Some elites take it a step further and argue that parents should have no role whatsoever in raising their children. In the meantime, they settle for eviscerating parental rights at every juncture.

"We're all in this together." Sounds reasonable. It is true that there are times when we need to depend on our fellow neighbors for support, so such appeals have a certain ring of truth to them. It is also true that parents need all the help they can get, and this is especially true of single parents. Going it alone is difficult, so making appeals to collective support systems sounds attractive. But not so fast.

It is true that we all have to live together, and parents need the assistance of non-family members, but such verities can never be used as an excuse to encroach on the rights of fathers and mothers. They are biologically vested in raising their children as they see fit (always allowing for extraordinary exceptions such as practices that endanger children) and should never be forced to surrender their rights to the state or to any other entity. Beware of those who sound empathic but are in reality pursuing a collectivist agenda for the purpose of exercising control of children.

When President Biden spoke at the Teacher of the Year event in 2022, he told teachers that their students belong to them. "They're all our children. . . . They're not somebody else's children; they're like yours when they're in the classroom."[247] What he said is patently untrue. To be certain, teachers are responsible for the welfare of their students while they are in school, but to say that "they're not somebody else's children" is to say that they do not belong to their parents. That smacks of authoritarianism.

The next year, Biden spoke at the National and State Teacher of the Year Celebration and spoke glowingly of the winner, Rebekah Peterson. He quoted her approvingly, saying, "Rebecca put a teacher's creed into words when she said, 'There is no such thing as someone else's child.'" Biden took the opportunity to second her by saying, "Our nation's children are all our children."[248] But having people believe that all children are our nation's children is a dangerous omen: it could whet the appetite to nationalize them.

Biden is particularly interested in casting LGBTQ kids as a collective responsibility. In 2023, after he denounced violence against these children, he took the opportunity to up the ante, saying, "These are our kids." He emphasized, "Not somebody else's kids, they're all our kids."[249] In other words, it is mistaken to believe that kids belong to their parents. White House Press Secretary Karine Jean-Pierre had the talking points down pat when she echoed the president by saying "we have to be very clear about" this issue, noting "these are *our* kids" and "they belong to all of us."[250]

When Kamala Harris served as vice president under Biden, she adopted the same policy. She told late night talk-show host Seth Meyers that "when you see our kids, I truly believe that they are our children, they are the children of our country, of our communities."[251] Once again, parental rights take a back seat to the interests of the collective. She did not call for state control of children, but the logic of her remarks is not inconsistent with it.

It may not matter much if these were just the rumblings of some left-wing politicians. But this is not the case. In 2025, Chicago Teachers Union President David Gates argued that "The children are always ours. Every single one of them. All over the globe." Others go even further, insisting that teachers should subvert parental rights. Rachel Wall is an Iowa school board member, and she contends: "The purpose of a public education is to not teach kids what the parents want. It is to teach them what society needs them to know. The client is not the parent, but the community."[252]

The notion that children belong to the community is a very old idea. Plato believed that children are best socialized and educated by the state, not their biological parents. He explicitly said in *The Republic* that the good society was one where "no parent shall know his own offspring nor any child his parent."[253]

Marx and Engels insisted that parents should not be allowed to raise their children. Their goal was to nurture in the very young a commitment to the state, the purpose of which was to facilitate the greatest transformation in history—to remake their nature and create the "New Man." They declared that the traditional family was "narrow and petty, where the parents quarrel and are only interested in their own offspring," thus making them incapable of "educating the 'new person.'"[254] In short, once the family is destroyed, thought control would abet behavioral control.

These were not empty words. In 1918, the year after the Russian Revolution, the Communists gave instructions to Soviet educators. "We must remove the children from the crude influence of their families. We must take them over and, to speak frankly, nationalize them."[255] They meant what they said. One year later, on March 1, 1919, a Soviet decree announced that "one month after birth, children will be placed in an institution entrusted with their care and education. They will remain there to complete their instruction and education at the expense of the national fund until they reach the age of seventeen." What happens if someone objects? They "shall be declared enemies of the people, anti-anarchists, and shall suffer the consequences."[256] We know from history what that meant.

This communist dream has also been entertained by Americans. Mary Jo Bane is a radical professor emerita at Harvard University and served as a member of the ruling class during the Clinton administration in the Department of Health and Human Services. Her specialty is the family. What makes her somewhat unique is that she wants to abolish the very institution she has studied throughout her academic career. An egalitarian zealot, she said that "in order to raise children with equality, we must take them away from families and communally raise them."[257]

Bane's sociology is accurate. Parents will always love their children more than someone else's children, and it is true that some may not have the will or the resources to nurture in them the requisites that make for success in school or the workplace. Hence, inequality is inevitable. But if her sociology is correct, her ethics are not. She is not the least bit bothered by the idea that the state has the right to effectively kidnap children and take them from their home. Too bad she didn't tell us what the punishment ought to be for those who resist. We can only guess.

Hillary Clinton believes "we are all part of one family, the American family." Nonsense. Families are, by nature, based on exclusivity, not inclusivity. The average Joe understands this intuitively. Now this may not sit well with those who want to collectivize it, but certain verities cannot be willed away. Nature is stubborn. Hillary wants us to believe that to raise a child, "it takes a family. It takes teachers. It takes clergy. It takes business people. It takes community leaders. It takes those who protect our health and safety. It takes all of us. Yes, it takes a village."[258] She should have stopped after making her first observation. Those who think she is just showing her caring and compassionate side ought to ask themselves what is going to happen once the "village" doesn't agree with the parents of the child.

It should come as no surprise that radical homosexual intellectuals also favor communal upbringing of children. Denied by nature from having their own children, they want an equal opportunity to raise the children of heterosexuals. In the early 1970s, Dennis Altman made the case that as long as heterosexuals raise their children, the youngsters will not learn that homosexuality is natural. The way to resolve this alleged problem is to create "a social system that provided instead an opportunity for children to grow up regarding *both* homo- and heterosexuality as part of the human condition." In short, homosexuals should not be denied "any role in child-rearing."[259] This is a crude example of usufruct—declaring that what belongs to others also belongs to me.

Forgetting for the moment that no one has a right to raise someone else's children, the fact is communal living is no panacea for what its enthusiasts seek. In the 1980s, two renowned sociologists, Brigitte Berger and Peter Berger, surveyed the research and concluded that "far from creating the non-authoritarian personalities dreamed of by their original proponents, the communes of recent decades have been the context of some of the most rigidly authoritarian and destructive movements of our time. If any phenomenon can, then the communes constitute the most telling empirical falsification of the theory that the destruction of the bourgeois family is the precondition of freedom."[260] This doesn't appear to be the utopian society it was cracked up to be. Just the opposite.

The Catholic Perspective

Catholic social teaching makes so much sense because it is in accordance with what human nature decrees. There is no tension between the two. The problem for many radicals, and their friends in the ruling class, is human nature itself: they are constantly at war with it. This explains their antipathy for the nuclear family, which is much older and more universal than frequently believed.

In 1983, the Holy See issued the *Charter of the Rights of the Family*," a document that made it very clear that the Church awards primacy to the family in the rearing of children. In the preamble, it says, "the family, a natural society, exists prior to the State or any other community, and possesses inherent rights which are inalienable."[261] In other words, agents of government take a back seat to the authority vested in parents—the family is *prior* to government and all other social institutions. To be clear, it does not say that government should adopt a laissez-faire position. No, it says government "must protect the family" through its policies, providing "the unity and stability of the family so that it can exercise its special function."[262] Its special function is the rearing of children. This obligation belongs to parents, not the state.

If the family is special, it must be treated as such in law, and this means that "non-married couples must not be placed on the same level as marriage duly contracted." Consider how different this is from what we hear today. Left-wing intellectuals and activists want to relativize marriage and the family, making them no more important than cohabiting arrangements. But children deserve better. Moreover, the Holy See holds that because "the spouses have the inalienable right to found a family,"[263] no government edict can order parents to give up their children to the state. Inalienable rights, by definition, cannot be compromised.

When it comes to educating children, the document makes it clear that the "it takes a village" approach is nonsense. "Since they have conferred life on their children, parents have the original, primary and inalienable right to educate them; hence they must be acknowledged as the first and foremost educators of their children."[264] The Soviet model so beloved by radicals—let's take the children from their parents and raise them communally—is rightly seen as subversive of the "original, primary and inalienable right" of parents to educate their children. Another way to look at it is this: all the talk about creating the "New Man" is an abomination.

The Catholic Church's emphasis on parental rights was upheld in a famous Supreme Court case in the 1920s. At that time, the Ku Klux Klan—which was anti-Catholic and anti-Jewish, as well as anti-black—supported an Oregon law that required all children to attend a public school (thus closing down Catholic schools). The Sisters of the Holy Names of Jesus and Mary sued, and in 1925, the Supreme Court sided with them. Justice James C. McReynolds wrote the famous words, "*The child is not the mere creature of the State*; those who nurture him and direct his destiny have the right, coupled with the high duty, to recognize and prepare him for additional obligations."[265]

One does not have to be Catholic to understand the ramifications of religious liberty and parental rights if the high court had ruled otherwise. But to this day, the enemies of these twin rights are still trying to pry children from their parents whenever the opportunity arises. They believe that children belong to the state, not to parents.

Elites' War on Parental Rights

In the Committee to Unleash Prosperity survey of American elites conducted by pollster Scott Rasmussen, "They vs. U.S.," it found that the top 1 percent of income earners were overwhelmingly in favor of teachers' rights v. parental rights. "Two-thirds (67%) say teachers and other educational professionals should decide what children are taught rather than letting parents decide."[266] The percentage was even higher when those with an Ivy League education were asked. In other words, the ruling class knows better than the average Joe what's best for his kids.

These elites reflect the thinking of the post-World War II Communist Party. Skousen wrote that the Communists argued that the origin of the controversy over parental rights lay in the Ten Commandments. "Honor thy Father and thy Mother," they said, "was created by the early Hebrews to emphasize to their children the fact that they were the private property of their parents."[267] It is this twisted thinking that accounts for the rage against parental rights.

In 2017, the *American Journal of Bioethics* published a piece by Johan Bester and Eric Kodish titled, "Children Are Not the Property of Their Parents: The Need for a Clear Statement of Ethical Obligations and Boundaries." The first sentence makes unmistakable their position: "Children do not belong to their parents."[268] They wrapped their child-grabbing scheme in clinical terms, saying that doctors (the pediatricians) have an obligation to do what is best for their patient. Who anointed them with these rights remains a mystery. This takes on more urgent meaning when we learn something that academicians are not inclined to discuss—namely, the fact that the American Academy of Pediatrics supports child gender-transition policies that include genital mutilation and chemical castration. These are the people the child grabbers want to empower.

There are some scholars who want to decimate parental rights by adopting the language of liberation. Children are oppressed, they say, and they need to be liberated from their parents.

Lorna Finlayson is a lecturer of philosophy at the University of Essex in England. She passionately believes that "it's time we took child liberation seriously—not only for children's sake, but for everybody's."[269] Unlike some of the other writers who share her view, she has a problem with teachers, as well as parents. She opposes compulsory schooling (this may have something to do with why she left school at age thirteen) and the idea that children need to be regulated by adults.

Americans have a longing for liberty and equality, so appeals to liberation are welcome. But to those in the children's rights movement, the "liberation" of children comes at the expense of the diminution of parental rights. That's their real goal. Parents cannot be trusted to nurture the compliant citizen, but the state can.

It was in the 1960s, when so many liberation movements took place, that the cause of children's rights was launched. According to two of the leading advocates, Beatrice and Ronald Gross, the movement was triggered by the need "to rectify the shameful conditions that lead to the damage and death of so many children." They were convinced that "young people are the most oppressed of all minorities. They are discriminated against on the basis of age in everything from movie admissions to sex. They are traditionally the subjects of ridicule, humiliation, and mental torture in homes, schools, and other institutions."[270]

The oppressors are obviously parents, teachers, and others who exercise authority over children. There is nothing nuanced about anything they say—they are cocksure they are right. Just as obvious is their goal: to encourage lawmakers and judges to deal forthrightly with this horrendous condition and do something to liberate children from their oppressors. Only then will the "mental torture" end and the kids can engage in all the sex they want.

It seems plain that the average Joe would conclude that these people are freaks. Yes, their ideas may make them freaks, but in some education circles, the average Joe is the freak. Consider what John Holt, a respected education author, and Richard Farson, a well-known psychologist, had to say about this subject in the 1970s. I mention them only because they reached a sizable and influential audience, and their ideas are popular with left-wing child liberationists today.

Holt wants children to have the right to vote. Just so we understand him, he says, "I am talking not just about the sixteen-year-old vote but about the six-year-old vote." He also wants children to be able to travel independent of their family. To those who say they may get lost, he replies, "Adults get lost right now. It may be a nuisance, but not a tragedy or disaster."[271] So if Johnny gets lost in the airport—while he is traveling alone looking for his flight to Bermuda—that's not a big deal.

Holt wants to get rid of compulsory education, leaving it to kids whether they want to go to school. All drugs should be legalized and there should be no age restriction. Should kids be allowed to drive? Or to have sex? You got it—a thumbs up to both.

Farson wants children to have the right to live where they want, and with whom, including residences run by kids. In the event a child elects to go to school, he should determine the curriculum. The right to vote and work for a living must also be observed.[272]

These radicals say their goal is child liberation. But this cannot be done without destroying the family. That's their real goal. Once children are "liberated" from their parents, the state can move in and socialize them. The ruling class will make sure that this "soft totalitarian" approach will breed an obedient citizenry.

Left-wing writers today are just as committed to waging war on parental rights, though these days they accuse its proponents of using the state to accrue power. Sarah Jones, an admitted socialist and atheist, is one such author. She maintains that the invocation of parental rights by conservative activists is a way "to the total capture of state power and the imposition of an authoritarian hierarchy on us all."[273]

This is perverse. Advocates for parental rights do not want to maximize the state—they want to pare it back so that it does not interfere with their rights. It is people like Jones who are upset with what she correctly notes is a "resurgence" of the parental rights movement. She is also calling the kettle black when she claims that conservatives treat children as private property. It is true that normal parents believe that childrearing is a private affair, but they do not see them as property. It is atheists like Jones who are projecting their materialist ideas onto others who think of humanity in terms of property. So when she says that children are a "public responsibility," what she really means is that they are public property.[274]

Ideas have consequences. It is one thing for nutty educators, psychologists, and writers to say that parents should not have the right to bring their children up the way they want; it is quite another when the state affirms them. Take the issue of parents and their transgender children. Here is a perfect example of how radicals have succeeded in winning over the ruling class.

Frederick Short sent his children to Cherry Hill West High School in New Jersey. One day he learned of a school policy that upset him. "A transgender student shall be addressed at school by the name and pronoun chosen by the student, regardless of whether a legal name change or change in official school records has occurred."[275]

What if the parents object? What if they insist that Sam should not be called Sally? They lose. The school agreed to consult the school board's attorney, but Sam must still be called Sally in school. Short's kids were not transgender, but he was angered by the policy and was forced to sue.

Let's say a young girl is suffering from some mental issues and wants to transition to the opposite sex (80 percent of those who do so are girls). Let's say she lives in the state of Washington and wants to get sex-reassignment surgery done behind the back of her parents. Let's say her parents find out anyway, and their afflicted daughter wants to flee her home and live with a family who will take her in. Can she do so? Yes. Does the host family have to tell her parents? No. When the girl decides to undergo chemical castration and get her genitals amputated, does the host family have to alert her family at this juncture? Not at all. The law in Washington has eviscerated parental rights in the name of transgenderism. A sane society would label this child abuse.

It gets worse. States are now kidnapping children in compliance with this pernicious ideology. And if it can happen in Montana, it can happen anywhere.

Krista and Todd Kolstad have a sexually confused daughter, Jennifer, who mistakenly thinks she is a boy. Jen had suicidal thoughts (it is not uncommon for these mentally challenged young people to be suicidal), and when her school found out about it, Child and Family Services (CFS) were called to deal with her condition. Bullied at school, her parents moved her to a new school district, doing everything they could to stabilize the situation. But CFS was unimpressed. They took Jen from them because they refused to affirm her delusional state.

It should come as no surprise to learn that support for transitioning children to the other sex, behind their parent's back, is something the Biden administration championed. It also endorsed a website that ensured that girls under the age of eighteen can get an abortion without the permission of their parents.

Where did school authorities get the idea that somehow they know better than parents what is in the best interest of children? It began with Horace Mann, generally regarded as the father of public education. The early nineteenth-century educator embodied the elitist attitude that "teachers know best." Parents, he believed, need to shed the idea that they know best how to raise their children. "We who are engaged in the sacred cause of education are entitled to look upon all parents as having given hostage to our cause."[276] There was no need for educators to seek the consent of parents—they were entitled to overrule them in pursuit of their "sacred cause." It doesn't get more arrogant than this.

Mann's vision was implemented in the second decade of the twenty-first century by Eskelsen García, president of the National Education Association. She said the union needed to expand its agenda by focusing on "the whole child." Gone were the days when teachers should concentrate on academic performance, she said, now they had to cast their net wide, recognizing that the "child's world is our business."[277] Not their parent's business. "Our" business.

In 2013, a year before García took over the NEA, MSNBC host Melissa Harris-Perry ignited a debate among parents and educators when she said that "we have to break through our kind of private idea that kids belong to their parents or kids belong to their families and recognize that kids belong to whole communities."[278] Move over mom and dad—teachers to the rescue. Now what if the educators are teaching values that are at odds with what parents are teaching?

According to political theorists Amy Gutmann and Stephen Macedo, that's a good thing. They argue that the state can and should demand that children be taught values that are inconsistent with the values of their parents. This is part of what they call "diversity education." They even go so far as to say the state should mandate "diversity education" in private schools and home schools.[279] This would obviously mean that government bureaucrats would be given the authority to police the homes of parents who homeschool their children, making sure the kids are learning values that their mothers and fathers find objectionable. Make no mistake, the values they want to checkmate are grounded in Christian moral theology.

Sounds like they lifted a page from Huxley and Orwell—crushing the family is the duty of the state. That way children can be taught to "think the right way."

Homeschooling

The Catholic Church has always given priority to parents in making decisions regarding their education. "Parents have the first responsibility for the education of their children." Those words, found in the *Catechism of the Catholic Church*, were punctuated by the Second Vatican Council's *Declaration on Christian Education* (*Gravissimus Educationis*). "Since parents have given children their life, they are bound by the most serious obligation to educate their offspring and therefore must be recognized as the primary and principal educators."[280]

Thus does the Catholic Church find homeschooling to be entirely acceptable. Indeed, it accords with the Church's principle of subsidiarity, which locates authority at the level closest to the people. This was explicitly noted in the declaration on education. It could not be more clear, then, that for the state to deny homeschooling is to eviscerate parental rights.

Homeschooling is legal throughout the United States, though for most of the twentieth century, it ran afoul of compulsory education laws. It clearly is on the rise. In fact, it is growing so quickly that the *Washington Post* found that it is the "fastest growing form of education."[281] To say its critics are nervous would be an understatement. They are worried that the average Joe's kids are slipping away from them.

TV talk show host John Oliver is opposed to homeschooling, citing the need for government oversight. He worries that this school choice initiative is "essentially unregulated," as if government regulation of the public schools has an envious record. When he claims that it "can result in enormous damage,"[282] he is not only making an unsubstantiated accusation, but he leaves himself defenseless when we consider that the sexual abuse of minors in the public schools is a serious and ongoing problem, one that persists despite government oversight.

Oliver may only be a pundit, but his position is shared by noted authors. No scholar is more famous for making the case against homeschooling than Elizabeth Bartholet, professor of law at Harvard Law School. She wants to crush the homeschooling movement. She made her case in a widely discussed article in the *Arizona Law Review*.[283]

Bartholet deeply resents the "near-absolute" power that parents exercise. The legal argument upon which parental power rests, she says, "is based on a dangerous idea about parent rights—that those with enormous physical and other power over infants and children should be subject to virtually no check on that power."

Of course, if children are to be reared by adults who are not their parents, those persons would, necessarily, have "enormous physical and other power" over them. But that kind of power imbalance is okay with her: it's the child's parents who are the problem. She objects to their "monopoly," as though this were somehow unfair. She believes it is.

What is really angering Bartholet is the fact that conservative Christians do most of the homeschooling: they are at least a majority and may account for as much as 90 percent. She calls them "religious ideologues." If the homeschoolers were secular left-wing ideologues, like her and her colleagues at Harvard, that would not be a problem.

She accuses these homeschooling Christian parents of "isolating their children from the majority culture and indoctrinating them in views and values that are in serious conflict with that culture." What they need, she contends, is "exposure to the values of tolerance and deliberative democracy."

Her chutzpah is astonishing.

It is certainly true that many parents who homeschool their children seek to protect them from the rot that marks much of the dominant culture: internet pornography, violent video games, obscene lyrics, anti-Christian fare, and the like. They also seek to provide an alternative to school curricula that teach their children to disdain our Judeo-Christian heritage and lie about our nation's historic fight for liberty. Moreover, it is not the parents who are promoting the sick idea that we can change our sex—it's the nutty ones in academia.

It must also be said that it is risible to hear anyone from higher education complain about intolerance. In no place in America is there less tolerance for free speech and heterodox views than on the typical college campus.

Bartholet maintains that parents who homeschool their children are a threat to their safety. Parents can "subject them to abuse and neglect free from scrutiny that helps protect children in regular schools." She really needs to do her homework before sounding so sophomoric.

To those who have written extensively on this subject, as I have, it is well known that the public schools not only tolerate unspeakably high rates of sexual abuse, but they have resisted, via their unions, the establishment of a nationwide data bank. It is this which allows molesting teachers to be moved from one school district to another—it is so common that it is called "passing the trash"—ensuring even further abuse.

The Catholic Church went through this problem from the mid-1960s to the mid-1980s (though it did not make headlines until 2002). Fortunately, so much progress has been made that this problem has all but been eradicated. But it is still extant in the public schools, and efforts to conceal it are legendary, though this comes as news to Bartholet.

"Teachers and other education personnel have long been responsible for a significant percentage of all reports to CPS [child protective services], larger than any other group." This flies in the face of all the evidence. She is apparently unaware of the U.S. Department of Education studies, and the reports by the Associated Press and *USA Today* on this subject.

Bartholet can get downright nasty. She says families that choose to homeschool their children do so "because it enables them to escape the attention of CPS." In other words, not only do these vile Christian parents abuse their children, but they choose homeschooling *because* they want to abuse them with impunity.

I say she is nasty because the source she cites does not support her outrageous claim. The source she names in a footnote says "anecdotal evidence" shows that "some abusive parents . . . have taken advantage of lax homeschooling laws to hide their children from mandatory reporters." That is very different from what she said. She said families deliberately choose to homeschool their children so they can escape scrutiny.

Bartholet really looks like an amateur when she cites *New York Times* columnist Michelle Goldberg as a source showing that abuse and neglect in homeschooling is ongoing. When Goldberg was in college, she advocated violence against innocent persons. To be specific, when she was at SUNY-Buffalo, she wrote a piece for the campus newspaper urging readers to "do your part and spit at [pro-life students]. Kick them in the head."

Some of Bartholet's recommendations are rich with hyperbole. We need to rid ourselves of homeschooling, she contends, because of what it allows. "Parents can choose to beat their children, starve them, or chain them up, free from scrutiny by any who are required to report suspected abuse and neglect." But homeschooling is not the issue: a small percentage of parents have always abused their children. So this is a red herring. What she is really getting at is pernicious. By creating a straw man, she is inviting the ruling class to send in a swat team of educrats to rescue the children.

To top things off, it is striking to read a Harvard law professor rail against the U.S. Constitution. She calls it "outdated and inadequate by the standards of the rest of the world." But most people worldwide, she fails to say, live under tyrannical regimes. What bothers her are "negative rights," such as "Congress shall pass no law." She wants this model supplanted by positive rights, such as "Everyone must." A better prescription for despotism could not be found—it's why dictators love to dictate.

Bartholet wants to bestow children with positive rights. This means that when children are given rights, they can insist that their parents accede to their demands. This has always been the dream of radical egalitarians.

Her number one recommendation is that there should be a "general presumption against homeschooling." The burden, she says, must fall on parents to justify their request. She allows for "exceptions," but in those instances, the parents need to jump through an array of hoops, all of which are designed to weaken their status and enhance the power of the state.

Parents must submit their "intended curriculum and education plan"; offer proof of their credentials; submit to testing "on a regular basis"; allow "home visits by school authorities"; allow background checks, etc.

In other words, if they make the cut, parents who are permitted to homeschool must give up their parental rights and bow to the edicts of the state.

This is just the beginning. Bartholet wants to extend the reach of the state to police the private schools, singling out religious ones. "Religious and other groups with views and values far outside the mainstream operate private schools with very little regulation." This means, she says, they are being deprived of "exposure to alternative perspectives."

Translated, this means that Christians who homeschool their children are not teaching the values Bartholet wants to instill in them. This would surely mean, for example, that children would learn that it is okay for boys and girls to rebel against their nature and switch their sex; all they need to do is obtain services from someone who will mutilate their genitals. No doubt, referrals would be offered.

Bartholet is upset because kids who are homeschooled are beyond the reach of the state and are being given values she abhors. She knows better than their parents what values they should have and wants to subject them to her tutoring. This is the mind of a despot.

It all boils down to one thing: In the mind of radical egalitarians, the number one enemy is the family. The family is the heart of inequality and the source of traditional values. It must therefore be weakened, if not annihilated.

All the radicals need to win is to secure the blessings of the ruling class, which thus far has been reluctant to push their agenda too far. But one thing is for sure—the anti-Christian scholars and activists who hate homeschooling will continue their anti-family crusade. They need to be resisted and defeated at every turn.

CHAPTER 7

POPULATION CONTROL

Elites and Catholics Diverge

When Pharaoh felt threatened by the growth of the Hebrew population, he ordered every infant boy to be put to death. As population expert Steven Mosher notes, this was the beginning of population control in recorded history.[284] It has been a concern of the ruling class ever since.

The ruling class wants to stay in power, whether it be in democratic or non-democratic nations, and one of their perennial concerns is the size and the profile of the masses. It likes its subjects compliant and is prepared to take all necessary steps to ensure this outcome.

Population growth is always a worry for the ruling class, but those who specialize in family planning are also concerned about the characteristics of the population. Some people are seen as more desirable than others, and those labeled undesirable cannot be ignored. If it is decided that some may not fit in, that has to be dealt with forthrightly.

Elites are often drawn to a purist profile of America. It's another way they can exercise control. They run into opposition, however, from the Catholic Church. This explains why many of them are anti-Catholic: they resent the Church's teachings on eugenics, reproductive technology, euthanasia, and assisted suicide. These matters have long been key elements in the portfolio of the ruling class. They are wrong on these issues, but they are not wrong in casting the Church as the enemy.

In the late nineteenth century, social Darwinism became all the rage among elites. Following Darwin's work, they applied his principles to the various groups, particularly as they affected their ability to succeed. The fascination with natural selection did not sit well with Catholic observers and eventually led to an official rebuke of population control. In 1930, Pope Pius XI issued an encyclical, *Casti Connubii*, that reaffirmed the Church's teaching against artificial birth control, sterilization, abortion, and eugenics. The pope held that the state could not "tamper with the integrity of the body."[285]

In 1987, the Congregation for the Doctrine of the Faith issued *Donum Vitae*, a document that clarified Church teachings on reproductive technologies. The Church maintained that it was acceptable to use these developments to assist in helping a couple in reaching the natural objective of generating life, but it was morally wrong to try to replace the conjugal act. The document made clear that respect for the human person begins at conception, thus treating abortion as an illicit act. This encyclical was important for another reason: it reflected the thinking of Pope Saint John Paul II's Theology of the Body.

It was John Paul who also tackled euthanasia in his magnificent encyclical *Evangelium Vitae*. He did not mince words. "I confirm that euthanasia is a grave violation of the law of God, since it is the deliberate and morally unacceptable killing of a human person." He called it "murder."[286]

The Catholic way of handling the dying is not to kill the person but to do what Mother Teresa did so effectively and care for those in their last days.

The same moral logic is evident in the Church's response to assisted suicide. Assisted suicide is a great evil because it fundamentally alters the relationship between the doctor and his patients. Doctors are charged with tending to the living; they are not expected to hurry their death. It is also prone to massive abuse, despite the "safeguards" that its proponents advertise.

In August 2024, the Dicastery for the Doctrine of the Faith issued "Dignitas Infinita" on human dignity. Its section on euthanasia and assisted suicide was excellent.

It began by noting that these twin issues are "swiftly gaining ground." It took strong issue with the popular cause "death with dignity," the mistaken belief that euthanasia and assisted suicide are "somehow consistent with respect for the dignity of the human person." In response, the document asserts that "it must be strongly reiterated that suffering does not cause the sick to lose their dignity, which is intrinsically and inalienably their own." Instead, the document says, we should see suffering as "an opportunity to strengthen the bonds of mutual belonging" and to seize the moment to reaffirm our love for the dying.[287]

The utilitarian ethic that undergirds the movement to legitimize euthanasia and assisted suicide is based on a radical notion of autonomy. Such thinking does not speak to the welfare of the sick and dying and is therefore morally corrupt. It is the easy way out and should be resisted by those who put the human person at the center of their beliefs. That is the Catholic way.

Eugenics

There is no family more prominent among the population purists than the Rockefellers. Titans of the ruling class, they have spent more money founding, funding, and lobbying organizations in their quest for population control.

In the early twentieth century, John D. Rockefeller Jr. gave millions to eugenics organizations, hoping to inspire like-minded people to join his cause. He found a key ally in Margaret Sanger, founder of Planned Parenthood. Their joint goal was to weed out the undesirables, those who contributed to the dumbing down of the population. Eugenics would allow for more of the "right kind" of children to be born, the fittest of them all. Sanger pulled no punches, declaring, "We cannot improve the race until we first cut down production of its least desirable members." She opened birth-control clinics to ensure "the elimination of the unfit."[288] Angela Franks, who authored a book on Sanger, said, "She believed that if you eliminated the poor, then there would be no more poverty. Instead of eliminating the problem, she would eliminate the people who had the problem."[289]

In case there is any doubt about whom she meant by the "undesirables," Sanger's Planned Parenthood boasted in 1932 that "many of the colored citizens are fine specimens of humanity. A good share of them, however, constitute a large percentage of Kalamazoo's human scrap pile."[290] She brazenly admitted that "we don't want the word to get out that we want to exterminate the Negro population."[291] H. G. Wells, one of the most respected intellectuals of his day, agreed. "We want fewer and better children . . . and we cannot make the social life and the world-peace we are determined to make, with the ill-bred, ill-trained swarms of inferior citizens that you inflict upon us."[292]

John D. Rockefeller III held similar views; he believed that we could winnow the population by adopting purist measures. In 1969, he provided a large share of the money for the first bioethics research institute, called the Hastings Center. It would fund an array of population control initiatives, including euthanasia and genetic engineering. In 1988, the organization justified research using aborted fetal body parts.

Planned Parenthood, the Rockefeller's biggest prize, would eventually embrace abortion as an effective population control measure. Sanger was personally opposed to abortion, but she did not look kindly on the Catholic Church for opposing birth control. Her biographer, Ellen Chesler, admits that she was "rabidly anti-Catholic as she grew older." Indeed, Sanger compared the Church to communist regimes and argued that Catholics should stay out of politics. She said no Catholic "has any moral right to hold a position of authority for the State." The blacklist was necessary because Catholics "cannot help but give their first allegiance to the Church," thus giving life to the scurrilous canard about Catholics exercising dual loyalty.[293]

The Rockefellers are still prominent in promoting population control, but they are enjoying stiff competition from the World Economic Forum. Yuval Noah Harari, one of the central WEF figures, predicts that artificial intelligence and genetic engineering will "enable parents to create smarter or more attractive children."[294] This will lead, he says, to a society of gross inequality as the ruling class will find a way to create the fittest of the fit.

The kind of hi-tech society that Harari envisions was anticipated by Huxley when he spoke about severing the link between sex and procreation. It was also the central theme of *Humanae Vitae*, the 1968 encyclical by Pope Paul VI on artificial birth control. The difference is the ruling class has no problem with this development, and indeed welcomes it. But for Catholics, separating sex and reproduction has serious consequences, the most dramatic of which is to cheapen conjugal love. Here again, the ruling class and radicals are at one, uniting in their determination to further population control, whether it be by using birth control, abortion, or some other reproductive technology. Their answer to Catholic objections to birth control is that at least it doesn't result in abortion. This is completely misleading.

Mary Eberstadt has studied this issue as well as anyone, and it is her conclusion that "the old defense of birth control as the alternative to abortion has been overruled by facts. The reality that it is an accelerant to abortion has been confirmed by time."[295] The data backs her up. What *Humanae Vitae* predicted has come true. Contraceptive use and abortion have risen concomitantly. Why? Contraception sent the message to men that they could have their fun and escape responsibility for their behavior. In the event there is an unplanned pregnancy, there is always the option of abortion. Moreover, contraception has the effect of trivializing sex, and that abets the prospects of abortion. While radical feminists insist that contraception and abortion liberate women, the reality is quite the opposite—it liberates men from their obligations, leaving women to face the consequences alone.

Abortion

Daniel Patrick Moynihan said it seemed like we were witnessing a national nervous breakdown in 1968. Rev. Martin Luther King Jr. and Senator Bobby Kennedy were shot and killed, race riots exploded, mayhem took place in Chicago during the Democratic National Convention, and mass demonstrations protesting the Vietnam War were commonplace. Adding to this incendiary situation was the hysteria over population growth.

Stanford University entomologist Dr. Paul Ehrlich's book *The Population Bomb* was published that year, setting off a national debate. He predicted that there would be mass starvation and food riots by the end of the 1970s. He was wrong. As University of Tennessee law professor Glenn H. Reynolds observes, "Instead of mass starvation, the biggest nutritional problem on Earth is now obesity, a problem even in countries once associated with hunger."[296]

But at the time, Ehrlich was carrying the day, feeding the march to legalize abortion. Due to the influence of Dr. Mary Calderone, a radical sexologist, Planned Parenthood turned the corner and embraced the cause of abortion rights. But as recently as 1963, the organization Sanger founded was still opposed to abortion. When debating this issue with the late talk-show host Phil Donahue, I read on the air the following statement: "An abortion kills the life of a baby after it has begun. It is dangerous to your life and health." In an angry tone, Phil asked me who wrote that. I replied, "Planned Parenthood in 1963."[297] Sitting next to me was Gloria Feldt, president of Planned Parenthood. She was speechless.

There is no greater enemy of the family than abortion. That explains why the ruling class generously funds the abortion-rights industry, mostly through foundations and pro-abortion organizations. The elites are bent on control, and population control, via abortion, is one of their most prized methods of achieving it.

As important as Planned Parenthood has been in promoting this agenda, the organization that was most responsible for changing the landscape on the ethics of abortion was the National Abortion and Reproductive Rights Action League, or NARAL (now called Reproductive Freedom for All). How it prepared the American public to accept the morality of abortion is one of the great untold stories of this era. It was radical activists who eventually drove the Supreme Court decision to legalize abortion in its 1973 decision *Roe v. Wade*. They were not only left-wing influencers, but they were anti-Catholic bigots.

Two men, Dr. Bernard Nathanson and Lawrence Lader, were the driving force behind this movement; Lader was the most left-wing of the two. According to Nathanson, Lader "had a long history of being ultra-radical and anti-Catholic. He was for a time a political aide to Vito Marcantonio, who was the only card-carrying Communist ever elected to Congress."[298] Together, they forged a plan to promote the politics of abortion, but in order to be successful, they had to reckon with the Catholic Church. At that time, the Church stood alone against abortion (when *Roe* was decided, even evangelical Protestants were on the pro-abortion side, though that quickly changed).

In 1967, two years before Nathanson and Lader founded NARAL, they mapped out their strategy. According to Nathanson, Lader "brought out his favorite whipping boy," the Catholic Church. The goal was to "bring the Catholic hierarchy out where we can fight them. That's the real enemy." The trick was how to do this without alienating average-Joe Catholics. Nathanson reasoned that they needed to focus on "the Catholic hierarchy, not the Catholic Church. The Catholic Church was the ordinary man on the street Catholic. . . . We didn't want to antagonize the man on the street Catholic. So we focused on the hierarchy—the bishops, the priests, the cardinals, the pope. It was a clear shot and not many people were going to object to it."[299]

As Nathanson explained, the anti-Catholic strategy of NARAL "was not normally discussed in executive committee meetings. . . . But when Larry and I would go down to the Caribbean every six months or so to plot out the strategy for the next six months, of course we talked all about this. Lader was fixated on anti-Catholicism, he was obsessed with it."[300]

The strategy worked. Not only was the voice of the Catholic Church tarnished and abortion legalized, but the juxtaposition of radicals (Lader and Nathanson) and the ruling class (members of the Supreme Court) paid big dividends. The ruling in *Roe* was written by Justice Harry Blackmun, and he cited Lader's book, *Abortion*, eight times. The militant secular approach to abortion proved triumphant.

What did Blackmun learn from reading Lader's book? He learned that Lader relied on experts such as Dr. Garrett Hardin, professor of biology at the University of California at Santa Barbara, to draw his conclusions. Hardin bemoaned unwanted pregnancies and unwanted children. Instead of saying adopting babies is the answer, he said aborting them was the right thing to do. "Any woman at any time should be able to procure a legal abortion without ever giving a reason," he said.[301] He was such an extremist that his school's website describes him as a "white nationalist" and a eugenicist who believed that blacks were "intellectually, physically, and culturally inferior," which is why he supported racial segregation and sterilization of "people of color."[302] He also supported infanticide.

In Justice Blackmun's ruling on *Roe*, he said something that was rather amazing. Every honest person knows that abortion is controversial because it begs the question: When does life begin? Astonishingly, Blackmun said it didn't matter. "We need not resolve the difficult question of when life begins."[303] Thus did he lift a page out of Lader's playbook.

In his book, *Abortion*, Lader tried hard to skirt the issue of when life begins, focusing more on how people of different faiths view the subject. He was pleased to note that Protestants and Jews took a more pro-choice view, saving his criticism for Catholics. By casting the issue as one of theology, instead of science, he intentionally dismissed the central question of when life begins. Not surprisingly, he clearly misrepresented Catholic teachings several times. In short, Blackmun's agnosticism on when life begins is directly traceable to the book by Lader that he cited in his ruling.

There is one piece of good news. Following *Roe*, the pro-abortion movement lost one of its big players, and the pro-life side gained one, Dr. Nathanson. Once the Supreme Court decision was rendered, he took a job as an obstetrician in New York. It was there that he witnessed a child on the ultrasound screen, and it jarred him. He had presided over thousands of abortions, including one he performed on a girlfriend he impregnated, yet he thought nothing of it. But pictures don't lie. He met Fr. C. John McCloskey, a famous Opus Dei priest, and this relationship ended in Nathanson becoming a Catholic. Why did he choose Catholicism? Because, he said, it places a premium on forgiveness, and after what he had done, he needed all the forgiveness he could muster.

But some things never change. The ruling class continues to grease the pro-abortion industry like never before. Warren Buffett's choice vehicle, the Susan Thompson Buffett Foundation, has spent billions funding the pro-abortion cause. Even more disturbing is what happened to Melinda Gates. Raised a Catholic, she wanted nothing to do with abortion when she sat on the board of her husband's foundation. After she divorced Bill, she flipped sides and began spending a small fortune on "reproductive freedom." Unlike Nathanson, who gave a principled reason for changing his mind, Gates simply said that the decision overturning *Roe*, sending the issue back to the state to decide, made her switch sides. But the 2022 ruling in *Dobbs v. Jackson Women's Health Organization* was procedural—it did not touch on the morality of abortion. In other words, she did not give a principled reason for her change of heart.

Lying About Abortion

There is no public policy issue surrounded with more lies than abortion. It is one of the most infuriating aspects of this subject. Everyone is free to decide for himself whether to approve or disapprove of abortion, but no one is entitled to patently misrepresent the truth. To make matters worse, the media, overall, are so obviously on the side of abortion rights that it is no longer debatable. For those who are pro-life, it is a never-ending battle to set the record straight.

Robert P. George is a Princeton scholar, committed Catholic, and the nation's most persuasive proponent of the pro-life view. He not only makes the moral case for life, but he makes a scientifically astute analysis of when life begins.

In 2024, George engaged Ruth Marcus, a columnist for the *Washington Post*, on the question of when life begins.[304] She denied that human embryos and fetuses are human beings. George struck back saying that is "a flat denial of science." He conceded that gametes, sperm and egg, are not human beings. But, he hastened to say, "they are both genetically and functionally *parts* of other organisms—a man and a woman."[305]

Moreover, when they join, he says, "the resulting embryo has a new and complete genome of its own. More importantly, the embryo does not function as a mere part of anyone. He or she—for in humans, sex is established from the start—functions as a whole organism. Like infants, toddlers, or teens, embryos and fetuses will—unless prevented by disease, violence, lack of nutrition or warmth, etc.—develop by an internally directed and gapless process into later stages of the life cycle of a human being."[306]

His key point is this: "Embryos and fetuses do not 'gradually' *become* human beings. That *is* unscientific gibberish. Our *development to adulthood* is gradual, to be sure, but we come into existence *as* human beings—whole living members of the species *Homo sapiens*—and develop *as* (not into) human beings."[307]

George's analysis is unassailable—he is merely restating what human embryology and developmental biology teach. No wonder so few want to debate him on this issue.

As previously pointed out, Justice Blackmun's decision in *Roe* avoided the question of when life begins, so taken was he by Lader's view that the issue dealt more about theology than biology. Blackmun was wrong about this, but what makes *Roe* so troubling is that the case itself was based on a lie. The woman in *Roe*, Jane Roe (whose actual name is Norma McCorvey), was twenty-one when she became pregnant for the third time. She sought an abortion in Texas. But there was one problem: Texas did not allow for abortions except if the mother's life was endangered. So on the advice of feminist lawyers—who exploited her for their own ideological reasons—she lied and said she was raped.

In the run-up to *Roe*, Lader and Nathanson constantly lied. Indeed, their entire strategy was based on lies.

In the late 1960s and early 1970s, they coined phrases such as "Freedom of choice" and "Women must have control of their bodies." Nathanson said, "I remember laughing when we made up those slogans. We were looking for some sexy, catchy slogans to capture public opinion. They were very cynical slogans then, just as all these slogans today are very, very, cynical."[308]

The two were working with Betty Friedan, the most influential feminist of her era. They all agreed that if public opinion polls were taken at that time, it would not favor their side. "Knowing that if a true poll were taken, we would be soundly defeated, we simply fabricated the results of fictional polls. We announced to the media that we had taken polls and that 60 percent of Americans were in favor of permissive abortions. This is the tactic of the self-fulfilling lie. Few people care to be in the minority."[309]

They also lied about the data. They did so by "fabricating the number of illegal abortions done annually in the U.S. The actual figure was approaching 10,000, but the figure we gave to the media was 1 million. Repeating the big lie often enough convinces the public. The number of women dying from illegal abortions was around 200-250 annually. The figure we constantly fed to the media was 10,000."[310]

It should be noted that in 1972, the year before *Roe* legalized abortion, thirty-nine women died of an illegal or self-induced abortion. That's a far cry from ten thousand.

The lies never stop. In September 2024, former president Donald Trump debated vice president Kamala Harris, the late-chosen nominee to run for president. Trump was "fact checked" during and after the debate by the moderators and the media. They all claimed he lied about abortion. They were wrong. He got it right.

Harris was asked by Linsey Davis of ABC TV if she supported any restrictions on a woman's right to an abortion. "I absolutely support reinstating the protections of *Roe v. Wade*," she said. She added that "nowhere in America is a woman carrying a pregnancy to term and asking for an abortion. That is not happening. It's insulting to women of America."[311]

Trump responded by saying Harris "would allow abortion in the eighth month, ninth month, seventh month." She replied, "Come on." He followed by saying, "You could do abortions in the seventh month, the eighth month, the ninth month." She answered, "That's not true."[312]

Trump won the argument.

Late-term abortions, contrary to what Harris said, are more common than what she contends. In 1995, Dr. George Tiller told his fans, "We have some experience with late terminations; about 10,000 patients between 24 and 36 weeks and something like 800 fetal anomalies between 26 and 36 weeks in the past 5 years."[313]

Ron Fitzsimmons used to tell the media that partial-birth abortions—where the baby is 80 percent born—were extremely rare. Then in 1995, he went on national TV and admitted that he "lied through [his] teeth," saying he was just spouting "the party line."[314]

In 2019, the pro-abortion Guttmacher Institute admitted that at least twelve thousand late-term abortions take place annually in the United States. In 2023, a fact checker at the *Washington Post* conceded that at least ten thousand late-term abortions take place each year.

Quite frankly, under *Roe v. Wade*, abortion-on-demand, while not a *de jure* right (it was not permitted after viability except in limited cases), was a *de facto* right. For proof, consider *Doe v. Bolton*, the companion case to *Roe*; it opened the door to abortion-on-demand.

In *Roe*, the high court said the states may outlaw abortion "except where it is necessary, in appropriate medical judgment, for the preservation of the life or health of the mother." The ruling in *Doe* defined what an "appropriate medical judgment" was. It entailed the "physical, emotional, psychological, familial, and the women's age—relevant to the well-being of the patient."[315]

Not surprisingly, every state law that attempted to limit post-viability abortions to those necessary for the *physical* health of the women failed in court when challenged; the other reasons were so elastically defined that no one would be denied. In effect, the joint decisions in *Roe* and *Doe* legalized abortion up until birth. So when Harris said she accepts *Roe*, that means she wants to make all abortions legal, at any time during pregnancy.

Moreover, Harris voted against the "Pain-Capable Unborn Child Protection Act" that would protect unborn children by prohibiting abortion at twenty weeks, a point where the child is able to feel pain.

Then there is the matter of governors allowing babies to die after a botched abortion.

Trump addressed this issue by saying that the former governor of Virginia (Ralph Northam) was guilty of allowing this to happen. Substantively, what Trump said was basically right. He accused the governor of contending that "the baby will be born and we will decide what to do with the baby. In other words, we'll execute the baby."[316]

Here is what Virginia governor Northam opined in 2019. If a baby survived an abortion, he said, "the infant would be kept comfortable. The infant would be resuscitated if that's what the mother and the family decided, and then a discussion would ensure between the physicians and the mother."[317] So while the baby would not be "executed," per se, he could be put down, or left to die, after he was "kept comfortable." That's infanticide. There is no other word for it.

Northam is not alone among Democrats on this issue. Just prior to his stunning admission, New York governor Andrew Cuomo signed legislation that allowed premature babies who survive a chemical abortion to be denied treatment.

At the federal level in 2019, the Born-Alive Abortion Survivors Protection Act was blocked by Senate Democrats. It would require that a baby born alive during an abortion must be afforded the same care that would apply to all babies delivered at the same gestational age. Harris was one of the senators who voted to kill the bill. In 2023, all but two congressional Democrats voted against this same bill.

The family is under attack, and abortion is the most defined way of achieving this end. The pro-abortion movement was inspired by radical activists and put into practice by elites in government and healthcare. The anti-Christian venom they spill is designed to marginalize Christians, and to some extent, they have succeeded. But this chapter is not over.

CHAPTER 8

WHY RELIGION THREATENS ELITES AND RADICALS

The Problem That Religion Poses

If radical intellectuals and activists hate the family, they positively detest religion. Both are seen, quite correctly, as sources of allegiance, and therefore they compete with the interests of those who want all allegiances to be directed toward the state. In the eyes of elites, what makes religion so odious is that it takes the eyes of the masses off the here and now, thus diverting attention from existential conditions. By contrast, the only god that radicals worship is themselves.

The ruling class is generally more tolerant than their radical allies; however, this is only true of those who have not adopted the radical agenda. Increasingly in the West, they have. They are smart enough to know that religion can have a tight grip on the people, and that can be a problem: if the average Joe takes his primary cues from the clergy, that inexorably comes at the expense of the moral authority of the ruling class. Is this not what happened in Poland when

Pope Saint John Paul II took on the communist ruling class head-on? Hence, the need to keep religion in check.

What does the future hold for those of us in the West? Orwell predicted that religion would be outlawed. Personal loyalties must give way to Party loyalty, and this means that religion must be destroyed. Once Big Brother replaces God, there is no stopping the ruling class from achieving total dominance. It becomes the only source of truth.

For Huxley, Mustapha Mond, the Controller, takes the place of God. But this doesn't sit well with everyone. The Controller says to John Savage, a dissenter, "One believes things because one has been conditioned to believe them." He adds, "People believe in God because they've been conditioned to believe in God." Savage objects, noting that "it is natural to believe in God when you're alone—quite alone, in the night, thinking about death." "But people never are alone now," replies Mustapha Mond. "We make them hate solitude; and we arrange their lives so that it is impossible for them ever to have it."[318]

The state, whether it be the form of Big Brother or the Controller, has big shoes to fill given the void that religion's death entails. But the elites are omnipresent and omnivorous, leaving no traces of the past behind. This is what Orwell and Huxley said awaits us, and they were right. Radicals are now abetted by having many in the ruling class on their side. The elites who provide resistance are getting weaker, which is why Christianity is on the ropes.

As we saw in the first chapter, those who comprise the ruling class are the most secular segment of the population. Much of this has to do with education. College graduates are more secular than high school graduates, and those with postgraduate degrees are more secular than those with a college degree. While radicals really hate religion, the ruling class tends more towards cynicism: they are self-sufficient and have no need of God. Where they come together is in failing to see religion as a bedrock of democracy. So when radicals push back against religion, elites are disinclined to provide much in the way of resistance. The radicals know this, which is why they push so hard.

Those in the ruling class who are not overtly hostile to religion are more often than not uneasy with it. I have met many of them. They understand that religion can act as an antidote to moral decay, and many applaud that contribution. But they nonetheless feel awkward talking about religion. These are the communitarians, thoughtful Americans in high places who don't want to destroy religion as much as they simply dismiss it. In doing so, however, they are playing into the hands of radicals who harbor ill-feelings towards everything about religion. They certainly don't appreciate the defining role that religion plays in the development of a free society.

Edmund Burke and Alexis de Tocqueville saw things more clearly.

Burke went so far as to say that religion is "the basis of civil society, and the source of all good and of all comfort." He insisted that "man is by his constitution a religious animal" and that "atheism is against it." So we dispense with it at great peril, as happened during the French Revolution. We can rail against religion all we want, but in the end, we are destined to live with that which replaces it. It is the Christian religion, he said, that is "the one great source of civilization amongst us." Doing away with it is therefore costly. We are understandably "apprehensive," he cautioned, about the "void" it causes, beckoning some "uncouth, pernicious, and degrading superstition" that might take its place.[319]

For Tocqueville, religion is the guardian of the mores, those unwritten norms that distinguish right from wrong. A mature way of assessing religion's contribution to a free society, he wrote, is to acknowledge that religion is "the cradle of its infancy."[320] Tying mores, religion, and freedom together, he opined, meant that "one cannot establish the reign of liberty without that of mores, and mores cannot be firmly founded without beliefs."[321] What makes religion special, he said, is that it "sets limits to human sovereignty and therefore to the sovereignty of the people in a democracy."[322]

The elites know this to be true. Religion is a threat because it puts limits on their sovereignty, just as Tocqueville said. "Despotism may be able to do without faith," he aptly observed, "but freedom cannot." To put it differently, in a free society, we must police ourselves, lest the police do the job for us. To assure self-governing people, however, "moral ties" must be "tightened."[323]

Tightening moral ties, which are dependent on religious strictures, is anathema to radicals, as well as to many elites. The latter may not be viscerally opposed to a strong moral code the way radicals are, but they prefer morality to be grounded in some secular alternative. This explains why they incline toward the view that religious and secular norms and values should be seen as equals, even if the average Joe does not agree. But that is not what the Founders envisioned.

As law professor Patrick Garry explains, it was never their intent "to place religion and nonreligion on the same level." "Textually," he says, "the Constitution provides greater protection for religious practices than for any secular-belief-related activities."[324] This is true, but it is not what most of the ruling class believes, and it sure isn't what radicals believe.

The problem that religion poses for the ruling class becomes manifest when they pursue a radical secular agenda. It is in times of the Great Reset that it shines brightly.

John Tierney identifies four of the most prominent in history. The French Revolution sought to replace Catholicism with a state-sponsored secular religion based on the cult of reason; the Soviet antireligious campaign sought to destroy Russian Orthodox Christianity; the Nazis sought to crush Christianity; and the Chinese Communist Party targeted all religions. Tierney explains that "the motive for suppression in each case is similar: to remove the obstacle to the total commitment and faith required to remake the world."[325]

Yes, when the ruling class adopts radical ideologies, it invariably clashes with religion. Pope Saint John Paul II understood why. "The state or the party which claims to be able to lead history towards perfect goodness, and which sets itself above all values, cannot tolerate the affirmation of an *objective criterion of good and evil* beyond the will of those in power, since such a criterion, in given circumstances, could be used to judge their actions. This explains why totalitarianism attempts to destroy the Church, or at least to reduce her to submission, making her an instrument of its own ideological apparatus."[326]

The Communist Assault on Religion

When Karl Marx was a young man, Germany in the 1830s and 1840s was a hotbed of anti-Christian ideas: Jesus never existed, the Gospels were a fake, etc. He was particularly influenced by Ludwig Feuerbach. He not only disparaged Christianity, but he argued that man is the highest form of intelligence. This was music to Marx's ears. It explains why, when asked what his objective was in life, he answered, "To dethrone God and destroy capitalism."[327] This, in turn, was music to the ears of the Soviet communists.

Anatole Lunarcharsky was the Russian Commissar of Education under Lenin. His description of why religion must be destroyed underscores everything this book is about.

"We hate Christians and Christianity. Even the best of them must be considered our worst enemies. Christian love is an obstacle to the development of the revolution. Down with love of one's neighbor! What we want is hate. . . . Only then will we conquer the universe!"[328] The family—the other big threat to totalitarianism—was also targeted for destruction, and for the same reason: it is an obstacle to total rule.

If Lenin put Christianity on the ropes, it was left to Stalin to finish the job. His Five-Year Plan, launched in 1928, included an all-out assault on religion. Churches were converted into secular buildings, Christmas celebrations were banned, Sunday could no longer be observed as a day of worship, and the clergy were imprisoned, if not executed. Atheism was everywhere heralded. In 1937, Stalin boasted that they were closing in on the final destruction of religion, saying the day was approaching when "religion in the Soviet Union will exist only as a historical memory."[329]

Two years later, only an estimated two hundred churches remained open, out of a pre-revolution total of about forty-six thousand.

In his masterful analysis of the threat that communism poses to the United States, W. Cleon Skousen identified multiple goals, saying that "the general thrust of the 45 goals was to attack the Judeo-Christian underpinnings that had long prospered and protected freedom, and to replace them with the bricks, mortar and top-down force of a purely socialistic society."[330] Yes, a nation's religious heritage must be destroyed if communism is to win, but it is also true that many non-communist elites also see religion as a bulwark against their ambitions, which is why they seek to disable it.

Skousen was right to observe that a nation can be conquered in one of two ways. "The first is to attack it militarily and compel the people to obedience. The second is to corrupt the institutions that keep the people unified, and raise up leaders who promise to stabilize the chaos, establish order and return a sense of security."[331] As will be pointed out, while violence initiated by those abroad is not a looming threat, violence by radical activists is a preferred tactic within our nation. No matter, it is the second approach that poses the most existential threat. Many elites, and virtually all radicals, want to destabilize Christianity, making it easier for them to capture the allegiance of the average Joe.

Violent Attacks on Christianity

Theologian Thomas D. Williams has detailed violence against Christians. Most of us believe, he says, that Christian persecution is something that happened during the first three centuries, ending with the fall of the Roman Empire. "This is unfortunately far from reality," he says. "The troubling fact is that a full 75 percent of religiously motivated violence today occurs against Christians and some 300 million Christians around the world live in situation of serious persecution, meaning they fear for their lives and well-being on a daily basis."[332]

We are lucky in the United States that violence against Christians is not a major factor. But hatred of them is not uncommon, and when violence occurs, the media go mute.

In 2015, an Oregon man, Chris Harper-Mercer, said to his victims before he killed them: "Are you Christian?" After they stood up, he said, "Good, because you're Christian, you are going to see God in just about one second." He then shot them.[333]

The media covered this story as a mass shooting, but most never mentioned that Christians were singled out. The evening news shows on ABC, CBS, NBC, and PBS were all guilty, as was the Associated Press, the *New York Times*, *USA Today*. Prominent internet outlets, such as Yahoo, also failed to mention that Christians were killed because they were Christians.

This was not a mistake. It was not a gaffe. It was intentional. The Catholic League has long provided evidence that media elites harbor a strong animus against Christianity. If gays were killed because they were gay, or blacks because they were black, every media outlet would say so.

This is not to say that these elites want Christians to die, but it is to say that they see Christians as victimizers, so to run a story which casts them as victims is disconcerting to their narrative.

In August 2022, the Catholic League issued an eighteen-page report on hundreds of anti-Catholic crimes across the nation that had taken place since the urban riots took place in 2020.[334] Monuments were destroyed, iconic statues were bludgeoned, gravesites were desecrated, Catholic Masses were interrupted, graffiti was spray-painted on church walls, windows were smashed, churches were torched, schools were vandalized, chalices were stolen, etc. In some cases, messages were left indicating that the offenses were a payback to Catholics for their strong pro-life stand. Many wild-eyed charges were levied against the Church, seeking to justify the violence. In some cases, the guilty were caught and charged with a hate crime. In most cases, they were either not apprehended or were not prosecuted. In short, the average Joe who was victimized was treated like dirt.

The Family Research Council released a report in 2024 detailing attacks on churches that included vandalism, arson, gun-related incidents, bomb threats, and more; it covered incidents from January 2018 to November 2023.[335] In 2023, the organization identified 436 incidents—more than double the number identified in 2022 and more than eight times the number identified in 2018. The same entity, run by Tony Perkins, issued another report in 2024 detailing the intensification of intolerance against Christians in the West. The hostility to Christianity in Europe is astonishing.

Political Attacks on Christianity

Cardinal Robert Sarah is a well-known champion of religious liberty. An African, he is particularly concerned about the precarious state of Christianity in the West. He maintains that "the violence against Christians is not just physical, it is also political, ideological and cultural. This form of religious persecution is equally damaging, yet more hidden. It does not destroy physically but spiritually; it demolishes the teachings of Jesus and His Church and, hence, the foundations of faith by leading souls astray." He adds that this outcome is "the will of the Evil One."[336]

Pope Benedict XVI shared Cardinal Sarah's concern. He identified secularization as "the greatest challenge of our time."[337] Yes, when the clergy are barred from speaking at 9/11 ceremonies by the mayor of New York City, the effects of militant secularization are real. This matters all the more when the source of the animus is government; no organization wields more power.

One of the vilest expressions of militant secularization occurred in 2022 when the assistant principal of a Connecticut public school in Greenwich was caught on tape admitting that he doesn't hire Catholics. When he was asked by a journalist, who secretly taped him, what he did when he found out that a person looking for a teaching job was Catholic, he replied, "You don't hire them." He further explained that "if someone is raised hardcore Catholic, it's like they're brainwashed. You can never change their mind."[338] Of course, if someone is a committed secularist, that would make him open-minded and suitable for the job.

There are anti-Christian bigots in both political parties, but over the past half century the Democratic Party has become home to the most secular segment of the population. To be sure, it is wrong to say that because someone is a secularist he is therefore a religious bigot. That's nonsense. But it remains true that the more militant a secularist is, the more likely he is to be anti-Christian. Invariably, they are registered Democrats.

For example, when government officials threaten to pull the tax-exempt status of the Catholic Church, it is a sure bet it will not be a Republican. In 2001, Representative Jared Huffman, a Democrat from California, did just that when he said, "If they're [the Catholic bishops] going to politically weaponize religion by 'rebuking' Democrats who support women's reproductive choice, then a 'rebuke' of their tax-exempt status may be in order." His passion for abortion rights led him to totally dismiss the First Amendment rights of freedom of speech and freedom of religion as exercised by the bishops.[339]

Anti-Catholicism was not evident in the Democratic Party in any serious way until the administration of Bill Clinton, though he himself was innocent of this charge.

When he was elected president in 1992, he appointed Dr. Joycelyn Elders as surgeon general. It was a mistake. She had a history of bashing Christians, especially Catholics, over issues like abortion. Even the *Washington Post* called her out for her malicious words. She, however, was not alone in expressing her bigotry. In 1994, Clinton's ambassador to the Vatican, former Boston mayor Ray Flynn, blasted the administration for being anti-Catholic. He said he was "embarrassed" about the "ugly anti-Catholic bias that is shown by prominent members of Congress and the administration."[340]

John Kerry ran for president in 2004. Four years later, John Edwards sought the Democratic nomination. In both cases, they had anti-Catholics on their team. Though they were forced out, it was still surprising.

When I was growing up, it would have been unheard of for Democrats to hire anti-Catholics. After all, Catholics were one of their key constituencies. But things changed in the 1990s, and they haven't gotten any better.

In 2008, when Barack Obama was a presidential candidate, he made a disparaging comment about white working-class Christians. "It's not surprising," he said "[that] they get bitter, they cling to guns or religion or antipathy to people who aren't like them or anti-immigrant sentiment or anti-trade sentiment as a way to explain their frustrations."[341] What proved to be so revealing about this admission was the venue: in a closed-door session, he addressed a forum of wealthy, left-leaning secularists in San Francisco. Although no average Joes were there, they were the subject of his remarks.

In his first Christmas in the White House, the president and his wife, Michelle, planned to have a "non-religious Christmas."[342] It was one thing to learn that they don't give their children Christmas gifts; it was quite another to learn that they were not going to permit a nativity scene in the

White House. After this was leaked to the media, they had to reverse themselves and allow a manger scene.

Obama was in office for only a few months when he spoke at Georgetown University. Before the event, university officials were told to put a drape over all religious symbols that might appear as a backdrop to where the president was going to speak. To drive the point home, they made sure that the IHS symbol, a monogram of the name Jesus Christ, was not in sight. Who might be offended to see Christian symbols in a Catholic university was not explained.

Obama also had a habit of leaving out any reference to God, or the "Creator," when citing the Declaration of Independence. Similarly, he could not bring himself to utter the words "In God We Trust" when speaking about our national motto. In keeping with his secular ideology, in 2010, he became the first president in history to welcome a gathering of atheists, many of whom belonged to organizations with a history of Christian bashing.[343]

Obama's secular deeds were more consequential. He wasted no time trying to secularize the faith-based programs initiated by President George W. Bush. Under Bush, these programs were designed to allow religious social service organizations to receive public funds. This was a good move. We know from a mountain of evidence that faith-based programs do a better job than government ones in serving the needy. Whether working with juvenile delinquents or drug users, or providing counseling services and foster care programs, faith-based initiatives have a stellar record. Obama, however, was in denial. "I'm not saying that faith-based groups are an alternative to government or secular nonprofits," he said, "and I'm not saying that they're somehow better at lifting people up."[344] Not surprisingly, faith-based programs under Obama floundered. His heart was never in it.

A more serious issue evolved when Obama rolled out his Affordable Care Act in 2010. He promised that it wouldn't be used to provide federal funds for abortion, but that was said only because he needed to get a few pro-life Democratic congressmen on board. Once the law was passed, the Department of Health and Human Services sought to make every employer, including Catholic ones, provide abortion coverage in their insurance plans. Enter the Little Sisters of the Poor, and many other Catholic nonprofits. They were not about to fund abortions, however indirectly.

It was widely reported in the media that Obama's healthcare plan only made employers pay for contraceptives. Not true. It also required funding for abortion-inducing drugs, and that was something no Catholic organization could do in good conscience. The mission of the Little Sisters of the Poor is to tend to the needs of the elderly of every race and religion. They do so in the name of Jesus Christ. There was no way they would drop a dime to pay for abortion-inducing drugs. Eventually, their case won in the Supreme Court. In 2020, the high court ruled that the Trump administration was within its authority to expand exemptions to the Affordable Care Act, thus concluding that the Little Sisters of the Poor did not have to abide by the Obama mandate.

The most drastic anti-Catholic policies ever promoted by a presidential administration occurred under a self-professed "devout" Catholic—namely, Joe Biden. Under his rule, the

FBI was weaponized against practicing Catholics in a way never before seen in American history.

In early 2023, news reports surfaced about the FBI investigating orthodox Catholics. The agency cited the far-left, and scandal ridden, Southern Poverty Law Center as its source. In an important whistle-blowing article published by Kyle Seraphin, a former FBI special agent, the Richmond Field Office of the FBI released a report on "Radical-Traditionalist Catholics," or what they called RTCs. While some of these Catholics reject Vatican II, and have expressed controversial views, none have a history of violence. So why the probe?

As Seraphin noted, "The FBI is forbidden from opening cases or publishing products based solely on First Amendment-protected activities."[345] Why then the war on RTCs? Worse still was the FBI's war on mainline Catholic parishes and those in diocesan leadership positions: they were both selected for investigation. It was obvious that an anti-Catholic cell group had taken root in the FBI.

What was particularly odious about the FBI witch-hunt is that the agents had nothing to do with dissident Catholics—their entire focus was on Catholics who were "pro-life" and who "support the biological basis for sex and gender distinction." These practicing Catholics were labeled "domestic terrorists."[346]

Pro-life Catholics and Protestants were constantly harassed by Biden's Department of Justice (DOJ). Instead of cracking down on Jane's Revenge, a radical pro-abortion group that uses domestic terrorists' tactics, the DOJ went after pro-life Catholic activists like Mark Houck. The FBI sent two dozen agents to his house with guns drawn simply because he allegedly violated the Freedom of Access to Clinic Entrances Act (the FACE Act). In other words, violence against pro-life crisis pregnancy centers went unchecked, but nonviolent protests in front of abortion clinics were pursued. A twelve-person jury eventually found Houck not guilty of violating the FACE Act.

This becomes all the more infuriating when we consider that in November 2023, FBI Director Christopher Wray admitted that 70 percent of the FACE offenses were committed by abortion-rights activists. Moreover, we learned from Associate Attorney General Vanita Gupta that pro-lifers were disproportionately targeted. Everyone knew why: the Biden administration was angry over the Supreme Court ruling overturning *Roe v. Wade*.

Given its priorities, it is hardly surprising to learn that the Biden administration did not have a great religious liberty record. In fact, a Catholic League study comparing the Trump administration's record on this issue to that of Biden's found that in Trump's first term, his administration upheld religious liberty 117 times. The figure for Biden was 33.[347] This explains why Biden's Office of Faith-Based and Neighborhood Partnerships announced early on in his administration that it "will not prefer one faith over another *or favor religious over secular organizations* (my italics)."[348] The latter admission essentially eviscerated its raison d'être.

In more recent years, the Democrats, beginning with Obama, have tried to push legislation requiring Catholic hospitals to perform abortions. Obama failed with getting the Freedom of Choice Act passed, though he pledged to sign it. The Biden administration pushed hard with two bills, the Equality Act and the Do No Harm Act. The ruling class was rubber stamping the radical agenda.

Both of these laws would not only have forced Catholic doctors and hospitals to perform abortions, but they would have mandated that they perform sex-reassignment surgery as well. To get the job done, the Equality Act included a provision exempting the legislation from abiding by the 1993 Religious Freedom Restoration Act (RFRA). The Do No Harm Act amended RFRA, putting so many restrictions on it that it effectively gutted its application. Though these laws were not passed, it is clear that most Democrats want to weaken religious liberty protections. This is especially true when religious liberty clashes with the radical LGBTQ agenda, as it has in many states.

Gay lawmakers in Connecticut tried to take over the administrative affairs of the Catholic Church in 2009, and in the first decade of the twenty-first century, the San Francisco Board of Supervisors sought to intimidate Catholics from exercising their religious liberty and free speech rights. It accused the Vatican of "meddling" in its affairs. What did Rome do to merit this charge?[349] The radical ruling class declared that because the Church teaches that marriage is the exclusive union of a man and a woman, that meant it was interfering in the internal affairs of San Franciscans. According to this logic, San Francisco's extreme secular policies on marriage and the family were "meddling" in the affairs of the Catholic Church.

While attacks on Christianity are most worrisome when they stem from government, they are still invidious when they stem from individuals and organizations in the private sector. Smearing Christianity is something radicals and the ruling class have been doing for a long time, and not all their efforts stem from government.

Chapter 9

Smearing Christianity

When Denigration Turns Evil

If the goal is to weaken the moral authority of an organization, a time-tested strategy is to denigrate its mission, policies, and persons of influence. This is particularly true when the target is a religious organization. Radicals are very good at this, and when they enlist the power of the ruling class, they are an awesome force. Once the object of their venom is trashed and beaten down, they can proceed to finish the job.

Mother Teresa is not only a Catholic icon, but she is revered by millions who are not Catholic. A Gallup survey at the end of the last century found that she was voted the most admired person in the world in the twentieth century. This angers militant secularists. Some, like the late Christopher Hitchens, maligned her in words. Others, like Al Goldstein, depicted her in an extremely vulgar and obscene way: an illustration of her was made to look like she was having intercourse with a man portrayed as Jesus. Another image was a picture of her face superimposed on the naked body of a woman who sat with her legs spread. There was also a cartoon of her sitting on a toilet. As I said at the time, "This isn't just bigotry—it's Satanism."[350]

That was in the 1990s. More recently, Bill Maher, John Stewart, Trevor Noah, and Samantha Bee have routinely resorted to obscenities when commenting on Jesus, Our Blessed Mother, priests, nuns, popes, and the sacraments. Nothing is out of bounds for these bigots. They have but one goal, and it is not comedic—it is to smear and malign everything that matters to Catholics.

The same is true of many in the artistic community. Their idea of being creative is to attack Catholicism. But what is creative about putting a crucifix in a jar of one's urine? What is creative about portraying Christ having sex with the apostles? What is creative about putting elephant dung on a portrait of Our Blessed Mother, surrounded with porn pictures? What is creative about depicting large ants crawling over Jesus on the cross? And why is it that it is always our religion that these "artists" decide needs a creative touch?

When those who complain about artwork that was clearly designed to insult Catholics, they are typically told that they don't understand the meaning of the exhibit. This has certainly been my experience. Yet if someone were to put a picture of that same person's mother in a jar of urine, he would no doubt be taken aback. Lying is commonplace among offending artists. Many of them received grants from the ruling class, forcing the average Joe to pay for their masterpieces.

If these vile acts were the work of third-rate artists, it may not matter that much. But they are not—they are the work of some of the most prominent in their field. What is worse is that the ruling class is responsible for some of these antics: the Smithsonian hosted the ants-crawling-on-Jesus stunt.

In 2018, the elites who run the National Endowment for the Arts provided funding for the production company that supported "Jerry Springer: The Opera." The play was vulgar beyond belief. The crucifixion was mocked, the Eucharist was trashed, the Virgin Mary was introduced as a woman who was "raped by an angel," and Jesus was portrayed as a fat effeminate character; the Christ-like figure also had his genitals fondled by Eve. The play ended by saying, "Nothing is wrong and nothing is right," and "there are no absolutes of good and evil."[351]

The closing lines are emblematic of what is really at the heart of these attacks on Catholicism: it's a celebration of moral relativism. Those who blur the line between right and wrong are incensed that our Judeo-Christian moral code teaches that some acts are intrinsically evil. The relativists hate moral absolutes, the very font of the Ten Commandments. So did the Nazis.

Getting Under the Skin of Secularists

The hatred that radical secularists have for religion, especially Christianity, cannot be exaggerated. It takes practically nothing to set them off.

Clara Jeffrey is the editor-in-chief of *Mother Jones*, a far-left political tabloid. The nicest thing we can say about her is that she has a phobia about Christianity. Here is what happened in 2024.

When the plane she was on was about to land, the Alaska Airlines attendant wished the passengers on board a "blessed" evening. Most of them probably thought that was a sweet thing to say. But not her. She was so enraged that she issued an "alert" on X accusing the attendant of fostering "Creeping Christian nationalism." She berated the employee for not using adjectives such as "great, awesome, fabulous, amazing, fantastic."[352]

What kind of person is offended by an airline stewardess wishing everyone a "blessed" evening? Someone who frequently writes condemnatory articles about the Catholic Church. Figures.

At the end of 2024, a Catholic League member asked the property managers who run a cooperative where he lives if he could put a nativity scene in the lobby of his building. He was denied. When he was told that the nativity scene was a religious symbol and could not be displayed, he pointed out that the menorah is a religious symbol as well. He was told they didn't see it that way.

I wrote to the property officials letting them know that the menorah is clearly a religious symbol—it represents a miracle—and is cited in Exodus 25 as such. I also noted that the Supreme Court regards the menorah as a religious symbol. So if the religious symbol of one religion is okayed but another is prohibited, that constitutes discrimination. I sent a copy to Erin Mersino, a lawyer on our board of directors who at the time worked for the Thomas More Law Center. I also gave the officials a deadline.

The lawyers for the cooperative decided to end the issue by banning the menorah.[353]

This is so telling. There are two ways to be neutral: allow both the nativity scene and the menorah or ban both. The former is the tolerant way; the latter is the intolerant way.

They chose the intolerant way, and that is because they would rather deny Jews the right to display a menorah before also allowing Christians to display a nativity scene. Christianity clearly gets under their skin.

This kind of secular mania is also commonplace in big corporations. In 2021, Cigna asked employees to "Check Your Privilege"; it was part of their "Societal Norms" checklist. Among the choices were "Christian," "White," and "Cis-Male" (meaning biological males).[354]

Telling Christians that they are the beneficiaries of "religious privilege," and that they need to admit this, is outrageously false and demeaning. Are those Hispanic Catholics who work in groundskeeping at Cigna, the global insurance company, "privileged"? Are Asian Christians who clean the toilets of the corporate brass "privileged"? What about the African American Christians who work in security? And why is it that atheist executives who are filthy rich are not considered "privileged"?

This kind of game is designed to make Christians feel like they are members of an oppressive class. That's the way many of the corporate elite think. They have adopted the thinking of radicals and are willing to punish those who don't buy into their ideological agenda.

Gay Radicals Denigrate Catholicism

Admittedly, Catholicism is an easy target. A two-thousand-year-old institution, with a hierarchal structure, that proclaims the truth and admonishes sinners is out of step with the secular vision of man and society as entertained by radicals and the ruling class. Those who see libertinism as liberating are naturally drawn to oppose the Catholic Church, and this is especially true of gay activists. This hardly justifies denigrating Catholicism.

The Sisters of Perpetual Indulgence is a San Francisco-based group of homosexual men who dress as nuns. What animates them is a desire to mock nuns and the sacraments. Founded in 1979, the ruling class gave the radicals a tax-exempt status. This came just after they trashed Pope John Paul II's visit to San Francisco: the "Sisters" held an "exorcism" and a "Condom Savior Mass" in Union Square. At the event, they featured "the Latex Host" and referred to Jesus as the "Condom Savior." They also burned the pope in effigy.[355]

The "Sisters" are bad enough, but when the ruling class eggs them on, we are dealing with something much more serious. In 2023, the elites who run the Los Angeles Dodgers gave an award to the drag queen "Sisters" at its "10th Annual LGBTQ+ Night" in 2023.[356]

When news of this first broke in mid-May, I wrote a letter to the head of Major League Baseball, Commissioner Rob Manfred, asking, "If a group of white boys in black face—a modern day Al Jolson ensemble—were to be honored by an MLB team, there is little doubt that the event would be cancelled and sanctions would be forthcoming. There is no difference between this and the hateful farce of awarding the 'Sisters.'"[357]

Manfred felt the pressure building. He called Cardinal Timothy Dolan, Archbishop of New York, to complain about me. Dolan told him to take it up with me, saying

"Bill will be happy to talk to you." Manfred never called. But he did make sure that the Dodgers disinvited the "Sisters."

But it didn't take long—I predicted this would happen—before gay and trans activists, along with local government officials, blasted the Dodgers. The "Sisters" were then reinvited. This only goes to prove my thesis: the ruling class has gotten into bed with radical activists.

The "Sisters" are bad enough, but the homosexual radicals who comprise ACT-UP are worse. On December 10, 1989, hundreds of them invaded St. Patrick's Cathedral in New York City during a Sunday Mass to protest the Church's teachings on sexuality. They chained themselves to the pews, shouted and waved their fists, tossed condoms into the air, and spat a consecrated Host on the floor.[358] If this isn't Satanic, the word has no meaning.

St. Patrick's Cathedral was also the site of an incredibly vulgar attack in 1994 during the 25th anniversary of the Stonewall riot. There was a mostly well-behaved march up First Avenue, but there was an illegal march up Fifth Avenue that was surreal. The marchers had been denied a permit, yet they marched anyway. The demonstrators wore dresses and plaid skirts, as well as jockstraps—some were entirely naked—and one guy masturbated in front of the cathedral. They did Satanic dances and screamed obscenities on command. This is not a matter of dispute—I hired a professional photographer to record it.[359]

In 2024, at a funeral service at St. Patrick's Cathedral, men dressed as women and women dressed as men attended a service to honor Cecilia Gentili. Gentili was a man who falsely claimed to be a woman. He was an illegal alien, a drug addict, prostitute, transgender activist, and an atheist. At the service, many of those in attendance dressed as hookers, danced in the aisles, sang "Ave Cecilia" when "Ave Maria" was sung, and shouted, "St. Cecilia, Mother of All Whores."[360]

Radical gays, often supported by elites, choose St. Patrick's Cathedral to denigrate Catholicism because it is a symbol of everything they hate. If they can weaken its stature, they will be well on their way to victory. Which is all the more reason why they need to be defeated.

Government Smear Merchants

As previously indicated, Democrats are more likely to bash Christians than Republicans are, though it would be a mistake to think all Republicans are squeaky clean. Marjorie Taylor Greene, a former Catholic turned evangelical, went off the rails in 2022 when she said the Catholic Church was run by Satan. She objected to Catholic Charities working with illegal aliens, but instead of simply registering an objection, she got down and dirty. "I thought we had a separation of church and state, right? No, what it is, is Satan's controlling the church."[361]

At the close of Obama's second term, a report was issued by the U.S. Commission on Civil Rights that was a scathing assault on religious liberty. Titled "Peaceful Coexistence: Reconciling Nondiscrimination Principles with Civil Liberties," the findings made it clear that whenever there is a conflict between religious liberty and nondiscrimination, the former should be subordinate to the latter. Never mind that religious liberty is enshrined in the First Amendment and the latter is mostly encoded in statutes. Not surprisingly, the issue of discrimination that the document was absorbed with revolved around LGBTQ rights.

Rights are not absolute, so when two rights conflict, decisions to favor one over the other must be made; this requires sound jurisprudential reasoning. For example, the Bill of Rights explicitly protects religious liberty, and it says absolutely nothing about gay rights or gay marriage. Why, then, was this federal body awarding preferential treatment to rights nowhere found in the Constitution while diminishing rights plainly encoded in it?

If there were any doubt that this report was motivated by an animus against religious liberty, it was completely removed by Martin R. Castro, an Obama appointee, who chaired the commission. "The phrases 'religious liberty' and 'religious freedom' will stand for nothing except for hypocrisy so long as they remain code words for discrimination, intolerance, racism, sexism, homophobia, Islamophobia, Christian supremacy or any other form of intolerance."[362] We might expect such expressions of hatred from a left-wing pundit, but when it comes from a federal official—charged with overseeing civil rights—it is astounding.

Militant secularists go for the jugular when they smear all priests. Most priests are good men who have given their life to serve the Catholic Church. As with any demographic group, there are rogues. Unfortunately, in recent years, many in the media and in state government have made incredibly sweeping statements and accusations against all priests, merely because a very small percentage of them molested minors. They have been smeared beyond belief.

The molesting priests, most of whom were homosexuals, have either been thrown out of the priesthood or are dead; the lion's share of the abuse occurred between 1965 and 1985. They knew this in Pennsylvania when the attorney general, Josh Shapiro (now the governor), launched a grand jury investigation of the state's Catholic clergy, but that didn't matter. However, it did matter to some priests, and that is why they sued.

On December 3, 2018, the Pennsylvania Supreme Court ruled in a 6–1 decision that the Pennsylvania grand jury report on the Catholic clergy cannot make public the names of eleven priests who challenged the release of their identities; they claimed that doing so would violate their reputational rights as guaranteed by the state constitution. The priests never had the opportunity to challenge the accusations made against them to the grand jury. Moreover, they said the report contained "false, misleading, incorrect and unsupported assertions." Thus, their reputations would be smeared if their names were not permanently redacted. The court agreed.[363]

Why would a prominent governor want to mock the Eucharist? That is exactly what Michigan governor Gretchen Whitmer did in 2024. She intentionally insulted Catholics nationwide when she ridiculed the Eucharist in a video. She then compounded the problem by lying about it.

The short video was posted by podcaster Liz Plank on her Instagram account. Whitmer, who was wearing a Harris-Walz hat, was standing above Plank, who was kneeling in front of her. Plank opened her mouth and Whitmer placed a Dorito chip on her tongue. Whitmer was shown staring into the camera with a blank look on her face.

Whitmer dug herself in deeper when she offered a dishonest apology, and then had her team lie about it. Whitmer said she would "never do something to denigrate someone's faith," which, of course, she did. Indeed, it was the reason why she was forced to say something.

Her press secretary lied when he said, "Liz is not kneeling in the video." Liz Plank also lied when she said, "No one was on their knees. I'm sitting on a couch that's visible in the shot." In fact, pictures showed that she was sitting on the couch for the interview but was kneeling when they mocked the Eucharist.[364]

We live in strange times when a sitting Democratic governor, who is often mentioned as a future presidential candidate, feels comfortable disparaging Catholics, who represent roughly a quarter of the electorate.

Bigotry in the Schools

We have made great progress in this country in making sure that African Americans, Asians, Hispanics, and Native Americans are treated fairly by educators. Not so with Christians. Smearing them is fair game.

Randi Weingarten is president of the American Federation of Teachers. What this member of the ruling class says filters down to teachers. In 2023, she ripped the average Joe, saying those Americans who are in favor of school choice and parental rights are no different from the segregationists of old. "They want to have," she said, "basically, a Christian ideology, their particular Christian ideology to dominate the country as opposed to those that was born on the freedom of the exercise of religion."[365] But support for school choice and parental rights are not exclusively of interest to Christians, and they certainly have nothing to do with Christian domination. Her anti-Christian sentiments are evidently deep-seated.

During the Covid pandemic, Mollie Paige Mumau, a Pennsylvania teacher, took umbrage with those persons of faith who sought an exemption from vaccine mandates. Fine, but what was not so fine was what she said had to be done about these people. She called for them to be shot.

"Screw this guy and screw them all who are all about hiding behind religious exemptions. . . . He and his ilk deserve whatever comes their way, including losing jobs, getting sick, and perhaps dying from this virus." She advised Republicans to "just start shooting all of their constituents who think this way."[366]

She was not just a public school teacher—she served on the board of directors of the National Education Association, the most powerful education agency in the country. When radicals ascend to the ruling class, the damage they can do is incalculable. Too often their victims are Christians.

Educators like this woman really hate it when parents find out what their agenda is. Take the case of Kelly Love, a teacher at Auburn School District 408 in Auburn, Washington. She was upset when a fellow teacher sought to alert some parents to school policies that were being kept from them. In reply, Love said, "I cannot disagree with this more.

So many students are not safe in this nation from these Christo-fascist parents."[367]

We have entered a new day when inquiring Christian parents are labeled fascists for exercising their rights. Behavior like this was unheard of throughout most of American history, including those times when Catholics were denied elementary rights. Smearing Christian parents is unfortunately not a freak thing anymore in our nation's schools.

Berating Catholics is not uncommon on our nation's college campuses, but what happened at Texas A&M University in 2020 went beyond that. A professor posted several vicious anti-Catholic comments on social media. He referred to the Catholic clergy as gangsters, sociopaths, rapists, fascists, and murderers, toyed with burning down a Catholic retirement home, and threatened a bishop.[368]

Incidents like this make a mockery of higher education. Colleges and universities are supposed to be places where reasoned debate thrives, but too often they have become places where bigoted anti-Christian rants are tolerated. The elites who staff the board of trustees are complicit with the radicals responsible for these vicious tirades.

Intimidation

Another weapon in the arsenal of radicals is intimidation. Those who denigrate Catholicism seek to belittle it; those who prefer intimidation want to silence it. They want to cancel the moral voice of prominent laymen and the clergy, as well as the average Joe who takes their side.

In 2019, an elderly Catholic woman was praying outside a Planned Parenthood abortion clinic in Pennsylvania. Brian Sims, a state legislator, saw her and got in her face, badgering her for eight uninterrupted minutes. She did nothing to provoke him. But here was a member of the political ruling class intimidating her nonetheless. He was incensed because of the issue—abortion is a lightning rod for radical members of the ruling class.

Abortion is also the reason why practicing Catholics who are nominated for a seat on the federal bench are verbally tarred and feathered. Consider what happened in 2003 when Alabama attorney general Bill Pryor was nominated to the Eleventh Circuit Court of Appeals. Those who wanted to defeat him couldn't find legitimate issues to disqualify him, so they went after his religion. Pryor was a practicing Catholic who opposed abortion. His opponents, knowing that the Constitution bars a religious test for public office, chose a more oblique approach: they questioned his suitability to be a federal judge based on his "deeply held beliefs." Senator Charles Schumer led the way, saying Pryor's beliefs "are so deeply held that it's very hard to believe that they're not going to influence" him.[369] "Deeply held beliefs" of a secular sort are never a problem. They are only problematic when they are grounded in Christianity.

In 2017, Amy Coney Barrett, a professor at Notre Dame Law School, was nominated for a seat on an appellate court. Senator Dianne Feinstein made an incredible remark trying to smear her. "When you read your speeches," the California senator said, "the conclusion one draws is that the dogma lives loudly within you. And that's of concern when you come to big issues that large numbers of people have fought for years in this country." This was not Feinstein's first rodeo. In 2005, she questioned John Roberts about his suitability to sit on the Supreme Court. She specifically asked him if he shared President John F. Kennedy's 1960 convictions about not mixing church and state.[370] Why is it that candidates for the federal bench from other religions are never asked these questions?

Barrett was confirmed and she was later selected to sit on the Supreme Court. Fortunately, this time around there were enough eyes on the hearing that traces of anti-Catholic bigotry never materialized.

Catholics have every reason to be proud of all the brilliant Catholics who have sought a career in law, many of whom have ascended to the federal bench. But to the bigots, we have had too many of them on the Supreme Court. "Is it appropriate to have six Catholic justices on the Supreme Court?" That's what a militant atheist wrote on a liberal website.[371] Many other pundits said the same. Yet no one complained that the other three justices were Jewish, making the high court more disproportionately Jewish than Catholic. The bias is one-sided.

It is one thing to protest outside the Supreme Court; it is quite another to protest outside the homes of the justices. The former is a well-protected First Amendment right; the latter is designed to intimidate and is illegal. But this is what happened to those justices who overturned *Roe v. Wade* in the *Dobbs v. Jackson Wyoming Health* decision.

After someone leaked the *Dobbs* ruling in May 2022, the homes of Justices Samuel Alito, Amy Coney Barrett, Brett

Kavanaugh, Neil Gorsuch, and Chief Justice John Roberts were targeted by protesters. They held signs, chanted, and marched through their suburban communities at times designed to anger their neighbors. President Biden cheered them on. Legal analyst Andrew McCarthy was astonished. He accused Biden of "encouraging people to violate federal law by protesting at Supreme Court justices' homes."[372]

This was striking, McCarthy said, because the president is bound to "execute the laws faithfully and to protect both the security of the courts and the administration of justice."[373] It got so bad that the chief security officer of the Supreme Court asked Virginia and Maryland officials to enforce the law and stop the protests. Some demonstrators carried guns; threats to kill Kavanaugh were made.

Christian Nationalism

Another intimidation tactic is to smear patriotic Christian activists and public figures by branding them as dangerous Christian nationalists. As it turns out, the danger is emanating from those who make these scurrilous charges, not their targets.

The majority of Americans have never heard of Christian nationalism. That is a good sign. It's a fiction. It may exist in faculty lounges—in their heads—and in left-wing activist circles, but nowhere else. So why are radicals pushing this myth? Because it serves to demonize conservative Christians. They have invented a bogeyman because it serves their cause.

According to the professors, pundits, and activists who promote this propaganda, Christian nationalists are people who believe that our freedoms were "granted by God to all Americans as our birthright." The Clemson sociologist who said this, Andrew Whitehead, is apparently unaware that this is not the voice of a Christian nationalist—it is the voice of Thomas Jefferson, author of the Declaration of Independence. Our unalienable rights, he said, come not from government but from our "Creator."[374]

Whitehead was asked if Christian nationalists "think you have to be Christian to be truly American?" He said yes, that's what they believe. He did not name anyone who supposedly entertains this view. He tries so hard to keep the Christian nationalist myth alive that he found fault with someone who argued that "our freedoms in this country are for every single citizen." The person did not say that our freedoms are for Christians—he emphatically said that they were for "every single citizen."[375] So how is this the voice of Christian nationalism? Is it not simply the voice of the average Joe?

In 1892, the Supreme Court said, "This is a Christian nation." It was simply acknowledging that our nation's heritage is rooted in Christianity. Not to recognize this historical fact is plain stupidity. What is worse is the attempt to silence those who proudly proclaim this verity.

It would be wrong to suggest that these false accusations of Christian nationalism have no traction. Ask Representative Mike Johnson, a practicing evangelical who was elected Speaker of the House in 2023. Anti-Christian bigots couldn't stop him from being elected, so they went into high gear following the vote seeking to malign him. Their most serious charge: he was a "Christian nationalist."

In Johnson's first speech as House Speaker, he quoted G. K. Chesterton. "America is the only nation in the world that is founded on a creed," one that is "listed with almost theological lucidity in the Declaration of Independence."[376] That set off a fury with radicals. The mere mention of the word "creed" is seen by them as fighting words. Their argument has less to do with Johnson than with the Founders. They really hate the Judeo-Christian ethos that the United States was founded on.

On cue, radicals branded Johnson a "hard-core theocrat" and "one of the most extreme members of the House." Comedian Bill Maher, a vicious anti-Christian bigot, compared him to a mass shooter. Others called him a "Christofascist" and a "Bigger Threat to America than Hamas Could Ever Be."[377] What they really objected to was Johnson's opposition to abortion, gay marriage, and transgenderism, all of which are at the heart of Christian beliefs. It's also what the average Joe believes. But instead of finding fault with his policy views, they sought to personally destroy him by hurling their vile "Christian nationalist" slogan at him.

Those who smear conservative Christians have failed to persuade Americans to the alleged danger of Christian nationalism. If anything, it has driven them to become more extreme in their attempts to silence Christian activists. The most serious charge they make is to accuse them of violence. I decided to get to the heart of this charge in 2024.

The most prominent person floating this accusation is Amanda Tyler, executive director of the Baptist Joint Committee for Religious Liberty (BJC) and lead organizer of Christians Against Christian Nationalism. She testified before the U.S. House Oversight Committee's Subcommittee on National Security, the Border, and Foreign Affairs in October 2023.

In early 2024, I emailed Christians Against Christian Nationalism, asking them to provide me with the evidence that Christian nationalism "inspires acts of violence and intimidation." They wrote back referencing Tyler's October 25, 2023, testimony and her written testimony on December 13, 2022, before the House Oversight Committee's Subcommittee on Civil Rights and Civil Liberties. What I found was revealing.[378]

In Tyler's testimony in 2023, she said, "The greatest threat to religious liberty in the United States today . . . is Christian nationalism." Such a sweeping statement would ordinarily be peppered with one example after another. She provided none. She simply made an assertion, providing no evidence.

Tyler's testimony in 2022 offered some examples to support her thesis about the violence of Christian nationalists. But upon examination, they imploded.

The first example she mentioned occurred in Charleston, South Carolina, in 2015. Dylann Storm Roof shot and killed nine people at Emanuel African Methodist Episcopal Church. By all accounts, he was a seriously disturbed neo-Nazi who wanted to start a race war.

Roof came from a troubled home. When he was born, his divorced parents got back together for a while, but it didn't last. His father remarried and allegedly beat his new wife, before getting divorced again. He dropped out of school, spending most of his time taking drugs, getting drunk, and playing video games. He was busted twice for narcotics. He was also known for burning the American flag.

No one doubts he was a racist. But no one ever accused him of being a Christian nationalist.

The second example cited by Tyler was the tragic Tree of Life Synagogue mass shooting in Pittsburgh in 2018. Robert Gregory Bowers killed eleven people and wounded six. It was the deadliest attack on any Jewish community in the nation's history.

His parents divorced when he was a year old. His father committed suicide while awaiting trial on a rape charge. Like Roof, Bowers was a disturbed racist and a right-wing nut. But no one who ever knew him said he was a Christian nationalist.

The third and fourth incidents mentioned by Tyler took place at Christchurch mosque in New Zealand on March 15, 2019. Brandon Harrison Tyler was charged with fifty-one counts of murder, forty counts of attempted murder, and one count of committing a terrorist act.

His parents separated when he was a young boy, and his home was destroyed by a fire. When his mother remarried, he went to live with her and her husband. The new husband beat her (Brandon's mom), Brandon, and his sister.

Brandon left home and went to live with his father. That didn't turn out too well: Brandon found his father dead by suicide. Those who knew him, which were only a few, said he was disturbed but none ever described him as a Christian nationalist.

The fifth example cited was a shooting that took place in 2019 at Chabad of Poway synagogue in Poway, California. John Timothy Earnest shot and killed one woman and injured three other persons. In an open letter that he wrote prior to the shooting, he said Jews were plotting to kill the European race.

Earnest was an evangelical. Church members were split on whether his religious beliefs had anything to do with his shooting rampage. There is no evidence that he identified as a Christian nationalist, nor is there evidence that he was branded as such by those who knew him.

The sixth killing spree took place at Tops Supermarket in Buffalo, New York, in 2022. It is located in a predominantly black neighborhood. Payton S. Gendron shot and killed ten black people.

He was a classic loner. His father was an alcoholic and a drug addict for forty years, resulting in the demise of two marriages. Gendron had no friends and was known to wear a hazmat suit in the classroom. He was fascinated by violence, even to the point of bragging how he stabbed his own cat and then smashed the animal's head on concrete. He finished the cat with a hatchet.

Not only was he not a Christian nationalist, but he wasn't even Christian. Tyler concedes this point but nonetheless lists him as a Christian nationalist. Apparently, she is unaware how this undermines her credibility, which is amazing in its own right.

The seventh, and last, incident was the January 6, 2021, Capitol rally that turned into a riot. It merited a separate report, "Christian Nationalism and the January 6, 2021, Insurrection." The report was sponsored by the BJC and the Freedom From Religion Foundation, an anti-Christian organization run by militant atheists. It was published in 2022.

There are seven chapters in the report, all supposedly chock full of evidence that the riot was a Christian nationalist event. Yet the first three chapters are merely a commentary on Christian nationalism and don't even attempt to tie the violence at the capitol to it. Of the other four chapters, two were written by Andrew Seidel, an attorney who works for the atheist group.

Katherine Stewart is an author and investigative journalist. Here is the first sentence in her chapter: "By now, most Americans understand that Christian nationalism played a role in last year's violent attack on the Capitol." She cites not a single source. It is simply an unsupported assertion. This is the extent of her "evidence."

Seidel wrote chapter 5 and 6. Chapter 5 covers events leading up to January 6, and chapter 6 claims to provide evidence that the riot was of Christian nationalist origin.

One of the two preceding events cited occurred on November 14, 2020. Seidel argues that after supporters of President Trump rallied that day, "violence erupted in D.C." It did. But the source he cites from the *Washington Post* simply said that Trump supporters clashed with counterdemonstrators. So what? The news story said not a word about Christian anything.

The December 12 incident saw another nighttime clash between two factions. The source cited notes that the Proud Boys, a right-wing group that supports Trump, were involved. They were. What Seidel doesn't mention is that four of them were stabbed.

The next chapter begins by saying Paula White, one of Trump's spiritual advisors, delivered "an explicitly Christian nationalist and openly militant prayer." What was it? "Blessed is the nation whose God is Lord" (Ps 33:12). That was it.

Other "evidence" that the riot was a Christian nationalist event included statements by Katrina Pierson, a Trump campaign spokesperson. She said, Trump "loves the United States of America. He loves God." Ergo, this is an invitation to Christian nationalist violence.

Seidel also says that some people carried a cross and a Christian flag, and some were even spotted singing, "God Bless America." That seals it—this is an extremist group. More "evidence" that this was a Christian nationalist event was the sight of men blowing shofars. A shofar is a Jewish musical instrument—not exactly a prop used by violent Christian nationalists.

Tyler wraps up the report with similar "evidence." Signs such as "In God We Trust" are considered proof that Christian nationalists were on a tear. She says that when the violence took place, something curious happened: Christian leaders who condemned it "for the most part did not name Christian nationalism as a contributing or driving factor." Once again, she is clueless how this undermines her thesis.

It is bad enough that anti-Christians engage in smear tactics; it is worse when they resort to total distortions, if not out-and-out lies. But this is what we are faced with. The ruling class are not merely taking a page out of the radical playbook—in too many instances they have merged with them.

Chapter 10

Stealth Maneuvers

Hoaxes

Maria Monk said that on the night that she was inducted into a Montreal convent, she came upon a tunnel that was used by priests and monks from a nearby monastery to sneak into the convent at night. She said they had sex with the sisters, leaving many of them pregnant. Once the child was born, the old sisters would smother the baby to death, but only after they baptized them first.

The story is a hoax. Monk made it all up. She wasn't even a Catholic (she was Protestant), much less a nun. But that didn't stop the book, *The Awful Disclosures of Maria Monk*, from being a best-seller. It sold over a million copies before the end of the nineteenth century.

This story is not an anomaly. Telling hoaxes is a popular weapon in the arsenal of those who want to destroy Christianity. Regrettably, by the time these false narratives are exposed as a lie, much damage has been done.

Pope Pius XII

After World War II, Jews from all over the world praised Pope Pius XII for his incredible efforts to save the lives of hundreds of thousands of Jews. Among those who lauded the pope were Albert Einstein, Gold Meir, the ADL, the Synagogue Council of America, the Rabbinical Council of America, the American Jewish Committee, and the World Jewish Congress. In 1958, when he died, Leonard Bernstein of the New York Philharmonic was so moved that once he learned of the pope's death, he called for a moment of silence during one of his performances.

The positive appraisal of Pope Pius XII was entirely justified. Indeed, the more we learn of his actions during World War II from the opening of the Vatican archives, the more we learn of his heroics. Nonetheless, there has been a consistent chorus from his critics mostly claiming that he was "silent" at that time. Yet it was none other than the *New York Times* that singled the pope out in two Christmas editorials in the early 1940s for *not being silent*! So what changed and when?

There was not one piece of new evidence that emerged in the early 1950s to change anyone's mind about Pius XII. But there was a play, "The Deputy," that maintained he was silent. Published in 1963 and performed on Broadway the following year, it was written by a Protestant left-wing radical from Germany, Rolf Hochhuth.

In 2007, Ion Mihai Pacepa, the highest-ranking defector from the Soviet intelligence bloc, revealed that in 1960, Nikita Khrushchev, the Soviet master, approved a plan to discredit Pope Pius XII. According to American scholar Ronald Rychlak, who has chronicled and debunked the attacks on Pius XII, Hochhuth was probably a Soviet dupe. He certainly collaborated with noted Holocaust denier David Irving. He even defended Irving after he was arrested in Austria for being a Holocaust denier. Hochhuth was then discredited as an anti-Semite.

Hochhuth was also an anti-Catholic. Moreover, he was a coward. In the early part of this century, circa 2002–2003, I learned that Rychlak had asked Hochhuth to see his archives and read his correspondence and research. I told Ron, who is a member of the board of advisors of the Catholic League, that we would pay for him to go to Germany. I asked him if he would agree to debate Hochhuth. Ron was on board but Hochhuth said no to the request to see his archives and no to the debate. He died in 2020.

In 1999, John Cornwell, an English author, wrote a book, *Hitler's Pope: The Secret History of Pius XII*, that was another flawed attack on this pope. He argued that the pope was bent on creating a strong, centralized papacy, one that in the end would be easy for Hitler to exploit. Kenneth Woodward, an astute religion editor at *Newsweek*, described the book as "a classic example of what happens when an ill-equipped journalist assumes the air of sober scholarship. . . . Errors of fact and ignorance of context appear on almost every page."[379]

When Cornwell was about to make his book tour in the fall of 1999, I relayed to him—via ABC TV of Philadelphia—an invitation. I promised to give him a one-week, all expenses paid vacation in New York provided he agree to debate me every day on radio and TV. He formally declined my offer on September 10.

The reason why Hochhuth wouldn't debate Rychlak, and Cornwell wouldn't debate me, is obvious: as the authors of a hoax, they knew we would expose them as the phonies they are.

Books and Movies

If Jesus can be discredited, then Christianity will no longer be on the ropes—it will be finished. This was tried in 2007 when Simcha Jacobovici and Charles Pellegrino co-authored the book *The Jesus Family Tomb*. By claiming that the Jesus tomb had been found, they were sending a message to Christians: game over, there was no Resurrection.

The foreword to the book was written by James Cameron, of "Titanic" fame. He said the authors succeeded in their efforts "beyond any reasonable doubt."[380] But the fact is the book was not based on serious scholarship. There was not one citation, footnote, or endnote in the book. Cameron was right about one thing: he said the book reads like a detective novel. That's basically what it was—a work of fiction. It should also be noted that Pellegrino, who said he had a doctorate, was lying. Victoria University said he was never awarded a Ph.D.

The Jacobovici-Pellegrino-Cameron claim extends back to 1980 when Israeli archeologist Amos Kloner led a probe of the tomb that they seized on twenty-seven years later. "The claim that the burial site has been found is not based on any proof," he said, "and is only an attempt to sell. I refute all claims and efforts to waken a renewed interest in the findings. With all due respect, they are not archeologists."[381]

Many experts ripped apart their thesis in 2007. David Mevoah, curator of the Israel Museum, said the chances of the filmmaker's claim being true "are more than remote. . . . They are closer to fantasy." William Dever, archeologist and professor emeritus at the University of Arizona, said that "it looks more like a publicity stunt than any kind of real discovery. . . . They're not scholars. They are not experts."[382]

More testimony from other scholars who took apart their farcical thesis could be given. The bottom line is that the Jesus tomb story is a hoax.

Movies are a powerful medium of truth and propaganda, and everything in between. To the average Joe, this can be maddening. All he wants to do is know truth from falsehoods, but in the hands of clever writers and producers, this is often difficult to discern. Author Dan Brown and producer Ron Howard are a perfect example. Brown's book *The Da Vinci Code* was made into a movie by Howard, as was *Angels & Demons*. Both men are masters of pitching hoaxes at the expense of the Catholic Church; their work was published in the 2000s.

If the *Da Vinci Code* were merely a novel, there would have been no reason to include a page at the beginning of the book titled "Facts." Listed as "facts" were demonstrably false and defamatory statements.

Brown's first "fact" alleged that a secret society, the Priory of Sion, kept alive the story that Jesus and Mary Magdalene married. But in fact, this tale was exposed as a hoax that was made up in the 1950s by an anti-Semite Frenchman (who was sent to prison for fraud). The second "fact" alleged that a "religious sect" called Opus Dei was an evil organization. In fact, it is a lay group that calls Catholics to holiness in their daily lives. The third "fact" was the most malicious: it claimed that the book was based on historical documents that show that the divinity of Jesus was forged in the fourth century. When the movie opened in 2006, even "60 Minutes," the

CBS investigative show (which is not known to be kind to the Catholic Church), concluded that the film was a hoax.[383]

The movie “Angels & Demons” was Howard’s rendition of Brown’s book by that name. The twin hoaxers seized on the existence of the Illuminati, a secret society that believed the monarchy of King George III and the Catholic Church were conspiring to take over the world. Brown and Howard maintained that “it is historical fact” that the Illuminati were founded in the 1600s. They were lying. They lied because they wanted to pitch Galileo—the ultimate bogeyman of anti-Catholic lore—as a member. But the fact is that the Illuminati didn’t exist until 1776, almost 150 years after Galileo died.[384]

In 2002, Peter Mullan, an Irish writer and director, released “The Magdalene Sisters.”[385] His hatred of the Catholic Church is undisputed: he compares the Church to the Taliban. The movie was a dishonest portrayal of nuns who cared for “fallen” girls in England and Ireland from the mid-eighteenth century to the late nineteenth century in what were called the laundries. Mullan contributed mightily to the popular perception that the laundries were horrible places.

When the movie debuted, there was a Facebook page dedicated to the laundries titled “Victims of the Irish Holocaust Unite.” Irish journalists talked about the “Irish gulag system.” But the fact is there was no holocaust, and there was no gulag. No one was murdered. No one was imprisoned nor forced to stay against her will. There was no slave labor. Not a single woman was sexually abused by a nun. Not one. It is all a lie.

How do we know? The evidence is fully documented in the McAleese Report on the Magdalene Laundries, formally known as "Report on the Inter-Developmental Committee to establish the facts of the State involvement with the Magdalene Laundries."

Information garnered for the McAleese Report constitutes the most comprehensive collection of data ever obtained on the Magdalene Laundries. A full statistical analysis of all available data was conducted by the McAleese Committee. Additionally, 118 women who lived in the asylums were interviewed, as were many doctors who worked there. Their testimony blows the "holocaust" and "gulag" charges to smithereens.

One of many myths is that the laundries were exclusively run by the Irish and Catholics. They were not. There were Protestant-run facilities, and the first ones were run by lay women. These were institutions that served prostitutes and women likely to join "the world's oldest profession." Unmarried women, especially those who gave birth out of wedlock, were likely candidates. Contrary to what is often said, the laundries were not "imposed" on them; the evidence is extremely strong on this measure. The women were free to go at any time. Most stayed, if for no other reason than their choices were slim. The street was the most likely alternative.

The two most serious accusations made against the nuns who operated the Magdalene Laundries were (a) they tortured the residents and (b) they sexually abused the girls and women. Both are totally inaccurate. Not once in the McAleese Report is the word "torture" even mentioned—the charges are a complete fabrication. Exactly one woman claimed to have been sexually abused, but it was committed by a lay woman auxiliary who decided to stay in the institution for life. *No nun ever abused anyone.*

This is not to say that the women never experienced sexual abuse. They did. But it was in their home, or in an Industrial School where they came from (the majority of women interviewed were previously housed in an Industrial School, places that housed neglected youths). Not only were these women not abused by a nun, but all of them said they had never even heard of another woman being molested by any member of the staff.

The doctors who worked in the laundries said most of the women were happy and taken care of by the nuns. They emphasized that without the nuns tending to them—some of the girls and women were retarded and almost all were poorly educated—they would not have been able to make it on their own.

Despite the evidence that the laundries were not a horror show, the lies continue. The movie "Philomena" received four Oscar nominations, though it did not win a single award. But it did poison the minds of many who saw it. After all, the average Joe is not in a position to debunk these tales.

According to the book (of the same name) upon which the movie is based, Philomena Lee got pregnant out of wedlock in Ireland in 1952 when she was eighteen years old. That part is true. But it is a malicious lie to say that the nuns stole her baby and then sold him to "the highest bidder." It is also a lie to say that Philomena went to the U.S. to find him.

In reality, Philomena's mother died when she was six, leaving her father to care for three boys and three girls. He put the girls in a convent and raised the boys. When Philomena got pregnant and could not provide for her child, her father contacted the nuns asking for assistance.

In other words, the nuns never "stole" the baby. Moreover, Philomena's baby was not sold to "the highest bidder": no fee of any sort was charged. The Wisconsin couple who adopted the boy offered a donation, which is customary, but it was entirely voluntary. And Philomena never set foot in the United States until the end of 2013, when she was hawking the movie—no attempt was ever made to find her son. Her son died of AIDS in the mid-1990s.[386]

Mass Graves

The lies about Irish nuns, in particular, have flourished in recent times, not only about caring for women whom no one else wanted, but also about burying children in mass graves. The big mass grave hoax is traceable to a story that appeared in the *Irish Daily Mail* on May 25, 2014. The headline of the story by Alison O'Reilly read, "A Mass Grave of 800 Babies." But her first sentence was more tentative. She said, "A former home for unmarried mothers *may* contain the bodies of almost 800 babies" (my emphasis).[387] Which means it may not. More important, it did not.

The mass grave story began innocently enough in 2010, but it took a strong ideological turn in early 2014. The key players are Catherine Corless and Martin Sixsmith.[388]

Research by Corless, a local historian, "suggested 796 babies were buried in a tank outside the former Tuam Mother and Baby Home, in Co. Galway, once ran by the Bon Secours nuns in Galway."

In 2010, Corless read an article in the *Tuam Herald* that caught her eye. The piece, "Stolen Childhoods," recounted the fate of a former resident in the Mother and Baby Home. She had already done research on this home, so she naturally followed up and contacted the man identified in the article. This provided her with other leads. Two years later, in November 2012, she published her findings in a local journal.

What was striking about Corless is not what she said in 2012 but what she said in 2014. In her journal article, there was no professed anger at nuns or the Catholic Church. But that didn't last. One thing that surely contributed to her change of attitude—she went from being content to a state of rage—was her encounter with Sixsmith.

Sixsmith is an English atheist who wrote the dishonest book about Philomena Lee; it was the basis for the movie about her. Once he hooked up with Corless, she became increasingly strident in her denunciations of the nuns and the Catholic Church.

Her previous comments about the possibility of a mass grave were cautious; now she was cocksure. "I am certain there are 796 children in the mass grave." Just as important, she was now convinced of the mendacity of the Catholic Church. "I do blame the Catholic Church," she said. "I blame the families as well but people were afraid of the parish priest. I think they were brainwashed." No longer a Catholic, she confessed, "I am very, very angry with the Catholic church."

The notion that a mass grave existed in the site of the home is oddly enough credited to the same person who said there never was one. His name is Barry Sweeney.

In 1975, when Sweeney was ten, he and a friend, Frannie Hopkins, twelve, were playing on the grounds where the home was when they stumbled on a hole with skeletons in it. Corless had heard about some boys who found skeletons there but did not know their identity until 2014. On St. Patrick's Day, Sweeney was drinking at Brownes Bar, on the Square in Tuam, when he learned of Corless's research. The two subsequently met.

In her journal article, Corless made mention of a "few local boys" who "came upon a sort of crypt in the ground, and on peering in they saw several small skulls." So how did she make the leap in 2014 that she was "certain" there were 796 bodies in a mass grave when just two years earlier she wrote about "several small skulls?" The leap was not made on the basis of the evidence.

More important, Corless did not jump to the conclusion that "the bones are still there" because she learned of some new evidence from Sweeney. We know this because he contradicted her fantastic story. He was quoted in the *Irish Times* saying, "There was no way there were about 800 skeletons down that hole. Nothing like that number." How many were there? "About 20," he said.

It is a credit to David Dalby of the *New York Times* that he did not bury this new information the way most other media outlets did. On June 10, 2014, he wrote that "some of the assumptions that led Ms. Corless to her conclusion [about the mass grave] have been challenged, not least by the man she cited, Barry Sweeney, now 48, who was questioned by detectives about what he saw when he was 10 years old. 'People are making out we saw a mass grave,' he said he had told the detectives. 'But we can only say what we seen [sic]: maybe 15 to 20 small skeletons.'"

It does not speak well for Corless that she was flatly contradicted by one of the few persons whose credibility was questioned by no one. She allowed Sixsmith to get the better of her.

More sensationalistic stories about "mass graves" being attributed to Catholics surfaced in Canada in 2021 and 2022. By the end of 2023, they, too, were proven to be hoaxes.[389]

The Catholic Church, in its public pronouncements and deeds, is clearly open to criticism. But it is shameful that it continues to be singled out for investigations into wrongdoing when other religious and secular institutions get a pass. Worse, it is malicious to attribute falsehoods of a serious nature to it, all designed to weaken its moral voice.

Infiltrating the Catholic Church

Radicals in the United States, often assisted by the ruling class, have sought to wreak havoc in the Catholic Church by infiltrating its ranks. That it still goes on in the twenty-first century is mindboggling.

In the 1950s, the Communist Party of the United States chose as one of its forty-five goals the need to "Infiltrate the churches and replace revealed religion with 'social' religion."[390] They had already done so, and more subversive tactics were planned.

In 1953, Bella Dodd, an immigrant from Italy, testified before a congressional committee about her work with the Communist Party. She was no longer a member, and she had made her way back to the Catholic Church (with the help of Monsignor Fulton J. Sheen). While that was commendable, what she told the congressional panel was startling.

In the late 1930s, Dodd, who had worked hard to subvert the teachers' unions in New York state by organizing Communists to penetrate them, applied the same tactics to the Catholic Church. She was responsible for planting "over a thousand communist men" in Catholic seminaries (some sources say she cited a figure of 1,100; others report she cited 1,200).[391]

A few years before Dodd died in 1969, she was interviewed by Dietrich von Hildebrand and his wife, Alice. He said to her, "Bella, at times I wonder whether the Church has not been infiltrated." She replied, "Dear professor, you fear it. I know it. When I was a fanatic Communist, I was in close contact with four cardinals in the Vatican working for us. They are still very active today."[392]

Dodd noted that the Communist Party used a variety of tactics to destroy the Catholic Church. Besides infiltrating the seminaries, they established Catholic "front groups" and succeeded in placing members in lay organizations, such as the Holy Name Society. Who did she ultimately blame for these outrageous conditions? "I would have to say and have to identify that person as Lucifer."[393]

Dodd was not the only former Communist who made statements like this, nor was the Catholic Church the only religious institution to be infiltrated—the mainline Protestant denominations were invaded as well. But the big prize was the Catholic Church. When Louis Budenz testified before the Congress in 1946, he said that "the Communists everywhere plan to wage war on the Catholic Church as the bases of obliterating all religion."[394] Ben Gitlow, another ex-Communist, testified that this agenda was set by Moscow.[395] As Mary Nicholas and Paul Kengor put it, this meant the Catholic Church was in the "crosshairs."[396]

Dissident Catholic Groups

Dissident Catholic groups have long sought to change the Church's teachings on an array of issues, but most of them focus on celibacy, women's ordination, marriage, the family, and sexuality. Their goal is to Protestantize the Catholic Church, essentially secularizing it. That hasn't worked out too well for the mainline Protestant denominations—they are in free fall—but Catholic dissidents simply don't care. They are bent on bringing their "progressive" views to bear, even if it means the Church regresses and the average Joe resists.

Catholic dissidents often work with secular radicals to achieve their aims. Their alliance with famed radical activist Saul Alinsky is a case in point.

Beginning in the late 1930s, and continuing well in the 1970s, Alinsky teamed with members of the Catholic hierarchy in Chicago to move the Church in a decidedly left-wing direction. He did so by working with neighborhood civic groups aligned with the Catholic clergy. Monsignor John Egan was a social justice advocate, the kind of cleric that Alinsky easily embraced. It was Alinsky's activism that inspired Egan to lead the first Call to Action conference in 1976; it was the most prominent dissident Catholic group at that time, and remained so for many years. In 1996, Bishop Fabian Bruskewitz of Lincoln, Nebraska, announced that any Catholic who joined Call to Action would be excommunicated. He branded it "an anti-Catholic sect composed mainly of aging fallen-away Catholics, including ex-priests and ex-nuns."[397]

Alinsky supporters scored another victory when they formed the Campaign for Human Development in 1969, a social justice agency that veered from Catholic teachings on moral issues. It quickly became a conduit for left-wing groups, providing manpower and money. To this day, some bishops refuse to participate in the annual collection, citing concerns over funding programs tied to radical causes.

Catholics who are regular church-goers are mostly accepting of the Church's pro-life stance; those who typically do not go to Mass are much more likely to disagree. But even those in the latter category might be surprised to learn that there are quite a few organizations that claim to be Catholic that are pro-abortion. Women-Church Convergence, We Are Church, Catholics Speak Out, and the National Coalition of American Nuns are all pro-abortion.

Perhaps the most famous organization with a Catholic name that champions abortion rights is Catholics for Choice. In truth, there is nothing Catholic about it—it is a well-funded letterhead that has no members. But it generates media attention and is closely aligned with some political elites. As such, it presents itself to the public as if it were a legitimate Catholic organization. The goal is to sow confusion in the minds of Americans by making the case that it is perfectly acceptable to be pro-abortion and a Catholic in good standing. It is a stealth maneuver.

In 2002, Catholics for Choice (then known as Catholics for a Free Choice) succeeded in getting the Democratic National Committee (DNC) to provide a link to its website. The DNC came under considerable criticism for doing so, but it continued its alignment over the next couple of years. After the Catholic League spent a considerable amount of time and money seeking to get the DNC to drop its association with this rogue entity, it finally did on April 8, 2004.

More extreme than Catholics for Choice is the founding of organizations with a Catholic name that seek to manipulate Catholics into thinking that it is perfectly okay to change the Church from within by challenging its teachings on moral issues. In short, they seek to normalize dissidence, pushing the Church to make a host of "progressive" reforms. What makes this so dangerous is the extent to which radical activists, supported by the ruling class, are literally trying to subvert the Catholic Church so that they can exercise greater control of the masses. The average Joe has no idea that such machinations exist, and would be surprised to learn about it.

If there is one person who epitomizes this master plan, it is John Podesta. He was chief of staff for President Bill Clinton and was chairman of Hillary Clinton's presidential campaign. He also founded the Center for American Progress, a left-wing think tank. When Wikileaks documents surfaced in 2016, his role in undermining the Catholic Church was disclosed.

Podesta, who identifies as Catholic, has long been concerned about the role of conservatives in the Church. That is why he created Catholics in Alliance for the Common Good and Catholics United. He used them to directly confront the Church on its teachings on abortion and same-sex marriage. They also protested the decision by some bishops to deny Communion to dissident Catholic politicians. These two phony Catholic groups, Podesta said, would set their sights on foisting changes in the Church from the "bottom up."[398]

The most explosive revelation in the Wikileaks batch were the email exchanges between Podesta and Sandy Newman, president of Voices for Progress.

Newman, who was not Catholic, wanted to create a "Catholic Spring" in the Church—forcing wholesale revisions in its teachings—in order to undermine the bishops. He was angry that they were opposed to the Health and Human Services mandate requiring Catholic entities to pay insurance premiums for abortion-inducing drugs and contraception. He explicitly said that it was his goal to rally Catholics to "demand the end of a middle ages dictatorship and the beginning of a little democracy and respect for gender equality in the Catholic church." Podesta wrote back saying, "We created Catholics in Alliance for the Common Good to organize for a moment like this."[399]

In 2013, the IRS revoked the tax-exempt status of Catholics in Alliance for the Common Good for failing to file a 990 form for three consecutive years. This was hardly surprising: it was a dummy Catholic letterhead established to do the work of left-wing operatives in the Democratic Party. In other words, it was founded in deceit and crashed in deceit.

Throughout my elementary school years, I was taught by nuns. They were dedicated women who gave their lives to the Church and contributed greatly in the formation of boys and girls. But many of the nuns that I met as an adult turned out to be angry, embittered women who not only openly defied Church teachings but also spoke with utter contempt about those nuns who remained faithful to tradition. They called the loyal nuns "dead wood."

Dissident nuns dislike traditional nuns so much that they even joined anti-Catholics in welcoming the decision of the owner of the Empire State Building not to honor Mother Teresa on the anniversary of her centenary. The owner refused to light the towers in blue and white, the colors of her order, though he had no problem shining red lights in honor of Communist China. The National Coalition of American Nuns sided with the owner against Mother Teresa, as did Call to Action, Catholics for Choice, New Ways Ministry, DignityUSA, Women's Ordination Conference, and several other pro-abortion activists.

There are dissident priests as well, and some are active in such organizations as the National Federation of Priests' Councils and the Association of United States Catholic Priests. But there are relatively few dissident priests compared to dissident nuns. And there are none that go as far as the National Coalition of American Nuns: in 1988, it joined with Catholics for Choice in filing an amicus brief in support of abortion rights.

It comes as a shock to the average Catholic Joe to learn that a man who identifies as a woman is welcome to enroll in Catholic women's colleges—almost all allow men to do so. These are institutions that were founded by Catholic women's religious orders and maintain an affiliation with their founding congregation. Mount Saint Mary's University in Los Angeles, which is associated with the Sisters of St. Joseph of Carondelet, not only welcomes men who identify as a woman to apply for admission but also encourages students with documents "that include a gender designation that does not accurately reflect their gender identity to bring this to the attention of the Office of Admission at the time of application."[400]

All of these institutions are in conflict with Church teachings and with the proclamations of Pope Francis, who denounced gender ideology as "demonic." The parents of the students obviously have no problem paying for their tuition and the Board of Trustees is also complicit, so this is a problem that extends beyond dissident nuns.

Some nuns are very open about wanting to destroy the Church. Former Harvard law professor and U.S. ambassador to the Holy See Mary Ann Glendon recalls a 1995 conference of an American organization that was founded to promote women's ordination in the 1970s, where one of the sisters described the organization she belonged to in stark terms. "We need persons with chisels inside, chiseling away at that institution or it's never going to come down." Another woman, a professor of religious studies, said, "To ordain women is to give this rotten totalitarian system the Roman Catholic Church has become the push into the grave."[401] These are not women promoting reform—their goal is to disable the Church.

The Leadership Conference of Women's Religious is so extreme that their heterodoxy caused the Vatican to conduct an investigation. They not only reject Church teachings on homosexuality but also question the salvific role of Jesus. Some say they have moved "beyond Jesus." In 2009, most of the nuns simply ignored the Vatican questionnaire and did so with impunity.[402] The average Catholic Joe never heard of this group, and he would be further astonished to learn that it claims to represent most nuns.

NETWORK is one of the better known dissident nun groups, and that is due largely to its former executive director, Sister Simone Campbell. It was founded in the early 1970s by extremist nuns and has clashed with the bishops as well as with the Vatican. "My life is politics," she said in an interview.[403] She was honest—it is not the Catholic Church.

Campbell got her start in 2010 with Rep. Nancy Pelosi, trying to convince Catholic members in Congress to support Obama's healthcare plan, despite its abortion-laden provisions. This was just the beginning of her work for the Democratic Party. She made quite a media splash with her "Nuns on the Bus" gimmick in 2012, taking nuns on a bus tour around the country pushing the Democratic agenda. Although influential news commentator Bill Moyers said that the bus was "filled with nuns," in actual fact, only two nuns made the whole trip and there were never more than six on it at any one time.[404]

Campbell, who was a registered Washington lobbyist, was rewarded for her work with pro-abortion Democrats by giving an address at the 2012 Democratic National Convention. In 2020, she said, "Catholics cannot be true to their faith and vote for Donald Trump in November,"[405] and in 2024, she worked for Kamala Harris, a pro-abortion extremist. Catholics overwhelmingly voted for Trump.

When asked in 2012 if abortion should be legal, the good nun answered, "That's beyond my pay grade. I don't know."[406] By 2024, she was no longer uncertain. "I don't think it's a good policy to outlaw abortion."[407] Given what we know of her work, that was putting it mildly.

New Ways Ministry was founded in 1977 by Father Robert Nugent and Sister Jeannine Gramick. It was a homosexual outreach group, one that was denounced for its heretical views by priests, bishops, and cardinals. But in 2021, there was one notable priest who spoke highly of Sister Gramick—Pope Francis. He wrote a letter to her commending her for her work.

It didn't take long before New Ways Ministry was listed by the Vatican on its resource page for the upcoming synod. This moved me to write to Cardinal Mario Grech, secretary general of the Synod of Bishops, about the propriety of providing a link to this group's webinar on synodality. In my letter, I recounted that in 1999, Cardinal Joseph Ratzinger (Pope Benedict XVI), prefect of the Congregation for the Doctrine of the Faith, issued a document detailing how Sister Gramick and Father Nugent had been sanctioned by two major Church bodies for their public misrepresentations of Church teachings on sexuality. He never replied. On October

17, 2023, Pope Francis welcomed Catholic dissidents who were previously condemned by U.S. cardinals and bishops. He met for almost an hour with Sister Gramick.[408]

In other words, the ruling class working with radicals has also infested the Catholic Church.

The Donor Class

Radical "Catholic" groups can't depend on the faithful to support them, so they rely on wealthy benefactors, most of whom are not Catholic. These elites operate many foundations, and their goal is to undermine the Catholic Church by underwriting the work of these dissidents. Here's a look at the most prominent ones.

No organization in the nation has been working longer to undermine the Church than the Ford Foundation. It has consistently funded Catholics for Choice, trying to convince the public that it is okay to be a good Catholic and pro-abortion. Also funding this group are the Arcus Foundation, George Soros's Open Society Institute, the Susan Thompson Buffett Foundation, the John D. and Catherine T. MacArthur Foundation, the William & Flora Hewlett Foundation, and the David and Lucile Packard Foundation. The Ford Foundation also funded We Are Church, an organization trying to turn the Church topsy turvy, and NETWORK.

The super-rich Southern Poverty Law Center chooses a different tactic: it seeks to smear legitimate Christian organizations by labeling them "hate groups." Among its victims are Alliance Defending Freedom, American College of Pediatricians, Family Research Council, Liberty Counsel, the Pacific Justice Institute, and the Ruth Institute. All of them defend traditional moral values, and for this, they are treated as if they were Nazis. The media are ever too quick to pick up on their bullying. Perversely, Southern Poverty does not treat bona fide hate groups this way. Indeed, it defended Antifa, the urban terrorist group, complaining that it was "dangerous" to designate it as a "domestic terrorist organization." Doing so, it said, threatened civil liberties.[409] But Apple, the computer king, likes these radicals, providing millions, as does the George & Amal Clooney Foundation.

Tim Gill and John Stryker are two homosexual billionaires who hate the Catholic Church. The Gill Foundation does everything it can to discredit the Church's moral teachings and does not hesitate to directly attack the Magisterium. Stryker is the man behind the Arcus Foundation, one of the most prolific left-wing activist organizations in the nation. There is hardly a radical Catholic dissident group that it has not funded. Prominent among its recipients are We Are Church, DignityUSA, New Ways Ministry, Catholics for Choice, the Women's Alliance for Theology, Ethics and Ritual (WATER), the National Coalition of American Nuns, and Faith in Public Life.

George Soros is the kingpin of radical donors, which includes funding anti-Catholic groups. The mere fact that Soros is Jewish does not shield him from criticism. Indeed, he has earned the enmity of Jewish leaders. Defenders of Israel like the ADL have accused him of blaming anti-Semitism in Israel on the Israeli government, while the *Jerusalem Post* has accused him of weakening support for Israel in the Democratic Party. The editor of the *New Republic*, Martin Peretz, called him "a cog in the Hitlerite wheel."[410] These Jewish liberals are not wrong. Known as a "self-hating Jew" in many quarters, as a young man in Hungary, Soros became a Nazi collaborator. In a *60 Minutes* interview, he admitted that he helped confiscate property from Jews. He told Steve Kroft that he never regretted doing so. When asked if this was difficult, Soros said, "No, not at all." Stunned, Kroft said, "No feeling of guilt?" "No," came the reply.[411]

This needs to be said because when non-Jews criticize Soros for undermining Christianity, the media are quick to say such comments smack of anti-Semitism. Nonsense. If his name were O'Malley and he did the exact same things, such as funding the phony Catholic groups exposed by Wikileaks to create a "Catholic spring," does anyone believe he wouldn't be condemned for his work just as vigorously?

The enemies of Christianity have many weapons at their disposal, including stealth maneuvers. They have scored important victories, and they are far from quitting. They need to be put in their place if the good work done by Catholics and Protestants is to succeed.

Conclusion

If we have learned anything from history, it is that although Christianity has gone through cycles where it has been dealt severe blows, it always rebounds. The persecution is real and there are times like now when it appears to be on the ropes, but the victimizers never succeed in finishing the job. Christians are too resilient to be defeated.

That said, it behooves Christians not to be complacent. The forces aligned against them are formidable: when the ruling class teams with radical intellectuals and activists, as they do today, they make Christians look like wounded warriors. The average Joe wants nothing to do with them, preferring to mind his own business. But they will never respect his wishes, which is why vigilance and resistance are a must.

Huxley and Orwell warned us what was in motion and what was coming. They were right. Seduction and control are what motivate elites, especially those who occupy the command centers in the political arena. More than anything else, they want the creation of the compliant citizen. Unlike the tyrants of old, today's ruling class opts for democratic despotism, the soft version of totalitarianism. They are no less a threat to freedom.

The good news is that there are signs that the ruling class is being challenged in a way not seen for some time.

In 2024, Kevin Roberts, the president of the Heritage Foundation, spoke at the World Economic Forum in Davos. He took the occasion to give the elites a reality check. "Around the world," he said, "people distrust global elites because they hate us." If they want to regain trust, he said, "Davos must accept the moral virtues, practical benefits, and natural rights of individual nations (and, ultimately families and individuals) to govern themselves. No serious person believes that the global elites' grand moral stands over the last generation—bowing to China, erasing borders, worshipping climate extremism—*just so happened* to serve their class interests at the direct expense of ordinary people's sovereignty and economic opportunity" (emphasis in the original).[412]

Roberts zoned in on Covid, citing the elites' lockdown mandates. He nailed them for cracking down on "disinformation," all the while defending Harvard University's plagiarist president. And he slammed them for hypocritically promoting diversity, calling them "a hermetically insulated claque of race-hustling, anti-American, anti-Christian, anti-Semitic bigots."[413]

We have seen how the elites live in a bubble, looking down their noses at the average Joe. A case in point is how they reacted to the Trump victory in 2024. There were crying sessions in the State Department, primal scream exercises for distraught women, and canceled classes at some colleges and universities. All over the nation, the well-educated, liberal-left wealthy Americans were in mourning. Not the average Joe—he voted for Trump.

Some in elite quarters went berserk. The editor-in-chief of *Scientific American*, Laura Helmuth, exploded in anger, using obscenities to describe the "fascists" who supported Trump. She wrote one vicious social media post after another, blasting the American electorate, until her rants got so bad she couldn't take the pushback and resigned.[414] Rachel Zegler, of "Snow White" fame, resorted to threats, saying Trump supporters would "never know peace."[415] An instructor at the University of Kansas said that men should be killed for not backing women candidates. "We can line all those guys up and shoot them. They clearly don't understand the way the world works."[416]

That last comment is emblematic of the way radicals think. The average Joe just doesn't get it—he's too stupid to know how the world works. But professors do.

Thought control, which is what professors are very good at, always targets religion; religious convictions are the heart of conscience rights. They target religion for the same reason they target the family: both stand in the way of getting the average Joe to exercise fidelity to them, which explains why they must be disabled.

It is easier for us to understand why radicals take aim at the family, resenting the authority of the father. Less obvious is why the ruling class does. Their interest has less to do with patriarchy than it does population control, seeing to it that we have less of the "useless people" that the Davos crowd crows about. Eugenics, assisted suicide, and abortion are their weapons of choice.

The ruling class cannot achieve the compliant citizenry it wants unless they can have greater access to children. The war on parental rights is being waged to liberate children from their parents, giving them over to the social engineers in education. No revolution can succeed without this happening, which is why it is a priority for elites and radicals alike.

When John the Savage in Huxley's *Brave New World* was told that the ruling class would grant him comfort, he replied, "I don't want comfort." So what did he want? "I want God."[417] He also said he wanted freedom. This is reminiscent of a joke about a dog who sought to liberate himself from Communist Cuba. His masters asked, "Are you not taken care of?" "Yes." "Don't they feed you?" "Yes." "Then why do you want to leave?" "I want to bark."

Being free to commune with God is not something that radicals and the ruling class can identify with. Indeed, it scares them. They can't stand being subordinate to anyone, much less God Almighty. It is an obstacle to their control ambitions.

The Catholic Church is there to serve the needs of John the Savage. It stands in opposition to the cultivation of the compliant citizen, preferring an active clergy and laity. The U.S. bishops insist that "the obligation to teach the moral truths that should shape our lives, including our public lives, is central to the mission given to the Church of Jesus Christ." Moreover, the law should "protect the right of the Church and other institutions in civil society to participate in cultural, political and economic life without being forced to abandon or ignore their central moral convictions."[418]

Such thinking is anathema to elites. Their tolerance for religious liberty is slight, which is why they want to privatize it. They will tolerate old ladies in church saying the Rosary but don't take it outside. The outspoken German prelate Gerhard Cardinal Müller knows how they think. "The motto of secularism, 'religion is a private matter,' is a brutal violation of human rights, and furthermore of reason, since all man's essential acts accord with his communal nature and are correspondingly public."[419] As Pope Benedict XVI said, "Denying the right to profess one's religion in public and the right to bring the truths of faith to bear upon public life has negative consequences for true development."[420]

Fortunately, the clergy in the United States is not inclined to accept the second-class status that many elites and radicals want. Theologically and politically, they are not supportive of the "progressive" agenda, and neither, it appears, does Pope Leo XIV.

According to Brad Vermurlen, a sociology professor at the University of St. Thomas in Houston, priests ordained since 2010 "are clearly the most conservative cohort of priests we've seen in a long time." His observation is backed up by the data. According to a large survey of priests by the Catholic Project at the Catholic University of America, more than 80 percent of priests ordained since 2020 describe themselves as theologically "conservative/orthodox" or "very conservative/orthodox." Politically, almost all describe themselves as moderate or conservative.[421]

These are the kinds of men that are not going to passively watch the ruling class encroach on the rights of Catholics. They will be assisted by those in the laity who share their convictions. A more religion-friendly administration in Washington will bolster their efforts.

The elites and radicals may have succeeded in putting Christianity in the crosshairs, but they will not succeed in destroying it. This, however, should not give us comfort. We don't need Catholics who are compliant with the dictates of the ruling class—we need Catholics who will subvert them.

ENDNOTES

1 Charles McGrath, "Which Dystopian Novel Got It Right: Orwell's '1984' or Huxley's 'Brave New World'?", *New York Times*, February 13, 2017, https://www.nytimes.com/2017/02/13/books/review/which-dystopian-novel-got-it-right-orwells-or-huxleys-brave-new-world.html.

2 Victor Davis Hanson, "Billionaires Are Starting to Question Their Loyalty to Democrats," *Daily Signal,* March 27, 2025, https://www.dailysignal.com/2025/03/27/the-real-oligarchs-whove-been-running-our-country/.

3 "Pride and Humility," https//www.cslewisinstitute.org/resources/pride-and-humility/.

4 Rob Bluey, "'Most Terrifying Poll Result I've Ever Seen': Scott Rasmussen Surveys America's Elite 1%," *Daily Signal*, March 21, 2024, https://www.dailysignal.com.

5 Stephen Moore, "The Real Story of the Two Americas," Daily Caller, January 21, 2024, https://dailycaller.com/2024/01/21/opinion-the-real-story-of-the-two-americas-stephen-moore/.

6 Ibid.

7 Ibid.

8 Craig Bannister, "64% of Registered Democrats Want Their Party to 'Oppose Everything That Trump is Doing,'" February 25, 2025, https://mrctv.org/blog/craig-bannister/64-registered-democrats-want-their-party-oppose-everything-trump-doing#.

9 John Nolte, "55% of Leftists Believe It's Justifiable to Assassinate Trump Thanks to Apps Like Blue Sky," April 8, 2025, https://www.breitbart.com/politics/2025/04/08/nolte-55-of-leftists-believe-its-justifiable-to-assassinate-trumps-thanks-to-apps-like-bluesky/.

10 Pam Key, "NY Gov. Hochul: Trump Wasting Time in NYC While Biden Winning Over Battleground States," *Breitbart*, May 23, 2024, https://www.breitbart.com/clips/2024/05/23/ny-gov-hochul-wasting-time-in-nyc-while-biden-winning-over-battleground-states/.

11 Roger Kimball, "Restoring American Culture," *Imprimis*, February 2025, Vol. 54, No. 2. *Imprimis* is a publication of Hillsdale College.

12 Joe Concha, "Nancy Pelosi Yet Again Reveals Democrats' Disdain for Average Americas," *New York Post*, May 13, 2024, https://nypost.com/2024/05/13/opinion/nancy-pelosi-yet-again-reveals-democrats-disdain-for-average-americans/.

13 Oliver Darcy, "Fact Check on Hillary Clinton and 'Everyday Americans,'" October 2016, https://www.businessinsider.com/wikileaks-email-hillary-clinton-everyday-americans-2016-10.

14 Marco Rubio, "Elites Love The 'Deep State' Because They Loathe The People," April 16, 2024, *The Federalist*, https://thefederalist.com/2024/04/16/elites-love-the-deep-state-because-they-loathe-the-american-people/.

15 Robert F. Gorman, "Global Elites Put Christianity in the Crosshairs," Acton Institute, November 30, 2016, https://www.acton.org/pub/commentary/2016/11/30/global-elites-put-christianity-crosshairs.

16 Ibid.

17 Seamus Bruner, *Controligarchs: Exposing the Billionaire Class, Their Secret Deals, and the Globalist Plot to Dominate Your Life* (New York: Sentinel, 2003), pp. xi–xii.

18 Michael Rectenwald, "What Is The Great Reset?", *Imprimis*, December 2021, Vol. 50, No. 12.

19 His comment was aired on the "Ingraham Angle," Fox News Network, January 23, 2025.

20 Scott Walter, *Arabella: The Dark Money Network of Leftist Billionaires Secretly Transforming America* (New York: Encounter Books, 2024), xxiii.

21 Jason Chaffetz, *The Puppeteers: The People Who Control the People Who Control America* (New York: Broadside Books, 2023), xi.

22 Ibid., xix.

23 Marco Rubio, "Elites Love The 'Deep State' Because They Loathe The American People."

24 Daniel Payne, "Supreme Court Overturns 'Chevron' Doctrine with Big Implications for Religious Liberty," *Catholic New Agency*, June 28, 2024, https://www.catholicnewsagency.com/news/258141/supreme-court-overturns-chevron-doctrine-with-big-implications-for-religious-liberty.

25 C. Wright Mills, *The Power Elite* (New York: Oxford University Press, 1956), 4.

26 David Horowitz, *America Betrayed: How a Christian Monk Created America & Why the Left Is Determined to Destroy Her* (New York: Final Battle Books, 2024), 112.

27 W. Cleon Skousen, *The Naked Communist: Exposing Communism and Restoring Freedom* (Salt Lake City, Utah: Izzard Ink, 1958), 319.

28 Ibid., 317.

29 Ibid., 320.

30 Robert Stilson, "Big Philanthrophy's Most Radical Foundation?", Foundation Watch, Capital Research Center, May/June 2024, 9.

31 Skousen, *The Naked Communist*, 306.

32 Ibid., 308.

33 Ibid., 325.

34 Ibid., 321.

35 Kristina Wong, "'Blood Money': Leaked U.S. Federal Law Enforcement Documents Reveal How China Is Secretly Arming American Criminals with Machine Guns," *Breitbart*, February 26, 2024, https://breitbart.com/politics/2024/02/26/blood-money-leaked-u-s-federal-law-enforcement-documents-reveal-how-china-is-secretly-arming-american-criminals-with-machine-guns.

36 Bill Donohue, "Democrats Have a Catholic Problem," June 16, 2017, www.catholicleague.org/democrats-have-a-catholic-problem/.

37 Ibid.

38 Ibid.

39 Ibid.

40 Tom McGrath, "How 1980s Yuppies Gave Us Donald Trump," *Politico*, June 4, 2024, https://www.politico.com/new/magazine/2024/06/04/yuppies-donald-trump-book-excerpt-00160689.

41 Bruner, *Controligarchs*, 83.

42 Ibid.

43 Mike Gonzalez and Lindsey Burke, "The Root Cause of the Insanity on College Campuses Is Older Than You May Think," *Daily Signal*, November 20, 2023, https://www.dailysignal.com.

44 Eric A. Posner, Kathryn E. Spier & Adrian Vermeule, "Divide and Conquer," *Journal of Legal Analysis*, Fall 2010 (Vol. 2, No. 2), 450.

45 Joseph Ratzinger and Marcello Pera, *Without Roots: The West, Relativism, Christianity, Islam* (New York: Encounter Books, 2008), 3.

46 Ryan P. Williams, "Defend America—Defeat Multiculturalism," The American Mind, April 23, 2019, https://americanmind.org/memo/defend-america-defeat-multiculturalism/.

47 Eva Vlaardingerbroek at CPAC Hungary: "The Great Replacement Is No Longer A Theory, It's Reality," Real Clear Politics, April 27, 2024.

48 "Henry Kissinger on Hamas Attacks Fallout: Germany Let in Too

Many Foreigners," *Politico*, October 11, 2023, https://www.politico.eu/henry/kissinger-germany-let-in-way-too-many-foreigners/.

49 Carlon Howard and Allen Mendenhall, "What Does It Mean To Be A Woke Corporation? Experts Debate," Divided We Fall, February 8, 2023, https://dividedwefall.org/woke-corporations/.

50 "Attack on Chiefs' Butker; Bigotry in Play," *Catalyst* (June 2024), 1, https://www.catholicleague.org/attack-on-chiefs-butker-bigotry-in-play/.

51 Bill Donohue, "Our Pampered Elites," June 24, 2024, Catholic League, https://www.catholicleague.org/our-pampered-elites/.

52 Paul Kengor and Robert Orlando, *The Divine Plan: John Paul II, Ronald Reagan, and The Dramatic End of The Cold War* (Wilmington, Delaware: ISI Books, 2019), 53–54.

53 Lance Morrow, "Your Periodic Reminder That Evil Is Real," *Wall Street Journal*, October 24, 2023, https://www.wsj.com/articles/your-periodic-reminder-that-evil-is-real-rage-history-israel-hamas-6b255ebd.

54 Bombshell Email: Clinton Camp "Demands 'Complaint Citizenry' for Her Master Plan-Look!", October 12, 2016, https://2020conservative.com/bombshell-email-clinton-camp-demands-compliant-citizenry-master-plan-look.

55 Michael L. Coulter, Stephen M. Krason, Richard S. Myers, Joseph A. Varacalli, *Encyclopedia of Catholic Social Thought, Social Science, and Social Policy*, Vol. 2 (Lanham, Maryland: The Scarecrwo Press, Inc., 2007), 793.

56 Ibid., 793–94.

57 Ibid., 794.

58 Ibid., 693.

59 "Forming Consciences for Faithful Citizenship," November 2002, https://usccb.org/forming-consciences-for-faithful-citizenship.

60 George Weigel, *Evangelical Catholicism: Deep Reform In The 21st-Century Church* (New York: Basic Books, 2013), 223.

61 Rod Dreher, *Live Not By Lies: A Manual for Christian Dissidents* (New York: Sentinel, 2020), 7–8.

62 John Paul II, *Centesimus Annus*, 1991, https://www.vatican.va/content/john-paul-ii/en/encyclicals/documents.hf_jpii_enc_01051991_centesimus-annus.html.

63 John Keane, *The New Despotism* (Cambridge, MA: Harvard University Press, 2020), 215.

64 Alexis de Tocqueville, *Democracy in America*, edited by J.P. Mayer,

translated by George Lawrence (New York: Harper & Row, 1969), 539.

65 Ibid., 691.

66 Ibid., 692.

67 Richard K. Vedder, "Bread and Circuses Then and Now," *Independent*, October 9, 2023, https://www.independent.org/news/article.asp.

68 John Keane, *The New Despotism* (Cambridge, MA: Harvard University Press, 2020), 59–60.

69 Aldous Huxley, *Brave New World* (New York: HarperPerennial, 1932), 43.

70 Alexis de Tocqueville's *Memoir on Pauperism*, translated by Seymour Drescher (London: Civitas, 1997).

71 Kenneth Niemeyer, "Pope Francis Becomes Figurehead in the Universal Basic Income Movement," *Business Insider*, September 22, 2024, https://www.businessinsider.com/pope-francis-universal-basic-income-ai-jobs-automation-2024-9.

72 Nicholas Eberstadt and Evan Abramsky, "What Do Prime-Age 'NILF' Men Do All Day? A Cautionary on Universal Basic Income," Institute for Family Studies, February 8, 2021, https://ifstudies.org/blog.what-do-prime-age-men-do-all-day-a-cautionary-on-universal-basic-income.

73 Ibid.

74 Ibid.

75 Ibid.

76 Hannah Grossman, "Democratic Mayor Hands Out $10,800 for Economic Equity Program That Funds Lavish 5-day Trip to Miami," *Fox News*, February 24, 2024, https://www.foxnews.com/media/democratic-mayor-hands-10800-economic-equity-agenda-one-blows-60-lavish-5-day-trip-miami.

77 Ibid.

78 Pope Francis, Encyclical Letter *Fratelli Tutti* (3 October 2020), no. 162 AAS 112 (2020), 1025; quoting Francis, *Address to Members of the Diplomatic Corps Accredited to the Holy See* (12 January 2015), AAS 107 (2015), 165.

79 John Paul II, *Laborem Exercens*, September 14, 1981, https://www.vatican-va/content/john-paul-ii/en/encyclicals/documents.hf_jp_ii_enc_14091981_laborem-exercens.html#.

80 United States Catholic Bishops, "Economic Justice for All: Pastoral Letter on Catholic Social Teaching and the U.S. Economy," 1986, no. 88.

81 Bill Donohue, "Mother Teresa Earned Sainthood," October 20, 2016, Catholic League, www.catholicleague.org/mother-teresa-earned-sainthood-2/.

82 Thomas C. Reeves, "Mother Teresa's Critics Undone," Catholic League, September 20, 2016, https://www.catholicleague.org/mother-teresas-critics-undone/.

83 Ibid.

84 "Forming Consciences For Faithful Citizenship."

85 Huxley, *Brave New World*, 228.

86 Keane, *The New Despotism*, 117.

87 Lee Harding, "The WEF Wants To Build Trust-Good Luck With That," Frontier Centre For Public Policy, January 18, 2024.

88 Bruner, *Controligarchs*, 81.

89 Lyman Stone, "Bread and Circuses: The Replacement of American Community Life," American Enterprise Institute, April 2021.

90 Neil Postman, Quotes by Neil Postman: "When a population becomes distracted by trivia…," https://www.goodreads.com/quotes/286011-when-a-population-becomes-distracted-by-trivia-when-cultural-life.

91 Huxley, *Brave New World*, 23.

92 Douglas Hartmann, *Midnight Basketball: Race, Sports, and Neoliberal Social Policy* (Chicago: University of Chicago Press, 2016).

93 Huxley, *Brave New World*, 238.

94 Jason Breslow, "John Boehner, Once Opposed to Marijuana, Now Wants Legalization," National Public Radio, March 16, 2019, https://www.npr.org/2019/03/16/704086782/john-boehner-was-once-unalterably-opposed-to-marijuana-he-now-wants-it-to-be-leg.

95 Rachel Schilke, "House Report Details China's 'Abhorrent' Role Fueling the Fentanyl Epidemic Killing Americans," *Washington Examiner*, April 16, 2024, https://www.washingtonexaminer.com/news/house/2967072/house-report-details-chinas-abhorrent-role-fueling-the-fentanyl-epidemic-kiling-americans/.

96 Father John A. Hardon, S.J., "How to Be Truly Happy," Catholic Education, November 19, 2008, https://catholiceducation.org/en/culture/how-to-be-truly-happy.html.

97 Ibid.

98 Aldous Huxley, *Brave New World* (New York: HarperPerennial, 1932), pp. 34–35.

99 Ibid., 219.

100 George Orwell, *1984* (New York: Signet Classics, 1949), 6.
101 Ibid., 155.
102 Ibid., 248.
103 Jacob N. Shapiro and Chris Mattmann, "A.I. Is Coming for the Past, Too," *New York Times*, January 30, 2024, Section A, 21.
104 Bishop Donald J. Hying's "Statement on the Call for the Destruction of Christian Statues" June 23, 2020, is available on the Diocese of Madison website.
105 Father Seán Connolly, "The True Christopher Columbus and the Crisis of the West," *Catholic World Report*, October 11, 2021, https://www.catholicworldreport.com/2021/10/11/the-true-christopher-columbus-and-the-crisis-of-the-west/.
106 Gerald Korson, "Christopher Columbus and Fake History," kofc.org, September 1, 2017, https://www.kofc/en/news-room/columbia/2017/september/christopher-columus-fake-history.html.
107 Ibid.
108 Carol Delaney, *Columbus and the Quest for Jerusalem* (New York: Free Press, 2011), 107, 181.
109 Much of what follows is taken from my monograph, "The Noble Legacy of Fr. Serra," September 9, 2015. See "Special Reports" at the Catholic League website, www.catholicleague.org.
110 Ibid.
111 Ibid.
112 Laura M. Holson, "Sainthood of Serra Reopens Wounds of Colonialism in California," *New York Times*, September 30, 2015, p. A1.
113 Bill Donohue, "NY Times Piece on St. Serra Needs Correction," October 1, 2015, Catholic League, www.catholicleague.org/ny-times-piece-on-st-serra-needs-correction/.
114 Ibid.
115 Bill Donohue, "New York Times Smear of St. Serra Stands," October 7, 2015, Catholic League, www.catholicleague.org/new-york-times-smear-of-st-serra-stands/.
116 Bill Donohue, "NY Times Consistent Defiance On Serra," October 23, 2015, Catholic League, www.catholicleague.org/ny-times-consistent-defiance-on-serra/.
117 Ibid.
118 Elizabeth Bruenig, "'Racism Makes a Liar of God,'" *New York Times*, August 6, 2020.
119 Bill Donohue, "New York Times Addresses St. Serra Issue," August 17, 2020, Catholic League, www.catholicleague.org/new-york-times-addresses-st-serra-issue/.

120 Orwell, *1984*, 249.

121 Ibid.

122 Huxley, *Brave New World*. See P.S. section following the text of the book, "A Letter to George Orwell," 15–18.

123 Ibid.

124 Huxley, *Brave New World*. This quote is also in the P.S. section, titled, "Prophecies Fulfilled: The Contemporary Response to *Brave New World Revisited*" (1958), 12.

125 "Brave New World (1932)," Observation Blogger, December 2, 2020, https://observationblogger.com/2020/12/02/brave-new-world-1932-aldous-huxley/.

126 Lorraine Boissoneault, "The True Story of Brainwashing and How It Shaped America," *Smithsonian Magazine*, May 22, 2017, https://www.smithsonianmag.com/history/true-story-brainwashing-and-how-it-shaped-america-180963400/.

127 Samantha Aschieris, "Author Who Lived Under Mao Warns of Woke Revolution Here," *Daily Signal*, November 27, 2023, hpps://www.dailysignal.com/2023/11/27/communism-is-not-only-here-its-going-mainstream-survivor-of-mao-china-says/.

128 W. Cleon Skousen, *The Naked Communist* (Salt Lake City, Utah: Izzard Ink, 1958), 315.

129 Ibid.

130 Ibid., 316.

131 Ibid., 306.

132 Ibid., 310.

133 John Canaday, *Embattled Critic* (New York: Noonday Press, 1959), 31–33.

134 Skousen, *The Naked Communist*, 322.

135 Ibid., 307.

136 Michael L. Coulter, Stephen M. Krason, Richard S. Myers, Joseph A. Varacalli, *Encyclopedia of Catholic Social Thought, Social Science, and Social Policy*, Vol. 1 (Lanham, Maryland: The Scarecrow Press, Inc., 2007), 231.

137 "Forming Consciences for Faithful Citizenship," November 2023, usccb.org/forming-consciences-for-faithful-citizenship.

138 "Persecution of Christians Can Have a Polite Disguise, Pope Francis Warns," April 12, 2016, https://www.catholicagency.com/news/33718/persecution-of-christians-can-have-a-polite-disguise-pope-francis-warns.

139 Bill Donohue, "The Evil of Thought Control," October 13, 2022, Catholic League, https://www.catholicleague.org/the-evil-of-thought-control/.

140 Cal Thomas, "Jordan Peterson is Doomed to be a Victim of Woke Culture," *New York Post*, February 1, 2024, https://www.nypost.com/2024/01/31/opinion/jordan-peterson-is-doomed-to-be-a-victim-of-woke-culture/.

141 Tyler O'Neil, "Religious Freedom, Part 2: Lawyer Sounds Alarm Ahout 'Rise of Global Citizenship,'" *Daily Signal*, March 19, 2024, https://www.dailysignal.com.

142 Iwan Stone, "Dr Hilary Cass Reveals She Cannot Use Public Transport as She is Threatened by 'Unforgivable' Activists Over Her Hard-Hitting Report into Trans Medicine and Blast Labour MP Dawn Butler's 'Completely Wrong' Criticism," *Daily Mail*, April 20, 2024, https:/dailymail.co.uk/news/article-13330519/Dr-Hilary-Cass-public-transport-threatened-activists-hard-report-trans-medicine-Labour-MP-Dawn-Butlers.html.

143 "Police Scotland 'Can't Cope' with Flood of Hate Speech Reports as 8,000 Flood in During First Week of Draconian Law," *Breitbart*, April 9, 2024, https://brietbart.com/europe/2024/04/09/police-scotland-cant-cope-with-flood-of-hate-speech-reports/.

144 O'Neil, "Religious Freedom, Part 2: Lawyer Sounds Alarm About 'Rise of Global Censorship.'"

145 Nate Hochman, "Free Speech Is Dead in Europe," *Spectator*, March 14, 2024, https://spectator.org/free-speech-is-dead-in-europe-belgium/.

146 Edward Pentin, "Free Speech Wins! Belgian Court Overturns Ban on Conservative Conference," *National Catholic Register*, April 17, 2024, https://www.ncregister.com/blog/free-speech-wins-belgian-court-overturns-ban-on-conservative-conference.

147 "The 'G' in ESG: How the Left Institutionalizes Its Agenda in Corporate America," *Breitbart*, May 29, 2024, https://www.breibart.com/politics/2024/05/29/the-g-in-esg-how-the-left-institutionalizes-its-agenda-in-corporate-america-2/.

148 Carl M. Cannon, "Poll: Is Censorship a Partisan Issue?", *Real Clear Politics*, September 22, 2023, https://www.realclearpolitics.com/real_clear_opinion_research/poll_is_censorship_a_partisan-issue_149790.html.

149 Ibid.

150 William A. Donohue, *The Politics of the American Civil Liberties Union* (New Brunswick, N.J., 1985), 229–38.

151 Ibid., 306–7.

152 Elizabeth Troutman and Tyler O'Neil, "AP Bans 'Crisis Pregnancy Centers,' Directs Journalists to Use Negative Term Instead," *Daily Signal*, February 3, 2023.

153 Oliver Darcy, "James Bennet Resigns from New York Times after Cotton Op-ed Backlash," CNN, June 7, 2020, https://www.cnn.com/2020/06/07/media/james-bennet-new-york-times-resigns/index.html.

154 Matt Walsh, "New CEO Of NPR is Everything Wrong With The News Media," *Daily Wire*, April 18, 2024, https://www.dailywire.com/news/new-ceo-of-npr-is-everything-wrong-with-the-news-media.

155 Daniel Nuccio, "USSR-born scientist: DEI Dogma in STEM 'Reminiscent of What I Experienced in Soviet Union," *The College Fix*, December 12, 2024, https://www.thecollegefix.com/ussr-born-scientist-dei-dogma-in-stem-reminiscent-of-what-i-experienced-in-soviet-union/.

156 Bill Donohue, "Campuses Sponsor Gay Thought Control," July 29, 2010, Catholic League, https://www.catholicleague.org/campuses-sponsor-gay-thought-control/.

157 Bill Donohue, "Why The Left Defends Islamists," August 8, 2017, Catholic League, https//www.catholicleague.org/why-the-left-defends-islamists/.

158 Stanley K. Ridgley, "The Critical Race Speech Tribunal," *Academic Questions*, 2022 (35.4), 132–35.

159 Kurt Zindulka, "WEF: EU Chief Von Der Leyen Demands Censorship of 'Industrial Scale Disinformation' at Davos," January 17, 2024, *Breitbart*, https://www.breitbart.com/europe/2024/01/17/wef-eu-chief-von-der-leyen-demands-censorship-of-industrial-scale-disinformation-at-davos/.

160 Seamus Bruner, *Controligarchs* (New York: Sentinel, 2023), 191–93.

161 Jonathan Turley, "A Judge Rules, Yes, the Biden Administration Was Trying to Censor People Online," *New York Post*, July 23, 2024, https://www.nypost.com/2024/07/23/opinion/a-judge-rules-that-yes-the-biden-administration-was-trying-to-censor-people-online/.

162 "Catholic League Report: Biden Administration and Thought Control," Catalyst, May 2024. It is available on the Catholic League website under Archives.
163 Ibid.
164 "Reports Show Trump Shared Nuke Secrets with Foreign Billionaire; Hillary Clinton Speaks Out On GOP Chaos, Trump, 2024 Race," CNN Live, Special, October 5, 2023.
165 Joseph Wulfshon, "Katie Couric 'Condescending, Elitist' Remarks Calling to 'Deprogram' GOP Retires Journo Label, Critics Say," Fox News, January 18, 2021, https://www.foxnews.com/media/katie-couric-condescending-elitist-remarks-calling-to-deprogram-gop-retires-journo-label-critics-say.
166 Bill Donohue, "Maoist Roots of Deprogramming," January 27, 2021, Catholic League, https://www.catholicleague.org/maoist-roots-of-deprogramming/.
167 Ibid.
168 Ibid.
169 Bill Donohue, "Look Who's A Domestic Threat?", June 25, 2024, Catholic League, www.catholicleague.org/look-whose-a-domestic-threat/.
170 Ibid.
171 Ibid.
172 Seamus Bruner, *Controligarchs* (New York: Sentinel, 2023), 67–68.
173 Michael Woronoff, "Put a Stake in Stakeholder Capitalism," Commentary, May 2023, https://www.commentary.org/articles/mworonoff/profit-motive-stakeholder-capitalism/.
174 Ibid.
175 Charles Gasparino, *Go Woke, Go Broke: The Inside Story of the Radicalization of Corporate America* (New York: Center Street, 2024), 17–18.
176 Michael Rectenwald, "What Is the Great Reset?," *Imprimis*, December 2021, Vol. 50, No. 12.
177 Bruner, *Controligarchs*, 62.
178 John Tierney, "The Shape of Things to Come: The Tyranny of Covid-19," in *Against the Great Reset: Eighteen Theses Contra the New World Order*, Michael Walsh, ed., (New York: Bombardier, 2022), 268.
179 Mattias Desmet, *The Psychology of Totalitarianism*, translated by Els

Vanbrabant, (White River Junction, VT: Chelsea Green Publishing, 2022), 6-7.

180 Peter Morici, "Be Wary of the Leviathan; Democrats Will Never Let a Good Crisis Go To Waste," *Washington Times*, July 21, 2021.

181 Victor Davis Hanson, "The Great Regression," in *Against the Great Reset*, 25.

182 Ibid.

183 Ibid., 24.

184 Jeffrey J. Anderson, "Covid Catastrophies," *Claremont Review of Books*, Winter 2023/24, https://claremontreviewofbooks.com/covid-catastrophes/.

185 Ibid.

186 Bruner, *Controligarchs*, 37.

187 Ibid., 38.

188 Matthew Impelli and Alex Backus, "Dr. Fauci Testifies: Unvaccinated American Caused Additional '200-300k Deaths,'" *Newsweek*, June 3, 2024, https://www.newsweek.com/live-updates-dr-anthony-fauci-testify-before-congress-origins-covid-19-1907497.

189 James Bovard, "Fauci's Returning to Congress—Will He Continue His COVID Coverup?", *New York Post*, January 4, 2024, https://nypost.com/2024/01/04/opinion/faucis-returning-to-congress-will-he-continue-his-covid-coverage/.

190 Ibid.

191 Ibid.

192 Ibid.

193 "Anthony Fauci Fessus Up," *Wall Street Journal*, January 11, 2024, https://www.wsj.com/articles/anthony-fauci-covid-social-distancing-six-feet-rule-house-subcommittee-hearing-442890850.

194 "Moral Considerations Regarding the New COVID-19 Vaccines," United States Conference of Catholic Bishops, December 11, 2020, www.usccb.org, moral-considerations-covid-vaccines.

195 Katherine Stewart, "The Religious Right's Hostility to Science Is Crippling Our Coronavirus Response," *New York Times*, March 27, 2020, https://www.nytimes.com/2020/03/27/opinion/coronavirus-trump-evangelicals.html.

196 Bill Donohue, "Eucharist Ban in MD County Must Be Repealed," May 28, 2020, Catholic League, www.catholicleague.org/eucharist-ban-in-md-county-must-be-repealed/.

197 Bill Donohue, "Abortion Activists Endanger Public Health," March

25, 2020, Catholic League, www.catholicleague.org/abortion-activists-endanger-public-health/.

198 Bill Donohue, *Cultural Meltdown: The Secular Roots of Our Moral Crisis* (Manchester, New Hampshire: Sophia Institute Press, 2024), 16.

199 Bill Donohue, "COVID-19 Concerns Jettisoned For Protesters," July 15, 2020, Catholic League, www.catholicleague.org/covid-19-concerns-jettisoned-for-protesters/.

200 Ibid.

201 Michael Powell, "Are Protests Dangerous? What Experts Say May Depend on Who's Protesting What," *New York Times*, July 6, 2020.

202 Bill Donohue, "Cuomo's Tyrannical Edict," October 6, 2020, Catholic League, www.catholicleague.org/cuomos-tyrannical-edict/.

203 Ibid.

204 Bill Donohue, "Critics Object to Religious Liberty Gains," June 9, 2020, Catholic League, www.catholicleague.org/critics-object-to-religious-gains/.

205 Michael Deegan, "Is NYC's Department of Education Trying to Sabotage Catholic Schools?", *NY Post*, November 30, 2020, https://nypost.com/2020/11/30/is-nycs-department-of-education-trying-to-sabotage-catholic-schools/.

206 Salvatore Joseph Cordileone, "Catholics Must Resist Government's Unjust Repression of Our Right to Worship," *Washington Post*, September 16, 2020, www.washingtonpost.com/opinions/2020/09/16/archbishop-salvatore-cordileone-right-to-worship.

207 "Rendering Unto Caesars Palace," *Wall Street Journal*, July 26, 2020, https://www.wsj.com/articles/rendering-unto-caesars-palace-1159578141?mod=opinion_lead_pos2.

208 Bill Donohue, "SCOTUS Ruling On Religious Rights Is Illuminating," November 30, 2020, Catholic League, www.catholicleague.org/scotus-ruling-on-religious-rights-is-illuminating/.

209 Bill Donohue, "Masketeers Are Not Doing Us Any Favors," September 20, 2021, Catholic League, www.catholicleague/masketeeers-are-not-doing-us-any-favors/.

210 Ibid.

211 Tyler Cowen, "Politics & Policy; Elites Are Unmasked. What About the Servers?", The Westerly Sun (Rhode Island), October 9, 2021.

212 Ben Weingarten, "2021: The Year of the Ruling Class' Crackdown on Dissent," *Newsweek*, January 3, 2022, https://www.newsweek.com/2021-year-ruling-class-crackdown-dissent-opinion-1664757.

213 Desmet, *The Psychology of Totalitarianism*, 103.

214 David Zimmermann, "Former Harvard Medical Professor Claims He Was Fired for Opposing Covid Lockdowns, Vaccine Mandates," *National Review*, March 18, 2024, https://www.nationalreview.com/news/former-harvard-medical-professor-claims-he-was-fired-for-opposing-covid-lockdowns-vaccine-mandates/.

215 Ibid.

216 Jason Cohen, "Mark Zuckerberg Tells Joe Rogan That Biden Admin Would 'Scream' and 'Curse' At Meta Employees To Censor 'True' Content," *Daily Caller*, January 10, 2025, dailycaller.com/2025/01/10/mark-zuckerberg-joe-rogan-biden-admin-censorship.

217 Bill Donohue, "Making Sense of the ACLU's Covid-19 Response," July 31, 2020, Catholic League, www.catholicleague.org/making-sense-of-the-aclus-covid-19-response-2/.

218 Ibid.

219 Ibid.

220 Ibid.

221 Sarah Mervosh, et al., "What the Data Says About Pandemic School Closures, Four Years Later," *New York Times*, March 18, 2024.

222 Rich Lowry, "Francis Collins's Covid Confession," *National Review*, December 29, 2023, https//www.nationalreview.com/2023/12/francis-collinss-covid-confession/.

223 Anderson, "Covid Catastrophies."

224 Tierney, "The Shape of Things to Come: The Tyranny of Covid-19," 269–70.

225 Laura Ingraham, "The Ingraham Angle," Fox News, December 13, 2023.

226 Victor Davis Hanson, "The Great Regression," in Michael Walsh, ed., *Against the Great Reset* (New York: Bombardier, 2022), 15.

227 Janice Fiamengo, "The Great Reset, Feminist Style," in Walsh, *Against the Great Reset*, 243, 252–53.

228 W. Cleon Skousen, *The Naked Communist* (Salt Lake City, Utah: Izzard Ink, 1958), 323.

229 Ibid., 311.

230 Ibid.

231 "The Family and the New Totalitarianism," editorial, *Inside the Vatican*, November 1, 2015, https://insidethevatican.com/magazine/editorial/reflection/reflections-on-the-synod/.

232 Pope Benedict XVI, *God Is Ever New: Meditations on Life, Love, and Freedom*, Luca Caruso, ed. (San Francisco: Ignatius Press, 2024), 89, 96.

233 Bill Donohue, *War on Virtue: How the Ruling Class is Killing the American Dream* (Manchester, New Hampshire: Sophia Institute Press, 2023), 125.

234 Scott Hogenson, "Why the Left Hates God, Family and Country," Townhall, October 22, 2022, https://townhall.com/columnists/scotthogenson/2022/10/22/why-the-left-hates-god-family-and-country-n2614871.

235 "13 Guiding Principles," Black Lives Matter, https://www.blacklivesmatteratschool.com/13-guiding-principles.html.

236 Pope Benedict XVI, *God Is Ever New*, 144.

237 Cardinal Robert Sarah, "Full Text: Cardinal Sarah at the National Catholic Prayer Breakfast," *Catholic World Report*, May 18, 2016, https://www.catholicworldreport.com/2016/05/18/full-text-cardinal-sarah-at-the-national-catholic-prayer-breakfast/.

238 Mallory Millett, "Marxist Feminism's Ruined Lives," *Front Page*, September 1, 2014, https://www.frontpagemag.com/marxist-feminisms-ruined-lives-mallory-millett/.

239 Steven Goldberg, *The Inevitability of Patriarchy: Why the Biological Difference Between Men and Women Always Produces Male Domination* (New York: William Morrow, 1973).

240 Bill Donohue, *Common Sense Catholicism: How to Resolve Our Cultural Crisis* (San Francisco: Ignatius Press, 2019), 129.

241 Ibid.

242 Goldberg, *The Inevitability of Patriarchy*, 93.

243 William A. Donohue, *The New Freedom: Individualism and Collectivism in the Social Lives of Americans* (New Brunswick, New Jersey: Transaction Press, 1990), 59.

244 William A. Donohue, *The Politics of the American Civil Liberties Union* (New Brunswick, New Jersey: Transaction Press, 1985), 90–94.

245 Dusty Gates, "The Death of the Family Wage Culture," *Crisis*, October 15, 2014, https://www.crisismagazine.com/opinion/death-family-wage-culture.

246 Ibid.

247 Jason Chaffetz, *The Puppeteers: The People Who Control of the People Who Control America* (New York: Broadside Books, 2023), 114.

248 Lindsay Kornick, "'Parents, Do You Agree?' Biden Alarms with Assertion There's 'No Such Thing as Someone Else's Child,'" Fox

News, April 25, 2023, https://www.foxnews.com/media/parents-agree-biden-alarms-assertion-no-thing-someone-elses-child.

249 President Biden, "Remarks by President Biden and Prime Minister Rishi Sunak of the United Kingdom in Joint Press Conference," June 8, 2023, https:www.whitehouse.gov/briefing-room/speeches-remarks-by-president-biden-and-prime-minister-rishi-sunak-of-the-united-kingdom-in-joint-press-conference.

250 Rebecca Downs, "KJP Says the Quiet Part Out Loud on the Disturbing Plans Democrats Have for Kids," May 18, 2023, https://townhall.com/tipsheet/rebeccadowns/2023/05/23/kjp-says-the-quiet-part-out-loud-at-glaad-awards-show-n2623368.

251 Lindsay Kornick, "'Parents, Do You Agree?' Biden Alarms with Assertion There's 'No Such Thing as Someone Else's Child.'"

252 Brett T, "School Board Member Says the 'Client' of Public Schools Is 'Not the Parent, But the Community,'" June 28, 2025, twitchy.com/brett/2025/06/28/school-board-member-says-the-client-of-public-schools-is-not-the-parent-but-the-community-n2414903.

253 Plato, Republic, Book 5, Section 457, https://www.perseus.tufts.edu/hopper/text.

254 Mike Gonzalez, "Commentary: Marriage and Family," March 1, 2022, https://www.heritage.org/marriage-and-family/commentary/socialism-and-family.

255 William Norman Grigg, "Nationalizing Children," April 8, 2013, https://www.lewrockwell.com/2013/04/william-norman-grigg/to-whom-do-children-belong/.

256 W. Cleon Skousen, *The Naked Communist: Exposing Communism and Restoring Freedom* (Salt Lake City, Utah: Izzard Ink, 1958), 97.

257 Grigg, "Nationalizing Children."

258 Hillary Clinton, "It Takes a Village," DNC Address, delivered August 27, 1996, Chicago, Illinois, https://www.americanrhetoric.com/speeches/hillaryclintontakesavillage.htm.

259 Dennis Altman, *Homosexual: Oppression and Liberation* (New York: Discus Book, 1971), 83.

260 Brigette Berger and Peter Berger, *The War Over The Family* (Garden City, New York: Anchor Books, 1984), 173–74.

261 "Charter of the Rights of the Family," October 22, 1983, Presented by the Holy See, October 22, 1983, Preamble, Section D.

262 Ibid., Section I.

263 Ibid., Article 3.

264 Ibid., Article 5.

265 Robert Pondiscio, "Schoolchildren Are Not 'Mere Creatures of the State,'" *Commentary*, September 2022, https://www.commentary.org/articles/robert-pondiscio/schools-vs-parents/.

266 Stephen Moore, "The Real Story of the Two Americans," January 21, 2024, https://dailycaller.com/2024/01/21/opinion-the-real-story-of-the-two-americas-stephen-moore/.

267 Skousen, *The Naked Communist*, 96.

268 Johan Bester & Eric Kodish, "Children Are Not the Property of Their Parents: The Need for a Clear Statement of Ethical Obligations and Boundaries," *The American Journal of Bioethics*, Vol. 17, 2017 – Issue 11, https://doi.org/10.1080/15265161.2017.1378768.

269 Colleen Dean, "Children Need 'Liberation' From Parents, Scholar Argues," June 21, 2024, https://www.thecollegefix.com/children-need-liberation-from-parents-scholar-argues/.

270 William A. Donohue, *The New Freedom: Individualism and Collectivism in the Social Lives of Americans* (New Brunswick, New Jersey: Transaction Press, 1990), 80.

271 Ibid., 85.

272 Ibid.

273 Sarah Jones, "Children Are Not Property," *New York Magazine*, April 8, 2023, https://nymag.com/intelligencer/2023/04/children-are-not-property.html.

274 Ibid.

275 Melissa Koenig, "New Jersey Dad Sues Cherry Hill Public Schools Over Transgender Policy that Allows Children to Change Names and Gender Without Parental Consent," *New York Post*, October 26, 2023, https://nypost.com/2023/10/25/news/new-jersey-dad-sues-school-over-transgender-policy/.

276 Kaylee McGhee White, "Biden Admits Why the Left Opposes Parental Rights in Education," April 25, 2023, https://www.washingtonexaminer.com/restoring-america/community-family/biden-admits-why-the-left-opposes-parental-rights-in-education.

277 Chaffetz, *The Puppeteers*, p. 107.

278 Melissa Moschella, "To Whom Do Children Belong?", April 16, 2013, https://www.thepublicdiscourse.com/2013/04/9880/.

279 Ibid.

280 Michael L. Coulter, Stephen M. Krason, Richard S. Myers, Joseph A. Varacalli, *Encyclopedia of Catholic Social Thought, Social Science, and Social Policy*, Vol 1, (Lanham, Maryland: The Scarecrow Press, Inc., 2007), 512.

281 Peter Jamison, et al., "Home Schooling's Rise from Fringe to Fastest-Growing Form of Education," *Washington Post*, October 31, 2023, https://www.washingtonpost.com/education/interactive/2023/homeschooling-growth-data-by-district/.

282 Jordan Boyd, "John Oliver Calls for States to Crack Down On Homeschool Wave," *The Federalist*, October 10, 2023, https://thefederalist.com.2023/10/10/clueless-john-oliver-calls-for-states-to-crack-down-on-post-covid-homeschooling-wave/.

283 Everything that follows about Bartholet can be found in my article, "The War on Homeschooling," September 21, 2020, Catholic League, https://catholicleague.org/the-war-on-homeschooling/.

284 Steven W. Mosher, *Population Control: Real Costs, Illusory Benefits* (New Brunswick, New Jersey: Transaction Press, 2008), 136.

285 Michael L. Coulter, Stephen M. Krason, Richard S. Myers, Joseph A. Varacalli, *Encyclopedia of Catholic Social Thought, Social Science, and Social Policy*, Vol. 3, (Lanham, Maryland: The Scarecrow Press, Inc., 2012), 336.

286 Ibid., Vol 1, p. 377. Vol 1 edition was published in 2007.

287 "Declaration of the Dicastery for the Doctrine of the Faith 'Dignitas Infinita' on Human Dignity," April 8, 2024 https://press.vatican.va/content/salastampa/en/bollettino/pubblico/2024/04/08/240408c.html.

288 Mosher, *Population Control*, 33–34.

289 Bill Donohue, "Margaret Sanger's Racism Still Defended," August 26, 2020, Catholic League, www.catholicleague.org/margaret-sangers-racism-still-defended/.

290 Bill Donohue, *Secular Sabotage: How Liberals Are Destroying Religion and Culture in America* (New York: FaithWords, 2009), 41–42.

291 Donohue, "Margaret Sanger's Racism Still Defended."

292 Ibid.

293 Donohue, *Secular Sabotage*, 42.

294 Seamus Bruner, *Controligarchs: Exposing the Billionaire Class, Their Secret Deals, and the Globalist Plot to Dominate Your Life* (New York: Sentinel, 2023), 82–83.

295 Mary Eberstadt, "The Prophetic Power of *Humanae Vitae*," in *Why Humanae vitae Is Still Right*, Janet E. Smith, ed., (San Francisco: Ignatius Press, 2018), 19.

296 Glenn H. Reynolds, "'The Population Bomb' Was Wrong: The World Now Struggling to Make More Babies," *New York Post*, April 3, 2024, https://nypost.com/2024/opinion/the-world-struggling-to-make-more-babies-the-population-bomb-was-wrong/.

297 Bill Donohue, "Taking the Bait," March 22, 2003, Catholic League, www.catholicleague.org/taking-the-bait/.

298 Robert P. Lockwood, "NARAL, Anti-Catholicism & the Roots of the Pro-Abortion Campaign," June 19, 2001, Catholic League, https://www.catholicleague.org/naral-anti-catholicism-the-roots-of-the-pro-abortion-campaign.

299 Ibid.

300 Ibid.

301 Lawrence Lader, *Abortion* (Boston: Beacon Press, 1966), 169.

302 Garrett Hardin, Environmental Studies Program, "UCSB Environmental Studies Program Statement on Garrett Hardin," 2024, https://es.ucsb.edu/index.php/people/garrett-hardin.

303 *Roe v. Wade*, 410 U.S. 113 (1973), https://supreme.justia.com/cases/federal/us/410/113/.

304 Ruth Marcus, "How Pushing 'Fetal Personhood' Could Backfire," *Washington Post*, March 6, 2024, https://www.washingtonpost.com/opinions/2024/03/06/fetal-personhood-embryo-ivf-alabama-supreme-court-backfire/.

305 Robert P. George, "Are Human Embryos Human Beings?", March 18, 2024, https://www.nationalreview.com/2024/03/are-human-embryos-human-beings/.

306 Ibid.

307 Ibid.

308 Bill Donohue, "Who Wants Abortion Without Restrictions?" Catalyst, December 2023, https://www.catholicleague.org/who-wants-abortion-without-restrictions/.

309 Ibid.

310 Ibid.

311 Bill Donohue, "Trump Was Right About Abortion," September 11, 2024, Catholic League, https://www.catholicleague.org/trump-was-right-about-abortion/.

312 Ibid.

313 Dr. Susan Berry, "NBC News: 'Elective Abortions Do Not Occur Up Until Moment of Birth,'" *Breitbart*, August 27, 2020, https://www.breitbart.com/politics/2020/08/27/nbc-news-elective-abortions-do-not-occur-up-until-moment-birth/.

314 Bill Donohue, "Supremes Ban Infanticide," April 18, 2007, Catholic League, https://www.catholicleague.org/supremes-ban-infanticide/.

315 *Doe v. Bolton*, 410 U.S. 179 (1973)

316 Bill Donohue, "Media Distort Trump on Abortion," September 13, 2024, Catholic League, www.catholicleague.org/media-distort-trump-on-abortion/.

317 Bill Donohue, "Virginia Governor Justifies Infanticide," January 30, 2019, Catholic League, www.catholicleague.org/virginia-governor-justifies-infanticide/.

318 Aldous Huxley, *Brave New World* (New York: HarperPerennial, 1932), 234–35.

319 Edmund Burke, *Reflections on the Revolution in France* (New York: Penguin Books, 1968), 186–88.

320 Alexis de Tocqueville, *Democracy in America*, J.P. Mayer, ed., translated by George Lawrence (New York: Pernnial Library, 1969), 47.

321 Ibid., 17.

322 Ibid., 30.

323 Ibid., 294.

324 Patrick M. Garry, *Wrestling with God: The Courts' Tortuous Treatment of Religion* (Washington, D.C.: Catholic University Press of America, 2006), 22–23, 100.

325 John Tierney, "The Shape of Things to Come: The Tyranny of Covid-19," in Michael Walsh, ed., *Against the Great Reset: Eighteen Theses Contra the New World Order* (New York: Bombardier, 2022), 431–32.

326 John Paul II, *Centesimus Annus*, Encyclical Letter, 1991, https://www.vatican.va/content/john-paulii/en/encyclicals/documents/hf_jp-ii_enc_-01051991_centesimus-annus.html.

327 W. Cleon Skousen, *The Naked Communist: Exposing Communism and Restoring Freedom* (Salt Lake City, Utah: Izzard Ink, 1958), 63.

328 Ibid., 382–83.

329 John Horsch, *Modern Religious Liberalism: The Destructiveness and Irrationality of Modernist Theology* (Chicago: The Bible Institute Colportage Association, 1938), 248.

330 Skousen, *The Naked Communist*, 297–98.

331 Ibid., 298.

332 Thomas D. Williams, "The Coming Christian Persecution," April 21, 2023, Catholic League, www.catholicleague.org. It is based on his book by the same name published by Sophia Institute Press in 2023.

333 Bill Donohue, "'Christian Lives Don't Matter,'" October 2, 2016, Catholic League, www.catholicleague.org/christian-lives-dont-matter/.

334 Bill Donohue, "Church Vandalism," August 8, 2022, Catholic League, www.catholicleague.org/church-vandalism/.

335 Arielle Del Turco, "Hostility Against Churches Is on the Rise in the United States: Analyzing Incidents from 2018-2023," Family Research Council, Issue Analysis, February 2024, No. IS24801. See frc.org/HostilityAgainstChurches.

336 Cardinal Robert Sarah, "Full Text: Cardinal Sarah at the National Catholic Prayer Breakfast," May 18, 2016, https://www.catholicworldreport.com/2016/05/18/full-text-cardinal-sarah-at-the-national-catholic-prayer-breakfast/.

337 Pope Benedict XVI, *God Is Ever New: Meditations on Life, Love, and Freedom*, Luca Caruso, ed. (San Francisco: Ignatius Press, 2024), 19.

338 Bill Donohue, "Bigoted Teacher Under Fire; State Officials," Catalyst, October 2022, Catholic League, www.catholicleague.org/bigoted-teacher-under-fire-state-officials-contacted.

339 Bill Donohue, "Church's Tax-Exempt Status Threatened," Catalyst, July/August 2021, Catholic League, www.catholicleague.org/churchs-tax-exempt-status-threatened-2.

340 Bill Donohue, *Secular Sabotage: How Liberals Are Destroying Religion and Culture in America* (New York: FaithWords, 2009), 147-48.

341 Bill Donohue, "Obama's War on Religion," September 10, 2012, Catholic League, www.catholicleague.org/obamas-war-on-religion/.

342 Ibid.

343 Ibid.

344 Bill Donohe, "Obama's War on Religion," October 19, 2012, Catholic League, www.catholicleague.org/obamas-war-on-religion/.

345 Bill Donohue, "Western World At War With Catholics," February 9, 2023, Catholic League, https://www.catholicleague.org/western-world-at-war-with-catholics/.

346 William A. Donohue, "FBI Sources On Catholic Church Are Foul," Catalyst, January/February 2024. Available on Catholic League website, www.catholicleague.org.

347 Bill Donohue, "Biden and Trump on Religious Liberty," June 24, 2024, Catholic League, www.catholicleague.org/biden-and-trump-on-religious-liberty-2/.

348 "Fact Sheet: President Biden Reestablishes the White House Office of Faith-Based and Neighborhood Partnerships," February 14,

2021, whitehouse.gov/briefing-room-statements-releases/2021/02/14/fact-sheet-president-biden-reestablishes-the-white-house-office-of-faith-based-and-neighborhood-partnerships.

349 Bill Donohue, Executive Summary, Catholic League 2009 Annual Report on Anti-Catholicism, www.catholicleague.org.

350 Bill Donohue, Executive Summary, Catholic League 1997 Annual Report on Anti-Catholicism, www.catholicleague.org.

351 Bill Donohue, Executive Summary, Catholic League 2008 Annual Report on Anti-Catholicism, www.catholicleague.org.

352 Bill Donohue, "Christianity Terrifies Secular Left," Catalyst, November 2024, Catholic League, www.catholicleague.org.

353 Bill Donohue, "Menorah Pulled From Coop Lobby," December 17, 2024, Catholic League, www.catholicleague.org/menorah-pulled-from-coop-lobby/.

354 Bill Donohue, "Cigna's Top Officers Should Resign," Catalyst, May 2021, Catholic League, www.catholicleague.org.

355 Bill Donohue, "Historical Summary of 'Sisters' Bigotry," July 18, 2023, www.catholicleague.org/historical-summary-of-sisters-bigotry/.

356 Bill Donohue, "Dodgers Reinvite 'Sisters': L.A. Parishes Contacted," June 21, 2023, www.catholicleague.org/dodgers-reinvite-sisters-l-a-parishes-contacted/.

357 Ibid.

358 Donohue, *Secular Sabotage*, 45–47.

359 Ibid., 48–56.

360 "St. Patrick's Cathedral Defiled," Catalyst, March 2024. See www.catholicleague.org.

361 Bill Donohue, "Marjorie Taylor Greene Must Be Sanctioned," April 28, 2022, Catholic League, www.catholicleague.org.

362 Bill Donohue, "Federal Agency Trashes Religious Liberty," Catalyst, October 2016, Catholic League, www.catholicleague.org.

363 Bill Donohue, "Victory for Priests' Rights; Amicus Brief Prevails," Catalyst, January/February 2019, Catholic League, www.catholicleague.org.

364 "Whitmer Mocks Eucharist," Catalyst, November 2024, Catholic League, www.catholicleague.org.

365 Bill Donohue, "Union Head Rips Christians; She Should Resign," Catalyst, October 2023, Catholic League, www.catholicleague.org.

366 Bill Donohue, "NEA Board Member Ousted; Our Effort Paid

Off," Catalyst, January/February 2022, Catholic League, www.catholicleague.org.

367 Bill Donohue, "Students' Parents Called 'Christo-Fascists,'" Catalyst, April 2023, Catholic League, www.catholicleague.org.

368 Bill Donohue, "Texas A&M Prof Goes Beserk; Officials Contacted," Catalyst, October 2020, Catholic League, www.catholicleague.org.

369 Bill Donohue, Executive Summary, Catholic League 2003 Annual Report on Anti-Catholicism, www.catholicleague.org.

370 "Open Letter to Durban and Feinstein," September 7, 2017, www.catholicleague.org/open-letters-to-durbin-and-feinstein/.

371 Bill Donohue, "Too Many Catholics on the Bench?", September 18, 2014, www.catholicleague.org/catholics-bench-2/.

372 Andrew C. McCarthy, "Biden Encourages People to Violate the Law by Protesting at Justices' Homes," *The Hill*, May 11, 2022, www.thehill.com/opinion/judiciary/3483790-biden-encourages-people-to-violate-the-law-by-protesting-at-justices-homes.

373 Ibid.

374 Bill Donohue, "Making Bogeymen of Christian Nationals," Catalyst, January/February 2024, www.catholicleague.org.

375 Bill Donohue, "Christian Nationalism Is a Fiction, Part II," September 4, 2019, www.catholicleague.org.

376 Colin Woodward, "The Christian Nationalist Ideas That Made Mike Johnson," October 27, 2023, www.politico.com/news/magazine/2023/10/27/mike-johnson-christian-nationalist-ideas-qa-00123882

377 Bill Donohue, "Christian Bashers Aim Beyond Mike Johnson," November 9, 2023, www.catholicleague.org.

378 See the two-part series that I wrote, "The Myth of Christian Nationalism," September 3 and 4, 2024. Catholic League, www.catholicleague.org.

379 Bill Donohue, Executive Summary, Catholic League 2000 Annual Report on Anti-Catholicism, www.catholicleague.org.

380 Bill Donohue, "Science Channel Resurrects Jesus' Tomb Hoax," April 13, 2017, www.catholicleague.org/science-channel-resurrects-jesus-tomb-hoax-2/.

381 Ibid.

382 Ibid.

383 Bill Donohue, Executive Summary, Catholic League 2006 Annual Report on Anti-Catholicism, www.catholicleague.org.

384 Bill Donohue, Executive Summary, Catholic League 2009 Annual

Report on Anti-Catholicism, www.catholicleague.org.

385 The following discussion on the Magdalene Laundries is taken from Bill Donohue, "Myths of the Magdalene Laundries," July 15, 2013, Catholic League, www.catholicleague.org.

386 Bill Donohue, "More Lies About 'Philomena,'" April 22, 2014, Catholic League, www.catholicleague.org.

387 Bill Donohue, "Ireland's 'Mass Grave' Hysteria," 2014, Catholic League, www.catholicleague.org.

388 The following discussion of Ireland's Mass Grave story is taken from Bill Donohue, "Debunking the 'Mass Grave' Story," Catalyst, July/August 2014, Catholic League, www.catholicleague.org.

389 Bill Donohue, "Church Maligned In Canada And USA," October 30, 2023, Catholic League, www.catholicleague.org.

390 W. Cleon Skousen, *The Naked Communist: Exposing Communism and Restoring Freedom* (Salt Lake City, Utah, 1958), 313.

391 Mary A. Nicholas and Paul Kengor, *The Devil and Bella Dodd: One Woman's Struggle Against Communism and Her Redemption* (Gastonia, North Carolina: TAN Books), 260–61.

392 Ibid., 264.

393 Ibid., 2.

394 Ibid., 257.

395 Ibid., 252.

396 Ibid., 256.

397 Bob Reeves, "Catholic Group Calls for More Openness," Lincoln Journal Star, June 4, 2006, 1.

398 "Hillary Clinton Wikileaks: John Podesta Catholic Email," October 12, 2016, https://time.com/4528532/hillary-clinton-campaign-pushes-back-on-anti-catholic-charge.

399 Bill Donohue, *The Truth about Clergy Sexual Abuse: Clarifying the Facts and the Causes* (San Francisco, Ignatius Press, 2021), 245.

400 Matthew McDonald, "Almost All Catholic Women's Colleges Admit Men Who Identify as Women," National Catholic Register, February 16, 2024, https://www.ncregister.com/news/almost-all-catholic-women-s-colleges-admit-men-who-identify-as-women.

401 Mary Ann Glendon's Address, "Feminism and the Church" was given December 16, 2006 before the Centro di Orientamento Politico in Rome. See "The Pope's New Feminism," October 6, 2001, www.catholiceducation.org/en/controversy/the-pope-s-new-feminism.html.

402 Donohue, *The Truth about Clergy Sexual Abuse*, 224–25.

403 Ann Carey, "Sister Simone Campbell of 'Nuns on the Bus' Leaves $100K Job – But Abortion is Still 'Above Her Pay Grade,'" National Catholic Register, April 16, 2021, https://www.ncregister.com/blog/sister-simone-campbell-retires.

404 Ann Carey, "Nuns on the Bus' Media Stunt Detracts From Bishops' Fortnight for Freedom," *National Catholic Register*, July 13, 2012, http://www.ncregister.com/site/print_article/34124/.

405 "Catholic Lobby: Catholics Cannot Vote for Donald Trump," Targeted News Service, August 11, 2020.

406 John McCormack, "Catholic Nun & DNC Speaker Simone Campbell on Abortion: 'That's Beyond My Pay Grade,'" *Weekly Standard*, September 5, 2012, http://www.weeklystandard.com/print/blogs/catholic-nun-dnc-speaker-simone-campbell-abortioin-s-beyond-my-pay-grade_6651775.html.

407 Joshua Nelson, "Catholic College Defends Pro-Abortion Nun as Commencement Speaker Amid Backlash," Fox News, May 10, 2024, https://www.foxnews.com/media/catholic/college-defends-pro-abortion-nun-commencement-speaker.

408 William A. Donohue, "Pope Welcomes Catholic Dissidents," Catalyst, October 2023, Catholic League, www.catholicleague.org.

409 Bill Donohue, "Southern Poverty Law Center Is A Hate Group; Part II," March 26, 2024, Catholic League, www.catholicleague.org/southern-poverty-law-center-is-a-hate-group-2/.

410 Bill Donohue, "Soros Gets AP Whitewash," May 15, 2017, Catholic League, www.catholicleague.org/soros-gets-ap-whitewash-2/.

411 Bill Donohue, "The Hateful Legacy of George Soros," July 27, 2022, Catholic League, www.catholicleague.org/the-hateful-legacy-of-george-soros/.

412 Kevin D. Roberts, "Why I Am Going to Davos," January 12, 2024, www.heritage.org.node/25156532/.

413 Ibid.

414 Richard Pollina, "Editor-in-Chief of Scientific American Resigns Following Expletive-Filled Rant Against Trump Voters," *New York Post*, November 14, 2024, https://nypost.com/2024/11/15/us-news/editor-in-chief-of-scientific-american-laura-helmuth-resigns-following-expletive-filled-rant-against-trump-voters/.

415 Shane Galvin, "Megyn Kelly Calls Rachel Zegler 'A Pig' After 'Snow White' Star's Nasty Tirade About Trump Voters," *New York Post*, November 13, 2024, https://nypost.com/2024/11/14/us-news/megyn-kelly-rips-rachel-zegler-after-snow-white-stars-tirade-about-trump-voters/.

416 Caitlin Doornbos, "University of Kansas Instructor Out of Job After Saying Men Should be 'Lined Up and Shot' for Not Backing Female Candidates," *New York Post*, October 11, 2024, https://nypost.com/2024/10/11/us-news/university-of-kansas-lecturer-out-of-job-after-saying-men-should-be-lined-up-and-shot-for-not-backing-female-candidates/.

417 Aldous Huxley, *Brave New World* (New York: HarperPerennial, 1932), 240.

418 "Forming Consciences for Faithful Citizenship," USCCB, 2008, usccb.org/offices/justice-and-peace/forming-consciences-faithful-citizenship.

419 Gerhard Cardinal Müller, *God's Presence in the Eucharist and in the World* (Manchester, New Hampshire: Sophia Institute Press, 2024), 161.

420 Pope Benedict XVI, encyclical letter, *Caritas In Veritate*, June 29, 2009, vatican.va/content/benedict-xvi/en/encyclicals/documents/hf_ben-xvi_enc_20090629_caritas-in-veritate.html.

421 Ruth Graham and Nick Hagan, "Newly Ordained, and Leaning Right in Theology and Politics," *New York Times*, July 11, 2024.